Software Design Using Java 2

Kevin Lano, José Luiz Fiadeiro and Luís Andrade

First published 2002 by
PALGRAVE MACMILLAN
Houndmills, Basingstoke, Hampshire RG21 6XS and
175 Fifth Avenue, New York, N. Y. 10010
Companies and representatives throughout the world

PALGRAVE MACMILLAN is the global academic imprint of the Palgrave Macmillan division of St. Martin's Press, LLC and of Palgrave Macmillan Ltd. Macmillan® is a registered trademark in the United States, United Kingdom and other countries. Palgrave is a registered trademark in the European Union and other countries.

ISBN 1–4039–0230–5

This book is printed on paper suitable for recycling and made from fully managed and sustained forest sources.

A catalogue record for this book is available from the British Library.

10 9 8 7 6 5 4 3 2 1
11 10 09 08 07 06 05 04 03 02

Printed and bound in Great Britain by
J. W. Arrowsmith Ltd, Bristol

Contents

Preface

The use of Java as the first language in computer science courses is by now well established world-wide and supported by textbooks. Such courses typically cover the basic aspects of object-oriented programming with emphasis on the control structures made available in Java. This book contains an introduction to Java suitable for a first course in programming, and provides support materials including a computer-aided learning tool.

However, software engineering as a discipline requires another level of maturity to be attained: that of software design and "programming in the large", which covers the use of languages like Java for the development of complete and high-quality applications. This level is concerned with the development of *systems* as opposed to programs, in the sense that the complexity that is involved in their development is not of an algorithmic nature, but results from the need to construct and evolve applications as systems of interconnected components. This book covers all the essential techniques needed to design software systems using object technology: *design patterns, architectural, subsystem and module design, user interface design, web-based system design* and *database design*. The rapidly growing array of Java technology products across all areas of software development means that it is the natural language of choice for teaching these issues, so we use Java Swing for user interface construction, JavaScript, JSP and Servlets for web-based system design, and JDBC for database interfacing. We also introduce the industry-standard UML notation for analysis and design.

Unlike traditional engineering design, software design must produce systems which can be extended and modified relatively easily. There is an increasing need in industry for software to support *evolution* of requirements, the rapid addition of services, and a wide variety of customer needs. The book addresses this issue as a central design goal, and introduces an extension of object-oriented concepts, called *coordination contracts*, which supports flexibility by separating the program logic, or coordination of components, from the software components that this logic applies to. This approach has been developed and applied by the authors in a variety of application areas, from banking to telecommunications and control systems. On the CD we provide tools for implementing contracts in Java.

All material has been class tested in our own courses, and we include complete code as well as comprehensive instructions on how to construct the example systems presented. The book can be used throughout a computer science degree course, and is particularly aimed at supporting students embarking on a group or individual project – when the importance of design issues first becomes a serious matter for many future software developers.

Guidelines for Teaching

Chapter 1 introduces program design and the UML notation. Chapter 2 describes generic design steps and techniques, and guidelines for software project management. Chapter 3 covers GUI and database design. Chapter 4 describes 14 common design patterns. Chapters 5 and 6 cover the concept of coordination contracts and their application in design. Chapter 7 deals with design issues for reactive systems, and Chapter 8 gives programming and design techniques for web-based applications. Appendix A gives a rapid introduction to Java, and Appendix B gives a case study of software design.

We use the material in Appendix A in an introductory course in programming using Java, and Chapters 1 to 4, plus Chapter 8 and Appendix B, for a second year program design course. Chapters 5, 6 and 7 can be used in advanced design courses.

Acknowledgements

The introductory Java material presented in Appendix A was originally developed by Malcolm Bird at King's College London. Kelly Androutsopolous, David Clark, Arturo Sanchez and Pauline Kan contributed to the development of RSDS. The support of ATX Software, King's College London and Prof. Tom Maibaum in providing the resources for developing this book is gratefully acknowledged. Many of our students have also contributed to the development of the material in the book, in particular Gareth Davis (Chapter 8) and Depika Mistry (restaurant system case study).

João Gouveia, Georgios Koutsoukos, Antónia Lopes and Michel Wermelinger contributed to the development of the coordination contracts concept and the CDE tool.

Chapter 1

Software Design

This chapter describes the role of design in the software development process, and gives some desirable properties of software designs. It introduces three examples: a restaurant management system, an on-line football game, and a bank account management system, and describes what the design process consists of for these systems.

1.1 What is Software Design?

No-one would attempt to build an aeroplane or a bridge without careful planning of how the overall structure is going to be organised, what components and materials are needed and how they will fit together. For novel designs, such as the flat suspension bridge known as the "Millennium Bridge" over the river Thames in London, even more care is needed to ensure that the system when built will actually behave as expected[1].

For software the same principle applies: for small programs, under 100 lines, with one or two classes, we can often get away with hacking together some code at the terminal, and end up with something which, most of the time, works as intended. But this is far from the reality of industrial software production, where new systems have to be planned with care to ensure that they work correctly with existing systems, that they are reliable, and that they can be extended and maintained by people other than the original programmer. Software design is essential for any non-trivial program: unless care is taken to structure the code into sensible classes and methods, a program can quickly become very difficult to debug or extend.

In this book we will use the following practical definition which sets the scope of what we will be covering:

---

[1] Due to an error in the analysis of this footbridge, which ignored the fact that pedestrians produce lateral forces as well as vertical forces, the bridge started swaying excessively and had to be closed for over a year while expensive modifications were carried out.

> *Software design is the organisation of a software system into modules/subsystems/components/classes or other units; the definition of behaviour and data storage responsibilities for these units, and the definition of interactions and collaborations between them which together meet the required functionalities of the system.*

Therefore design involves some or all of the following activities:

- Breaking up a required service or group of services (from those identified during analysis) into methods of classes and compositions of these methods, or services provided by external software.
- Selecting algorithms for services.
- Representing data which is required to support the system services, as program data within classes or external data (e.g. held in a file or a database).
- Organising the connections and dependencies between modules to support the identified functionalities.
- Addressing the non-functional requirements of the system (performance, portability, maintainability, evolvability etc.) as appropriate at the design level.

Design is usually carried out in the context of some development method, such as the Rational Unified Process [47] for UML [51]. Each method has its own recommended techniques and strategies for design and emphasis on aspects of the activity. For example, scheduling analysis is an important part of design in real-time system development methods [12]. In this book we will cover general aspects of design which are common to many development methods. Our implicit underlying method is based on partitioning a system into "natural" (stable) subsystems, and simplifying the interfaces and assumptions made between these subsystems as much as possible in order to reduce complexity and enhance evolvability of the system. Chapter 5 explains the philosophy behind this approach in more detail.

1.1.1 Design is not just Elaborated Analysis

The analysis models of a system may already suggest some possible decompositions of data and functionality, but the design structure could be completely different to this: the analysis models simply describe *what* the required services of a system are, in the clearest possible way for human readers to understand (and possibly for some automated checking tools to process). In contrast, the design models describe *how* these services are to be carried out, in terms of a modular decomposition of the system and the responsibilities of these modules.

For example, in the restaurant management system of Section 1.1.3 we have a very clear analysis model of the data involved in the system, described in a UML class diagram. But during design we may decide to use an Access database to manage this data, which means converting the UML model into a relational data model. There is no simple mapping between the analysis and the design in this case.

1.1.2 Design is not Implementation

The design process may only define modules at the level of (language independent) pseudocode or method specifications, instead of filling in the details of the code of methods in some particular language. For completeness in this book we will often give the implementation of a module in Java, but in principle the two stages are distinct, and could (if the design description was precise enough and unambiguous) be carried out by separate individuals or teams.

1.1.3 Case Study 1: Restaurant Management System

In a popular London restaurant, the following computerised system is required to speed up the preparation of meals, manage stock and collect statistics on staff performance (Figure 1.1):

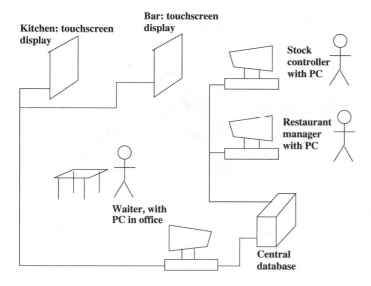

Figure 1.1: Restaurant Management System

- Waiters enter the orders (a list of dishes and drinks ordered by a diner or group of diners) into the system at their PC. Dishes to be prepared are sent to the kitchen, drink orders to the bar.
- Kitchen staff see the dish orders on their screen, prepare them in an appropriate sequence and confirm preparation to the system when complete, similarly with the bar.
- When the waiter sees the completion indications on his terminal he collects the items and takes them to the table.
- The system prints a bill at the end of the meal, and the waiter enters the details of payments for it. The manager can give discounts.

- The system keeps track of the number of customers served by each waiter, and the amount of money taken by each waiter. The manager can view these statistics, and keep track of staff details such as shift hours and timing.
- The stock management part of the system keeps a record of the stock level of all the ingredients which may be used in the dishes of the restaurant, and of all the drinks. When the stock level of an item goes below a set level, a warning is given to the stock manager, and a reorder can be set up.

We have been given the task to develop this system, using a standard PC platform where possible.

An analysis model of the data of the system, expressed in a UML class diagram (see Section 1.3), is given in Figure 1.2. Some of the use cases are given in diagrammatic form in Figure 1.3.

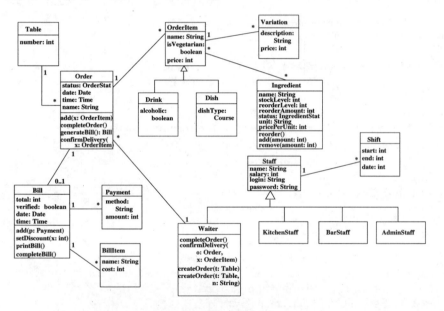

Figure 1.2: Class Diagram of Restaurant System

The corresponding textual specifications of functionality are (for the waiter/cook use cases only):

Create an order The waiter creates a new order instance, setting the table number and order name (optional).

Enter order item A dish or drink ordered is added to the current order, together with the number of copies required and any variations (e.g. no mayo).

Complete order The waiter closes the order.

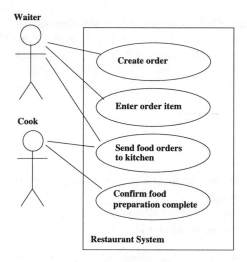

Figure 1.3: Selected Use Cases of Restaurant System

Send food orders to kitchen The system sends a list of the required dishes to the kitchen, displayed on the kitchen's terminal in the sequence in which they should be prepared (i.e. all starters first, then all mains).

Send drink orders to bar The system sends a list of the required drinks to the bar, where they are displayed on the terminal there.

Confirm preparation complete A cook confirms that preparation of a particular dish is complete and that it is ready for collection. Similarly for the bar.

Confirm delivery The waiter confirms that an order item has been delivered to the table. It is removed from the kitchen or bar display.

Bill order The system computes the charge for the order from the data on dish and drink prices, and discounts, and prints a bill.

Complete payment The waiter enters the details of how the bill is to be paid (e.g. a mixture of cash and cards). Once payment is confirmed the order ceases to be a current order and is stored in an archive of past orders.

What does the design process consist of for this system? Firstly some decisions about the implementation platform have to be made to guide the choice of design. For example our analysis class diagram, while an accurate and clear description of the conceptual entities and data that the application works with, is not appropriate as a database design (often called a *database schema*) for a relational database such as Microsoft Access.

There may be choices of implementation, in which case the alternatives should be clearly defined and costed and discussed with the customer before a decision is made. Alternatively a choice may already have been fixed at the requirements stage.

Let's assume in this case that MS Access has already been mandated, perhaps because existing systems in the restaurant use it so it is immediately available at no extra cost. In addition, that Java has been selected as the implementation language. So the design process has to include the development of a relational database schema and the definition of modules which store and retrieve data from this database, using the JDBC package of Java (http://www.java.sun.com/jdbc) which enables information to be moved between a database and a Java program using SQL statements.

The design must also:

- define components which provide the different GUI's required: for the waiter, kitchen, bar, manager and stock controller;
- define components which carry out computational tasks such as performance calculations and bill processing;
- define components which support the transmission of data between different terminals, e.g. the waiters console and the kitchen.

The first step in design is to map out the global *architecture* of the system: what major subsystems exist and what their responsibilities and connections are. We could draw an outline architecture (Figure 1.4) at this stage.

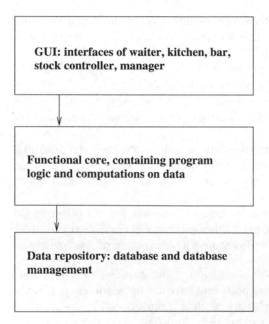

Figure 1.4: Restaurant Management System Architecture

Once the main subsystems are decided on, we can break down the functions identified by analysis into operations provided by one or more of these subsystems, so identifying *their* requirements more precisely. For example, the "enter order item" use case could become:

1. Waiter selects dish/drink from lists of available items shown on their GUI.
2. Waiter selects any variations available for this item, and number required.
3. Waiter presses "Add" button to add this order entry to a list showing the items presently in the order and their status (ordered/in preparation/ready/delivered).

Most of these are functional requirements on the GUI, although the database subsystem needs to provide the initial lists of data that are the available drinks and food dishes, and to store the current order data.

At this stage also we can begin to consider possible techniques for coordinating the interaction between subsystems. For example, the observer pattern (Chapter 4) is a possible candidate to use here, because there are several different "views" or presentations of completed orders: the separate displays of the order information used by waiters, the kitchen and the bar.

Finally, subsystem and module design repeats the process with each subsystem, until we obtain individual class and method definitions. In the case of this system specialised forms of design, such as GUI design and database design, will be needed in the corresponding subsystems.

1.1.4   Case Study 2: A Banking Application

The analysis model of a simple banking application involves three classes:

1. a **Customer** class with a method **withdraw(x: int)** which models the customer attempting to withdraw this amount from their current account, and **deposit(x: int)** modelling a deposit into the current account.
2. **CurrentAccount** with methods **debit(x: int)** and **credit(x: int)** and integer attribute **balance**.
3. **DepositAccount** with the same methods and attributes as **CurrentAccount**. The **balance** cannot be negative.

A UML class diagram of the application is shown in Figure 1.5.

Each customer has one current and one deposit account. If the **withdraw(m)** method executes, then their current account should be debited by amount **m**, if its balance is $\geq$ **m**. However if there are insufficient funds in the current account, but sufficient funds in their combined accounts, as much money as necessary is transferred from their deposit account in addition. Otherwise no debit or transfer is performed.

If **credit(m)** is invoked on the current account, and results in a balance of over 500 units in this account, then any surplus money is transferred to the deposit account, to reduce the current account balance to 500 units.

There are a number of ways we can design this system: we could use a design pattern such as Mediator (Chapter 4) to manage the interactions of the customer and their accounts, or simply hard-code the interactions within the customer or account classes. A third approach is given by the idea of a *coordination contract* between the components, as described in Chapter 5.

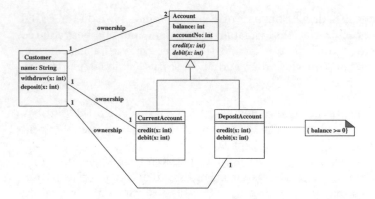

Figure 1.5: Analysis Model of Bank System

1.1.5   Case Study 3: Football Player System

The aim of this system is to control a simulated football player in order to guide their behaviour as part of a team of such players, in the *RoboCup* environment [45]. The system receives messages such as **(see step ((goal r) dist ang))** meaning that the player can see the right-hand goal at distance **dist** and angle **ang**. In response, the system can send commands such as **(kick power ang)** to the game simulator, to instruct the player to kick the ball with the specified force and angle.

Design of this system would start with an architectural decomposition into:

1. a communications interface responsible for receiving information and packaging this for use by the remainder of the application. This subsystem is also responsible for transforming commands issued by the application into messages for the external simulator.
2. A subsystem encapsulating the control algorithms for managing the players behaviour.

Further design stages would decompose the control algorithm for the player into different sub-algorithms depending on the state of the player (e.g. if they have possession of the ball their behaviour is different to when they do not have possession). The state pattern would be relevant to manage the different modes of behaviour of a playing agent depending on its position.

1.1.6   Planning the Design Process

Often people (especially students doing projects) talk about employing an "iterative, prototype-driven, design process". What this usually means in reality is "hack some code and debug it until it almost does what I want for one function, then do the same for another function, etc.". While this no doubt provides hours of entertainment, it can lead to an end product which is a patchwork quilt of different, inconsistent ideas, and that is much more complex than it needs to be[2].

An experimental approach can nevertheless be useful and even necessary, to explore different design possibilities and to test out a particular design approach. For example in the restaurant system it is not clear whether we should define a single class to act as the interface between the program logic and the database, or if we should define separate classes to manage different parts of this database. Trying to write the interface the first way, we could discover that it resulted in a huge class with dozens of methods, so leading us to the second approach. Similarly we could explore how the observer pattern would work in practice, etc.

But before experimentation starts, some overall architectural design should be carried out to give a coherent structure within which the design choices can be explored. A model such as that given in Figure 1.4 would be a suitable starting-point in the case of the restaurant management system.

1.2   What is a Good Design?

Some essential and desirable attributes of a design include:

- That it supports the given functional and non-functional requirements.
- That it is flexible and extensible – it can be effectively modified and extended to deal with changes to requirements and future enhancements.
- That it is comprehensible and verifiable – the system structure and components should be easy to understand and to test that they satisfy the requirements.
- It should be as simple as possible, given the need to fulfil the above properties.

1.2.1   Functional and Non-functional Requirements

This, of course, is the most important property: a design which fails to meet the functional requirements in particular will not be acceptable. By considering each use case and required service throughout development we can ensure that the stated functional requirements are met (there may be other implicit requirements which the customer/users expect but have not explicitly stated: these may be discovered during design as a result of preparing prototypes, for example. We then have to review the design and decide if it is still appropriate). By considering each of the non-functional requirements (e.g. that the system must run under Windows 2000) at all relevant stages of design, we can also select design choices which meet these requirements.

---

[2]This is pure "bottom up" design: solutions are found to individual functions, then these are pasted together in an attempt to give a solution for the whole system.

1.2.2   Design for Flexibility and Extension

Most real-world software applications are not simply written once and then stay frozen in place unchanged for the rest of their lives. Instead, if they are to remain useful, they must be extensible to new requirements and operating environments due to business and technological evolution. Therefore software design has to support such change.

At the most basic level this property of a design means you should avoid features of a language or external software which are *deprecated* (due to be phased out in the next upgrade of the language/software) or are likely to be deprecated in the foreseeable future. The users of your system will not appreciate it if they have to keep an antique version of Java or Microsoft Access just so they can run your software!

At a higher level this principle means that the design structure should support maintenance: changes to one module in the system should not affect other modules in an uncontrolled manner. It should be clear from the design structure what modules will need to be changed and how.

Design patterns (described in Chapter 4) can provide a structure into which new components can be slotted without affecting other components. For example we could add another view/observer component to a system following the observer pattern structure without needing to change any of the code of the elements being observed.

A more powerful means of achieving flexibility is by separating the components and subsystems which provide relatively stable functionality (e.g. essential bank account capabilities such as maintaining a balance and providing operations to modify this balance) from the business rules which describe how these components are to be combined and used. Chapter 5 describes the coordination contract approach to organising systems in this way. This organisation is particularly important for those systems where extensibility is part of the requirements, such as stock trading systems: the system design must be sufficiently "open" to allow new functionality to be rapidly added without affecting existing services.

1.2.3   Comprehensibility and Verifiability

Comprehensibility is important because if someone else needs to modify your code, to extend it or fix bugs, they have to understand at least part of the design (the more they understand, the more likely their changes will be correct). Even when revisiting a program you have yourself written, six months later, it is easy to be completely mystified by its structure.

One guideline for improving comprehensibility is to ensure that each component in the design has a clear purpose and meaning, so there is no ambiguity about what services it provides and how it fits into a larger component/system.

In the restaurant system, for example, a well-defined subsystem of the GUI could be the waiters GUI. This would contain the operations for creating and updating this display and dealing with the waiters input actions.

Additionally, a design should be well-commented, with comments (in a documentation production format such as *javadoc* [27]) embedded in each module. A description of each class and method should be given, including assumptions that each method makes about its parameters and starting state in order to execute correctly (e.g. that an object it invokes a method on is non-null).

For more critical systems, the same principles also enhance the degree to which a design can be formally checked for correctness with respect to the requirements.

Methods should have meaningful names which indicate what the method does. For example, a method that saves the state of an object to a backup memento object [43] should be called **saveToMemento** or similar, and the method which restores the object state from the memento should be **restoreFromMemento**. Java has several naming conventions for methods which should be used in most cases: if class **C** has attribute **att**, then the method to return the value of **att** is called **getAtt**, unless **att** is boolean, when the method is called **isAtt**. The method to set **att** to a new value is called **setAtt**. For example, the library class **JFrame** has methods **isResizable(): boolean** and **setResizable(r: boolean)**.

1.2.4 Simplicity

The design should minimise dependencies between components: component **M** *depends on* component **N** if **M** invokes methods of **N** (**M** may alternatively just use some types defined in **N**, this is termed *weak* dependence). Dependency of **M** on **N** is indicated by an arrow from **M** to **N** on a module dependency diagram, and this also means that if **N** is modified, **M** may need to be modified (because its behaviour may alter due to the possibly changed effect of **N**'s methods). Therefore minimising dependencies will, in principle, reduce the "knock-on" effect of a modification in a module.

Simplicity should also be aimed at within modules: an intricate and over-elaborate data structure or structure of object interactions will be fragile: one change to part of the structure could invalidate the entire module. A module may need to be rewritten during development to make it more simple and robust, if we find that the original idea we had for its design is leading to more and more complexity, need for special cases and flag variables, etc.

1.2.5 Design Principles

The following properties contribute to a good design:

- *Separation of responsibilities within an application*: for example, dividing the application into "tiers" which are relatively independent large subsystems of an application such as the GUI and interface to a database.

These tiers communicate via a small well-defined set of methods, and do not depend on the internal organisation or implementation of each other. Thus a GUI command to retrieve all records of a certain kind from a database should be independent of whether that database is implemented using internal Java structures such as maps, or by an external application such as MS Access.

This has the advantage that the tiers can be independently developed (once their interface is agreed) and are resilient to changes in other tiers.

- *Modularity*: the system (or its subsystems) are divided up into modules, which are coherent groups of operations and data. A module may correspond to a class, or to a group of closely related classes. For example in the restaurant management system there could be a module that deals with the data structure of an **Order** (and defines it, as a class) and defines all operations on this, such as adding or deleting order items from an order. Most likely there will be supplementary classes such as **OrderItem** and **Variation** also in this module to manage data that is closely connected with orders.

- *Low coupling and high cohesion*: modules will depend on other modules, for example a GUI module may invoke operations from another module to make a request for information or to enter data into the application. The GUI module is therefore dependent on the module whose services it uses. A design exhibits low coupling if there are relatively few dependencies between modules: only the minimum needed to carry out the functions of the system should exist and a system should be organised so that most method calls occur within modules instead of between them. High cohesion means that the modules are internally strongly related, they are not random collections of data and operations but have a single clear meaning and purpose.

- *Coding standards, tools and notations such as UML*: where possible an application should be developed with a uniform set of coding standards, such as the placement and style of comments (i.e. should they be javadoc or ESC [34] comments, etc.), naming conventions for methods, classes and variables, the layout of classes (location of { and } particularly: this may seem trivial but using a single convention can make a program much easier to read and maintain), and the use of exceptions, etc.

Similarly with documentation using UML or other notations: a single set of notations should be used for the design of a single application, such as (in this book) UML notations plus dependency diagrams.

1.3   Notations for Software Design

In this section we define some useful notations which are widely used in object-oriented software design. These are: use cases, class diagrams, statecharts and interaction diagrams from UML [51], and operation specifications based on the usual notion of pre and post condition contracts of methods [39].

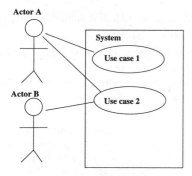

Figure 1.6: Simple Use Case Model

1.3.1   Use Cases

A use case model [26] describes (1) the system to be constructed, (2) the *actors* – representing a role played by a person or other entity that interacts with the system, and (3) the *use cases* – families of usage scenarios of the application, grouped into coherent cases of functionality. Figure 1.6 shows a generic use case diagram, where actor **A** participates in two use cases and actor **B** in one. Figure 1.7 gives the use cases for a share management system, where price changes are informed to the system from a stock exchange, and the trader using the system may receive alerts from it when share price changes pass some preset limits. The trader can also use the system to buy shares. Use cases may also have additional textual descriptions. A complete textual description of a use case includes:

1. *Start of the use case* – the trigger event: "the use case begins when *e* occurs".
2. *End of the use case* – the termination event: "when *f* occurs the use case terminates".

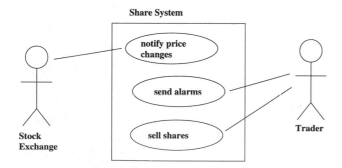

Figure 1.7: Share System Use Cases

3. *Interaction between the use case and the actors* – this identifies what activities should be inside the system and which outside.
4. *Exchanges of information* – what data items are passed between the system and the actors.
5. *Chronology and origin of information* – identifies when the system requires internal or external information and when it records it.
6. *Repetitions of behaviour.*
7. *Optional situations* – points where an actor or the system may choose different behaviours within the use case.

1.3.2   UML Class Diagrams

UML class diagrams define the data which an application deals with, as a set of entities (called classes) and relationships (called associations) between them. A simple UML class diagram, describing two entities and two relationships, is shown in Figure 1.8.

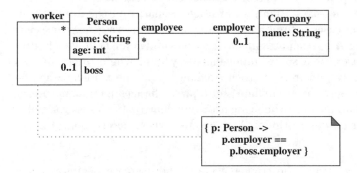

Figure 1.8: Simple UML Class Diagram

The basic elements of class diagrams are:

- *Classes*: displayed as rectangles with three components: name (using italic font for the name denotes an abstract class: one without direct instances); attributes; operations. Empty divisions are allowed.
- *Associations*: displayed as lines. Cardinality constraints are written on the end that they constrain: * means many (zero or more), the default (if no annotation is present) is 1.
  Associations can be "read" from one entity to another using the role names and cardinalities: each **Company** has *many* **employee**s (**Person**s); each **Person** has zero or one **employer** (a **Company**).
- *Constraints*: these give invariants which relate several elements in the diagram. They are written in *notes* presented as "dog-eared" boxes, and linked by dashed or dotted lines to the elements they relate. In the constraints we can use mathematical notation such as Z [36], *OCL* (Object Constraint Language [42]), or Java-like expressions.

For example, the constraint in Figure 1.8 relates the two associations in the diagram, and expresses that the boss of each employee works for the same company as themselves:

$$\forall \, \mathbf{p} : \mathbf{Person} \cdot \mathbf{p.employer} = \mathbf{p.boss.employer}$$

Attributes are written in the form **name** or **name: Type**, where **Type** is the type of the attribute **name**. Visibility constraints − (private), + (public) and # (protected) can also be used to annotate the attributes.

Operations are written in the form **op(params)** for operations that do not return a result, and **op(params): Type** for operations returning a result of type **Type**. **params** is a list of parameter declarations $\mathbf{p_1} : \mathbf{T_1}, \ldots, \mathbf{p_n} : \mathbf{T_n}$ which may be empty.

Associations can be directed: if there is an arrow at one end of an association it means that we need to navigate from the entity at the base of the arrowed association to the entity at the end with the arrowhead, in the design and implementation of the system. There is therefore a dependency in the direction of the arrow. For example if **Company** needed to call an operation on **Person** to change the boss of a person, there would need to be a navigation arrow from **Company** to **Person**. **Person** in such a situation would be called a *supplier* to **Company**, because it supplies operations and functionality to it. **Company** is called a *client* of **Person**. Figure 3.2 shows an example of a directed association.

Formal constraints are written between { and } brackets. Some formal constraints are pre-defined: **subset** (which asserts that the association at the source of the constraint arrow is a subset of that at the target); **exclusive or** (the two associations are mutually exclusive and exhaustive over the objects of one class). Informal constraints or comments are written without { and }.

Figure 1.9 gives some examples of constraints.

An association can express a strong form of binding/ownership between objects of one class and objects of another: this is termed *composition* and is represented by a filled diamond at the "whole" (owner) end. For example: a company owns a number of departments; the lifetime of each department is contained in that of the company. A composition association from **A** (whole) to **B** (part) should be:

1. transitive (a part of a part is also a part of the whole)
2. irreflexive (an object can't be a part of itself)
3. one-many (no sharing of parts between different wholes)
4. deletion propagating from **A** to **B**: deleting a whole deletes all its parts.

Parts are similar to attributes, hence the alternative notations of Figure 1.10.

Inheritance of class **A** by class **B** is represented by a line from **B** to **A** with an open-headed triangle at the **A** end (as with directed associations this helps to indicate that the entity **B** depends on entity **A** to an extent). **B** is called a *descendent* or *subclass* of **A**. If **A** represents an interface (a class which merely defines the signature of methods, not their implementations), then the

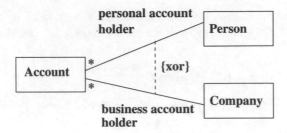

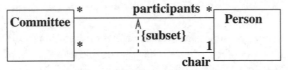

"Each account is either a personal or business account"

"The chair of a committee is always one of its participants"

Figure 1.9: Examples of Constraints

line may be dashed, indicating an *implements* or *realisation* relationship. Some predefined constraints on a family of descendants $\mathbf{D_1}, \ldots, \mathbf{D_n}$ of subclasses of a class $\mathbf{C}$ are (Figure 1.11):

- Overlapping – an object may belong to more than one subclass at the same time (e.g. **Student**, **Parent** as subclasses of **Person**).
- Disjoint – no object can belong to more than one subclass at the same time (e.g. **Square**, **Circle** as subclasses of **Shape**).
- Complete – all possible subclasses are present in the model.
- Incomplete – some additional subclasses may be added to the model.

Mathematically, disjoint subclasses satisfy:

$$\mathbf{Oak} \cap \mathbf{Elm} = \varnothing$$
$$\mathbf{Oak} \cap \mathbf{Birch} = \varnothing$$
$$\mathbf{Elm} \cap \mathbf{Birch} = \varnothing$$

where we use the class name to refer to the *set* of objects which currently exist in that class. So $\mathbf{Oak} \subseteq \mathbf{Tree}$, etc. Of course, these sets change over time (new trees grow, are entered in our database, etc.), but they are always pairwise disjoint. Overlapping subsets do not have such additional properties.

UML *object diagrams* use a variant of class diagram notation to show typical arrangements of objects (instances of classes) and links (pairs of objects, i.e. instances of associations). Objects are represented as rectangles, but their names are underlined and their class is also usually indicated: **wayne : Student**. Links are represented as lines between the objects they relate.

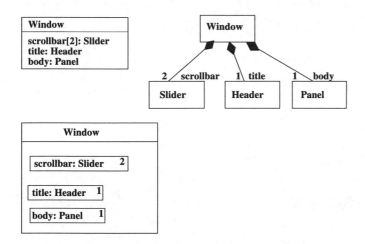

Figure 1.10: Alternative Notations for Composition

1.3.3 Statecharts

A class **C** may have a statechart describing the life history of its objects. Statecharts show all the possible states or "modes" of an object, as rounded boxes, connected by transition arrows: **Source** $\longrightarrow$ **Target**. States have names, and effectively represent (disjoint) subclasses of **C**. Transitions are labelled **event(params)[Condition]/action$_1$/action$_2$/.../action$_n$** where

- **event(params)** is the name of the event which triggers the transition (e.g. the name of the method which has been called on the object)
- **Condition** is a boolean test on **params** and attributes of **C**: if the condition is true when the trigger occurs then the transition is taken, otherwise it is not
- the **action$_i$** are actions, which can be assignments to attributes of **C** or method calls on its supplier objects
- states may contain activities, given by writing **do activity** in their box. These activities can include program code or specification of a maximum residence time **t** in the state: **wait(t)**.

A transition is only taken if the object is in the source state, and the trigger event happens with the condition true. The object then moves into the target state.

Example: Vending Machine Controller
The system to be controlled is a vending machine for drinks costing 15p each (this is an old example!). A customer can enter 5p and 10p coins only, the machine should dispense a drink once sufficient money has been entered, returning any excess change. The machine can also be refilled with 10 drink cans at any time.

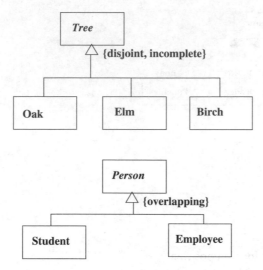

Figure 1.11: Examples of Inheritance Constraints

A class diagram of the system is shown in Figure 1.12, a statechart showing the required behaviour is given in Figure 1.13.

When we use statecharts to describe system behaviour:

- initial states are shown as the target of an arrow with no source. They represent the state the system is in when it starts up;
- trivial statecharts (e.g. **CashBox**) are usually not shown;
- a good design is one with clearly identified and separated responsibilities, and a pure client/supplier hierarchy: **Controller** sends commands to **Dispenser** and **CashBox**, no commands go in the opposite direction;
- Java notation is used for actions: we could alternatively use pseudocode or other kinds of notation: **stock := stock + 10**, **stock′ = stock + 10**, etc. provided we are consistent.

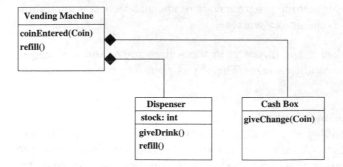

Figure 1.12: Class Diagram of Vending Machine System

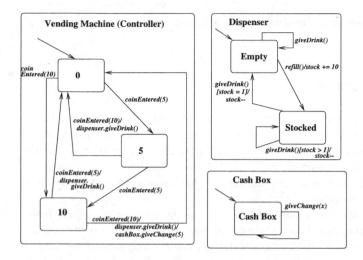

Figure 1.13: Statecharts of Vending Machine System

States may have other states nested within them, to describe further substates/subclasses (Figure 1.14).

Nested states have the properties:

- states can be nested in others (the inner states are analogous to subtypes of their enclosing state);
- an initial substate is given: a transition to the enclosing state actually goes to this substate (e.g. **testsFailed** goes to **Locate bug**);
- a transition whose source encloses other states implicitly represents a family of duplicate transitions from each enclosed state (unless these enclosed states have a more specific transition for the same event) to the target state: **giveUp** exits the whole debugging process and delivers code, regardless of its state ...;

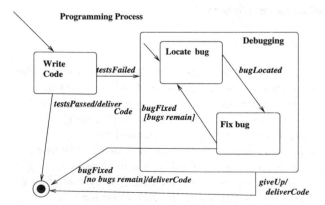

Figure 1.14: Example of Nested States

- a "bullseye" denotes the final state: the end of the life history of the object.

1.3.4 Interaction Diagrams

Interaction diagrams show examples (scenarios) of particular use cases. There are two forms of interaction diagram in UML: sequence and collaboration diagrams. *Sequence diagrams* emphasise timing and the history of objects. Sequence diagrams relate an interaction to statechart models of the classes involved, and can be used to give examples of the interactions involved in a particular use case scenario.

Collaboration diagrams in contrast emphasise the connection of the interaction to the class diagram. They show an interaction between objects as a set of messages sent from one object to another to achieve some required unit of functionality (e.g. a module operation execution). The diagrams consist of objects, links (instances of associations) and messages, they enhance UML object diagrams by showing explicitly what messages are passed between objects and the order of these messages. An example is given in Figure 1.15.

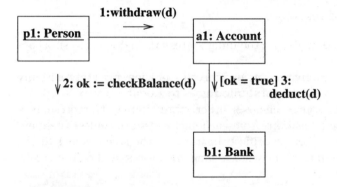

Figure 1.15: Example Collaboration Diagram

The features of collaboration diagrams are:

- Objects are represented by rectangles containing the name/identifier of the object, and the name of its class, all underlined: <u>object: Class</u>.
- Objects created during the operation execution are noted as {**new**}.
- Objects deleted during the execution are noted as {**destroyed**}.
- Objects both created and deleted are noted as {**transient**}.
- Links (instances of associations) often have arrows indicating their navigability direction: if a message is sent from object **a** of class **A** to object **b** of class **B** then **a** must have access to **b**, for example by means of an association from **A** to **B** which is navigable in that direction.

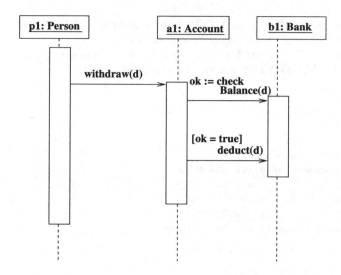

Figure 1.16: Example Sequence Diagram

- Messages are numbered consecutively starting at 1, nesting of messages is indicated by suffixes: e.g. 3.1.4 follows 3.1.3 within subprocedure 3.1.
- Conditions are given in square brackets: the associated message is only sent if the condition is true.

A sequence diagram corresponding to the collaboration diagram of Figure 1.15 is shown in Figure 1.16. In this diagram there are three objects, **p1**, **a1** and **b1**, which exist throughout the interaction (their lifelines are the vertical dashed lines). The vertical rectangles indicate an activity of the objects (usually an execution of a method on the object) and the duration of this activity. Arrows from one object lifeline to another represent messages, usually method invocations. Parameters, results and conditions are shown as in collaboration diagrams.

1.3.5   Method and Operation Specifications

These are used to describe abstractly what a method or operation does, without giving details of an algorithm or code. They consist of:

- *REQUIRES* – what conditions are needed on the input parameters and starting state to ensure that the operation or method executes without error, and to ensure that the EFFECTS are true at termination. The REQUIRES conditions are also called *preconditions* or "Assumes" conditions.
- *EFFECTS* – what is true of the outputs of the method/operation, and the final state at normal termination of the method/operation, if the precondition is true at its start. This is also called the *postcondition* of the method or operation.

Callers must ensure the precondition, and will then be guaranteed that the postcondition holds when the call of the operation completes.

If an operation parameter is modified within the method, we should explicitly declare it as such in a **MODIFIES** clause of the specification:

```
public class VectorUtil
{ // OVERVIEW: Provides useful utility procedures for
  // manipulating vectors

  public static void removeDups(Vector v)
  { // REQUIRES: All elements of v are not null
    // MODIFIES: v
    // EFFECTS: Removes all duplicate elements
    //          (under equals) from v. Order of
    //          remaining elements may be changed.
    if (v == null)
    { return; }
    for (int i = 0; i < v.size(); i++)
    { Object x = v.get(i);
      int j = i+1;
      // remove all duplicates of x from rest of v
      while (j < v.size())
      { if (x.equals(v.get(j)))
        { v.set(j, v.lastElement());
          v.remove(v.size() - 1);
        }
        else
        { j++; }
      }
    }
  }
}
```

Notice that we did not require **v != null** in the precondition, since this case is dealt with normally in the method body: it is valid to call the method with a null argument. Since **VectorUtil** is a utility package, it should work in the widest range of possible circumstances. Indeed it should ideally tolerate null elements inside the vector as well.

1.4 History and Background

The first design notations for software were *control flow graphs* showing the possible execution paths that could be taken through a piece of code, and *hierarchical structure charts*, which showed the decomposition of a program into procedures and sub-procedures. Popular in the 1960's and early 70's, these relatively primitive tools were gradually superseded by *structured analysis and design* [17]. Structured design was driven mainly by the needs of business information systems which required precise notations to describe their increasingly complex data and the designs of the databases that stored this data[3]. Structured design involved a number of interrelated notations, primarily: (i) Entity-relationship diagrams, describing the data of the system; (ii) data-flow diagrams, describing the processes of the system and how they communicated; (iii) state-transition diagrams, describing the life histories of entities and control aspects. By the mid 80s, versions of structured analysis and design adapted for engineering and real-time systems were developed, and a push towards the unification of the many different notations in use occurred, around the SSADM [23] notation and method, which could be regarded as a precursor of the unification efforts which led to UML. However this unification attempt was not very successful, and many variants of structured approaches are still in use, mainly for business information systems and for relational database design.

Object-oriented design methods began to appear during the 1980's. In some respects they were similar to the structured design notations, using class diagrams instead of entity-relationship diagrams (the concept of inheritance being the major difference between these), and interaction and sequence diagram notations instead of, or additional to, DFDs. By 1994 there were over 50 different OO modelling languages, and the so-called "method wars" between these were causing concerns in industry about the consequences of adopting methods which could soon become superseded and unsupported. At the same time the most popular methods, OMT, OOSE and Booch, were converging in terms of their modelling techniques, if not notationally. In 1994 work began on unifying the OMT and Booch methods into what became UML, with OOSE also integrated in 1995. From version 1.1 UML was endorsed by the Object Management Group (OMG) as a standard for object-oriented analysis and design, and it has now become the primary notation in this field.

Summary

This chapter has given an overview of what a software design is, and what its desirable properties should be. We've also defined UML and operation specification notations for documenting designs.

Exercises

1 Define a UML class diagram of the following system:

The system supports the playing of single or multiple-player board-based games. It is assumed that at most one piece may be on any board place (e.g. either an O or X is on each occupied position in a noughts and crosses game). A game consists of a board, a set of

---

[3]Engineering applications from this era often seemed to have been written without any use of design whatsoever. The first piece of software that directly caused loss of life, the Therac 25 control system, was a prime example of such practices [35].

players, and a history of moves in the game. A move is a set of single piece moves, represented by a start and end place and the piece to be moved (the start place may be null if a new piece is being added, the end may be null if a piece is being removed). A place is occupied by 0 or 1 pieces, and each piece has an owner (a player). A game board has an associated set of places describing the current situation in the game.

2   Define a UML statechart of the **Lift** class in the following system:

A lift system is designed to queue requests to serve floors in a first-come, first-served order. Initially the lift is idle and on the ground floor. If there are pending requests then the lift moves to the floor at the head of the request queue (a list of floors where the lift is requested to go). Having reached the floor, it stops, opens its doors, waits for 1 minute then closes its doors and goes to the next requested floor in the list. If there are no remaining requests it goes back to the ground floor.

3   Define a suitable REQUIRES/EFFECTS specification for the following method:

```
public int occurs(String s, Vector v)
{ int res = 0;
  for (int i = 0; i < v.size(); i++)
  { String ss = (String) v.get(i);
    if (ss.equals(s))
    { res++; }
  }
  return res;
}
```

4   Extend the **removeDups** method given above to deal with vectors which may have null items in them: the resulting vector should have only one null item in such a case.

5   Give a REQUIRES/EFFECTS specification for the **debit**(**x** : **int**) method of a deposit account in case study 2, given the restriction that the account should never have a negative balance.

Chapter 2

Design Techniques

This chapter describes some processes and techniques that can be used in software design, and specifically in object-oriented design. We illustrate the use of these techniques on the case study examples, and discuss management and design issues for software development projects.

2.1 Design Steps

The design process can be carried out in many ways, depending on the type of application and the requirements for rigour on the design. For instance, in a rigorous design process using UML, we may define several different design models (such as collaboration diagrams and statecharts) for each operation of each module, and check that one model of an operation is consistent with another. At an even more extreme level, in a formal design process such as B [32], the design models would be expressed in a formal design language, and mathematical proof used to compare one model with another.

In general the following steps in design can be distinguished, independent of notation and application:

1. *Architectural design*: define the global architecture of the system, as a set of major subsystems, and indicate the dependencies between them.
   For example, partitioning a system into a GUI, functional core, and data repository. The GUI depends on the core because it invokes operations of the core, and the core may depend on the GUI (if it invokes GUI operations to display the result of computations, for example). The core depends on the repository. There may be no other connections.
2. *Subsystem design*: decomposition of these global subsystems into smaller subsystems which each handle some well-defined subset of its responsibilities. This process continues until clearly identified *modules* emerge at the bottom of the subsystem hierarchy. A module typically consists of a single entity or group of closely related entities, and operations on instances of these entities. At this stage an initial module dependency

diagram can be drawn, although dependencies may change as we progress the design.

For example, in the restaurant system we can identify a subsystem of the functional core which deals with waiter operations only (creating, extending, modifying and completing orders, and bill payment). This in turn can be broken down into two subsystems, one for order processing and one for bill processing. These subsystems may be considered to be modules themselves or may possibly be broken down further.

3. *Module design*: define each of the modules, in terms of:

   (a) the data it encapsulates – e.g. a list of attributes and their types or structures;

   (b) the operations it provides (external services) – e.g. their names, input and output data, and specifications. This is called the *interface* of the module.

4. *Detailed design*: for each operation of the module, write down the list of tasks it has to carry out (not necessarily in the order they will be carried out, and not all executions of the method will carry out all these tasks, of course). From this we may identify *helper* methods which will be private methods of the module (perhaps belonging to auxiliary classes of the module) that carry out part of the functionality of the operation. This process is continued until an explicit and detailed definition of all data structures and operations within each module can be produced.

   In Java, for example, a module would usually consist of one main class whose public methods correspond to the module interface. There may be other subordinate classes within the module, especially if the data structures managed by the module are complex (e.g. a list whose members are lists: a helper class could be defined to represent the second-level lists).

In the following sections we describe these stages in more detail, and consider techniques which can be used at each of these stages. In each stage we aim to minimise dependencies between components, maximise the internal coherence of components, and maximise the flexibility and evolvability of the system. At the end of each stage we may carry out a *design review* to check that the decisions we have made are sensible ones and have met the desirable properties of a design such as low coupling, etc., and that the design supports the functional requirements of the system use cases.

2.2   Architectural Design

The global architecture of the system is something which is expected to be relatively stable over the lifetime of the system, and if it needs to change, this can (ideally) be achieved by replacing one or two subsystems without needing to change the others: a "pluggable" approach.

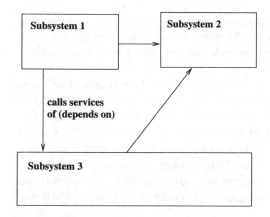

Figure 2.1: Architectural Design Notation

Thus we need to organise the architecture to minimise the effects of plausible anticipated or possible changes (this motto applies at all design levels in fact). For example, a system may be built originally to use a programmed file-based database, and may need to evolve to use an external commercial database. By separating the database management operations into a separate subsystem, this can be achieved without affecting any other subsystem: the subsystems which depended on the file database will invoke exactly the same operations, only the implementation of these operations will change.

The main notational tool we will use for architectural design is an architectural design diagram (see Figure 2.1) together with a textual list of the top-level subsystems and their responsibilities (including, for example, the list of use cases they are involved in implementing, and the list of services they provide). The detail of the subsystem descriptions may only become clear after later design steps. We can also list non-functional requirements that relate to the subsystem, e.g. a particular human-machine interface or database technology to be used. In an architectural design two subsystems **A** and **B** may be related either as:

1. Client and supplier – a one-directional dependency, for example where subsystem **A** depends on **B** but not vice-versa.
2. Peer-to-peer (P2P) – bi-directional dependency, **A** depending on **B** and **B** depending on **A**.

The client-supplier case is generally simpler and easier to test, analyse and develop separately, so is the preferred structure to adopt where possible.

2.2.1   Restaurant System Architectural Design

The architectural design description for the restaurant system consists of the design diagram (Figure 1.4) and the following subsystem descriptions:

GUI The user interface of the system, providing a means for the users of the system to: create an order; add items to an order, modify an order before it is confirmed; confirm an order as complete; create a bill for a terminated order, etc.

It participates in all use cases of the system. It is required to be as simple to use as possible, to be highly responsive and to be designed to minimise human error in high stress situations (particularly in the cases of waiter, bar and kitchen staff operations). Separate interfaces must be provided for the waiters, kitchen, bar, manager and stock controller. There must be security control so that waiters, kitchen staff, bar staff and stock controllers can only access the interface, data and operations specific to their role, whilst managers can access all interfaces, data and operations.

Functional core This performs all data processing and calculations involved in responding to updates and requests from the GUI, updating and retrieving data from the database, and generating data such as performance graphs for presentation in the GUI. It is involved in all use cases of the application.

Data repository This subsystem should store in a persistent manner all the data required by the application, as defined in the analysis class diagram, and provide operations to read and update this data. It is involved in all use cases of the application. It should not allow access to the stored data except via the interface of the restaurant management system application. It should run on a Windows 2000 platform.

2.3   Subsystem Design

The goal of subsystem design is to identify subsystems of existing subsystems of the system, dividing these in turn into subsystems until a level of basic modules is reached.

For example, in the restaurant system, subsystems of the GUI are the interfaces for the waiter, kitchen, bar, stock controller and manager. Subsystems of the functional core are groups of operations for these different users, plus other utility subsystems such as a graph production subsystem, or a communications subsystem (Figure 2.2). Documentation of this stage consists of the architecture diagrams plus textual descriptions of each subsystem. For example:

Waiter interface subsystem Provides a constructor to display the waiters interface on the waiters console. This interface provides a means for the waiter to initiate a new order for a specific table, to display the current order and other orders, to add items to an incomplete order, to complete an incomplete order, to confirm delivery of an order item, and to generate a bill for an order and record the payments for that bill. It also displays changes in the status of an ordered item.

It is involved in all use cases in which the waiter is an agent.

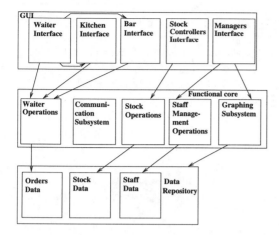

Figure 2.2: First Subsystem Architecture of Restaurant Management System

Waiter operations subsystem This supports operations

- **createOrder(t: Table, name: String)** and **createOrder(t: Table)** to construct a new order;

- operations **add(x: OrderItem)**, **addVariation(x: OrderItem, v: Variation)**, **removeVariation(x: OrderItem, v: Variation)** to modify the current order information,

- **completeOrder()** to complete the current order and initiate its sending to the kitchen and bar, and

- **confirmDelivery(x: Order, y: OrderItem)** to confirm delivery of item **y** from order **x**.

There are similar operations to view any named order and all orders, and to initiate and carry out bill processing.

Minimising dependencies at this design stage means reducing the number of dependencies between subsystems as much as possible. Design patterns may be applied as one means of doing this. For example we could initially consider having the **WaiterInterface** subsystem directly call the **BarInterface** and **KitchenInterface** subsystems when a **completeOrder** operation occurs. However, in practice a direct call may not be possible (these interfaces may reside on different computers) and a more systematic approach is to use the observer and proxy patterns with the order data being the observable (an entity whose changes need to be communicated to other entities) and the different interfaces being the observers, via a local proxy object and the communications subsystem. This is shown in Figure 2.3. Alternatively, coordination contracts could be used. In this case the contract would play the intermediary role between the interface modules and the waiter operation module, and its implementation would use the communication subsystem to carry out remote coordination.

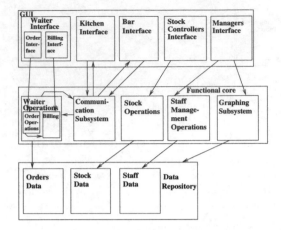

Figure 2.3: Enhanced Subsystem Architecture of Restaurant System

Figure 2.3 also shows a further stage of subsystem decomposition, where the components at the bottom of the subsystem hierarchy for the waiter are all basic modules. For example we have separated billing from order processing at both the interface and core functional levels. Splitting modules in this way is one approach for increasing flexibility: both order processing and billing may become more complex in future revisions of the system (e.g. billing over the internet may become necessary), so to make such changes easier we should reduce the amount of code in the module that is the subject of the change. In this case we achieve this by moving out all code for the billing use cases into its own module, and likewise for order processing use cases not involving billing.

2.4   Module Design

The goal of module design is to identify in detail the interface of individual modules, i.e. the set of operations/methods they offer as services to other modules, and the signatures of these operations. The data managed by the modules is also identified, i.e. the set of classes from the analysis model that it involves.

This stage starts with the outline module descriptions produced as an end result of subsystem design, which list the use cases the module is involved in satisfying, and indicate some of the operations it must provide. More operations may be discovered as a result of module and detailed design once we get into the process of identifying exactly how the module will carry out its operations.

In the case of the restaurant system, the billing module will manage the **Bill**, **BillItem** and **Payment** entities from the analysis model (Figure 1.2) and will provide operations:

- **generateBill(x : Order) : Bill**,
- **add(p : Payment)**,

- **setDiscount**(**amount** : int),
- **printBill**(),
- **completeBill**().

In terms of reducing dependencies between modules, we could examine the operations invoked from one module to another, and ask if they are really necessary. Similarly we can try to minimise the amount of information passed from one module to another. In the above case a complete **Order** object is passed from the orders module to the billing module via the **generateBill** operation. This can be reduced, since the bill is only likely to depend on the list **items** of order items which have actually been prepared. So the interface could be changed to: **generateBill(items: List): Bill**. This also reduces the amount of knowledge the billing module needs to know about the order items, for example, it will not need to access their status.

Similarly, the visibility scope of the **Payment** class could be restricted to be internal to **Billing** by replacing the **add** operation by **addPayment(method: String, amount: int)**.

Maximising flexibility on the other hand may imply enlarging the interface of a module to meet the potential requirements of future versions of the system. For example adding a **remove(p: Payment)** operation to the **Billing** module to cancel a payment already entered in the bill. Passing a complete **Order** to **generateBill** would make sense if one anticipated change is to handle pre-booked reservations over the internet, for example, and *Order* was extended to indicate if it is an order for a pre-booked reservation, and what deposit has been paid, to be taken off the bill total.

Having decided on the interface and outline functionality of each operation, we can provide specifications for the operations:

```
module: Billing
data: Bill, BillItem, Payment
use cases: Bill order, complete payment
operations:
  generateBill(items: List): Bill
  // REQUIRES: items is non-null and consists of
  //   those order items (all non-null) to be
  //   added to the bill
  // EFFECTS: returns a Bill which has a BillItem
  //   for each input order item, with cost
  //   set to item price plus the prices of any
  //   variations. The Bill total is the sum of
  //   the BillItem costs. The Bill is displayed
  //   on the billing interface and set as the
  //   current bill. Its date is set by
  //   the Bill constructor to the current date.

  add(p: Payment)
  // REQUIRES: current bill is non-null,
  //   and p non-null.
```

```
// EFFECTS: Adds p as a payment for
//    the current bill.
//    The display is updated to add this to
//    the list of payments, and to show the
//    amount still remaining to be paid.

setDiscount(amount: int)
// REQUIRES: current bill is non-null.
// EFFECTS: Removes amount from total of current
//    bill and shows this in list of discounts on
//    the bill display interface.

printBill()
// REQUIRES: current bill is non-null
// EFFECTS: displays printing menu on
//    billing interface and carries out
//    printing of all bill items, discounts
//    and total on the selected printer.

completeBill()
// REQUIRES: current bill is non-null
// EFFECTS: sets verified flag to true in the
//    current bill, adds this bill to archive of
//    bills and sets current bill to null.
```

2.5   Detailed Design

The goal of detailed design is to define in detail the data structures encapsulated by each module, and the classes and operations of the module.

This involves listing the tasks which each operation needs to carry out, and defining subordinate operations where necessary to perform parts of the tasks. In turn, this may lead to a separation of the module data into separate classes within the module, with helper operations becoming methods of the appropriate classes. A class is also defined to host the module operations themselves, and the data that remains in this module. The operations should be defined in enough detail (e.g. by using pseudocode) that all invoked operations are explicitly listed and therefore all module dependencies are completely identified at the end of this stage.

For example, for the **generateBill(items: List): Bill** operation of **Billing**, we could have the list of tasks:

- Check that the input **items** is non-null: if not, terminate with an alert to the user that something has gone wrong (or return a zero bill if we want to hide the error from the user).
- Set running total to 0.
- For each element of **items**, get the price, and the list of variations/extras for that element.

- Add the item price and prices of all its extras together, and create a **BillItem** with name equal to the item name, and cost equal to the sum. Add the sum to the running total.
- When all items have been processed, create a **Bill** with the accumulated total cost and set of **BillItem**s, and return this as the result of the operation. Display the bill on the billing interface.

This description is fairly explicit and algorithmic already, this may not be the case for all operations. In particular we have been able to directly use the analysis model entities here, without needing to define additional structures.

The corresponding pseudocode for this operation is:

```
public Bill generateBill(List items)
// REQUIRES: items is non-null and consists of
//    those order items (all non-null) to be
//    added to the bill
// EFFECTS: returns Bill which has a BillItem
//    for each input order item, with cost set
//    to item price plus the prices of any
//    variations. The Bill total is the sum of
//    the BillItem costs. The Bill is displayed
//    on the billing interface and set as the
//    current bill. Its date is set by
//    the Bill constructor to the current date.
{ int total = 0;
  List billItems = new Vector();

  if (items == null) // defensive programming
  { currentBill = new Bill(total,billItems);
    // display currentBill on billing interface
    return currentBill;
  }
  for (int i = 0; i < items.size(); i++)
  { OrderItem oi = (OrderItem) items.get(i);
    // if (oi == null) raise exception?
    String nme = oi.getName();
    int pr = oi.getPrice();
    List extras = oi.getVariations();
    int extrasTotal = 0;
    for (int j = 0; j < extras.size(); j++)
    { Variation ex = (Variation) extras.get(j);
      extrasTotal += ex.getPrice();
    }
    pr += extrasTotal;
    BillItem bi = new BillItem(nme,pr);
    billItems.add(bi);
    total += pr;
  }
  currentBill = new Bill(total,billItems);
  // display on billing interface
```

```
    return currentBill;
  }
```

This is 90% of the way to implementation, to polish things off we would need to consider how to handle exceptions such as null **Variation** objects, i.e. whether to raise a Java exception, simply give a warning message to the user and return some sensible result, or silently tolerate the error. Also we need to decide how the call to the (external) billing interface module is to be managed, i.e. whether it should be the responsibility of this module or a module that calls it. The latter choice is probably better as it is consistent with a client-supplier structure (the GUI depends on the billing module but not vice-versa) and is also consistent with our planned architecture (Figure 2.3). Modules will usually become packages in Java, in order to limit the visibility of their classes to only those other modules which explicitly import the package (i.e. which depend on the module). Defensive programming has been used to deal with the case of a **null** items list above.

For GUI components, detailed design involves user interface design, which we cover in Chapter 3. Database components require database design, also described in Chapter 3.

Guidelines for reducing dependencies in design

- Minimise the knowledge that one module has about another.
- Minimise the knowledge that a subsystem has about the internal details of the modules within it.
- Remove knowledge of how modules interact and how they are connected from the modules themselves.
- Minimise the number of methods provided by a module to others (its *public* methods).
- Use library classes (or preferably interfaces) and primitive types as parameter types for public methods of a module, if types from application modules must be used they should be interfaces and not classes.
- Optimise the conceptual and functional cohesion of modules: they should manage one entity type or a closely related set of entity types, a single resource, etc.
- Review and refactor designs at regular intervals during development to maintain design quality.

2.6   Generic Design Techniques

The following techniques can be used at any of the design stages described above.

- *Factoring* – splitting an element into subelements, such as splitting a large method/operation into "helper" methods, and identifying commonalities between different methods which can be factored into separate units.
- *Generalisation* – identification of how subsystems, modules, methods or classes can be generalised to be more widely useful within an application and more able to support changes or extensions in the application requirements.
- *Specification/layered design* – replacing a dependence of a client on a particular supplier by a dependence on a generalised interface, together with a specification of behaviour that clients can expect from this interface.

2.6.1 Factoring

At the architecture and subsystem design stages, this technique can be applied to identify additional subsystems which provide common services used in several other subsystems. For example, in the restaurant management system, both the staff management and order management subsystems are likely to need facilities for constructing graphs: performance graphs of staff in the first case, and graphs of numbers of customers per day in a week, or time period in a day, in the second. Rather than duplicating these facilities in the separate subsystems, we could define a **Graphing** subsystem which provides operations to define, display and print graphs:

Graphing Supports the definition of graphs as maps from labels (e.g. a staff name, or day of week) to values (integers, typically). Operations include:

- **createGraph(name : String)**,
- **addColumn(x : Label, y : Value)**,
- **removeColumn(x : Label)**,
- **setColumn(x : Label, y : Value)**,
- **printGraph(name : String)**,
- **displayGraph(name : String)**, etc.

In some cases suitable subsystems may already be available as library packages. For graph construction and display in Java, for example, the JSci [28] package can be used.

In module and detailed design factoring can be applied to split the data of a module into classes, and to split the operations of the module into suboperations and methods of classes in the module. The template method design pattern (Chapter 4) is particularly relevant as a factoring approach: it splits a method into a part which is independent of what subclass of the class is being used, and parts which may vary between subclasses. An example in the restaurant system is the completion of an order: each item in the order responds to this event by changing its status to **IN_PREPARATION**, but drinks and dishes behave differently in that their information is sent to different displays: bar and kitchen, respectively.

Factoring is also important in reducing the size and complexity of methods. If a method **m** involves a series of subtasks **P** followed by subtasks **Q**, etc., then it may make sense for **P** and **Q** to be placed in private methods of the class defining **m**, and these methods are then invoked from **m**. This reduces the depth of nesting in **P** and **Q** by at least one compared to **m**, but it is only worth doing if these are themselves significant pieces of code doing a coherent task, (e.g. if they are also subtasks of other current or prospective methods) and if **P** and **Q** do not use many local variables of **m** (which would have to be passed in and out of the new methods).

Finally, factoring can be used to package up a piece of code that appears in several places as a method in its own right. For example essentially the same code may occur in different places just working with different variables (e.g. `z = x*x + y*y` in one place, `s = p*p + q*q` in another). Replace the separate occurrences of this calculation by calls to a method for it: `z = sumSquares(x,y);` and `s = sumSquares(p,q);`. The advantage of this is that if the calculation needs to change, only the method needs to be modified, instead of all separate occurrences of the calculation.

The reverse of factoring (combining or absorbing) may also be necessary to rationalise a program structure, for example to replace a trivial class by an attribute.

2.6.2   Generalisation

At the architecture and subsystem design level an example of generalisation would be extending a subsystem to provide services which are natural additions to the operations already required, and which are likely to be required in future enhancements of the system.

For example, in the case of a one-many relation such as the **Order-OrderItem** association in the restaurant system, we may have a requirement for an operation to add a pair (x, y) to this relation but no requirement to remove a pair. In many cases removal would be a meaningful and potentially useful additional operation, so could be added to the interface of the subsystem that manages the relation. In the restaurant case, we could extend the **OrderOperations** subsystem with an operation to permit removal of an item from the order prior to completion of the order, and to cancel an item from a completed order if the item had not been delivered. If the item had not yet been prepared, then its preparation is cancelled and the status of the item in the order is set to **CANCELLED**. Otherwise the item is not delivered but is still charged for. Another generalisation would be to allow an order to be re-opened to add new items; these would then be notified separately to the bar or kitchen.

Data models may be generalised to deal with a wider range of possible situations than are handled by the current system, for example by generalising a 1-many association to be many-many.

2.6.3 Specification/Layered Design

Java, while a major advance on many previous programming languages, does not provide a formal way of recording pre and post-conditions of methods, or class invariants, other than as comments[1]. Where possible, REQUIRES and EFFECTS specifications should be added to methods, and invariants of class data or loops expressed. For example an essential property in most cases of list processing is the statement of what types of element are in the list:

```
public class Company
{ private List employees = new Vector();  // of Person objects
```

We can ensure that such an invariant is always true of **employees** by only permitting an addition **employees.add(obj)** of an element to this list if **obj instanceof Person** holds. Similarly we can express the type of object pairs in a **Map**:

```
public class UserDatabase
{ private Map users = new HashMap();  // String --> User
```

or that a variable recording someone's age can never be negative:

```
public class Person
{ private int age = 0;  // age >= 0 always
```

The keyword **final** in Java can be used to prevent redefinition of an element, particularly assignments to a variable:

```
public boolean equals(final Object obj)
{ ... }
```

indicates that the method will not assign to the **obj** variable in its text. However an updater method of **obj** may still be applied to it.

Layered design means that one module should only depend on the *specifications* of other modules (and specifications of classes in other modules, if absolutely necessary) not on their implementation details. Consider the common case in Java where we have a **Gui** class which depends on some back-end class:

```
public class Gui
{ private BackEnd b = new BackEnd();
   ...
}

public class BackEnd
{
...
}
```

---

[1] Although the *assert* statement can be used to check that these properties hold at expected places in the code during development

This makes **Gui** specific to exactly this one **BackEnd** class. Instead we can decouple the GUI from the back end by making **Gui** depend on an interface instead:

```
public class Gui
{ private BackEndInterface b;
  ...
  public void setBackEnd(BackEndInterface be)
  { b = be; }
  ...
}

public interface BackEndInterface
{ ...
  signatures and specifications of methods
  of back end used by Gui
}

public class BackEnd implements BackEndInterface
{
...
}
```

This allows any class that implements **BackEndInterface** to be used by the **Gui** class.

In the restaurant system, since the orders module invokes the **generateBill** operation of the billing module, it should only rely on the specification of this operation explicitly stated in its REQUIRES/EFFECTS clause and not on any other behaviour which may happen to be provided by the current implementation (e.g. that the order of items on the bill is the same as that in the order list) but which are not guaranteed by future revisions.

The benefit of this is that module implementations can change without requiring that the clients of that module also change, provided that the changes do not invalidate the specifications.

Similarly with data types: we should where possible use (in Java) *interface types* from other modules instead of actual classes within those modules, for the same reason that changes to the implementations of these types will not require changes in their users, provided the interface specification is still met.

For example, we used **List** as the input type to **generateBill(items: List)** instead of some concrete type such as **Vector**, therefore making this operation independent of any change in the representation of the list (an **ArrayList** being used in place of **Vector**, for instance).

The concept of layered design is illustrated in Figure 2.4. The implementation of component 1 depends only on the specification of component 2, not its implementation, and so forth. Each layer is a subsystem with an externally accessible part (its interface) and a private part (its implementation). An architecture of layers is called *closed* if each layer depends directly only on an immediate lower layer, and there are no "shortcuts" to layers beneath this one. It is *open* if a subsystem may use any lower layer. Generally open architectures

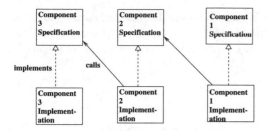

Figure 2.4: Layered Design

are more efficient (there is reduced nesting of method calls) but increase the number of dependencies between components.

Each layer may be divided up into *partitions*: modules or subsystems without dependencies on each other. For example in the restaurant system the stock operations subsystem and staff management subsystems are partitions of the functional core subsystem.

2.7   Software Development Projects

Any software development project, whether it is a five-person student project or fifty-person commercial effort, requires *project management* and *team management*. Project management includes the planning of the development into tasks and subtasks, with specified deadlines and deliverables to be produced by these deadlines. Team management includes the assignment of tasks and responsibilities to people, ensuring people have appropriate skills for their tasks, ensuring there is a fair balance of tasks between people, and that there is adequate communication and collaboration within the team, etc.

Software design plays a part in both these aspects:

- By splitting a system into subsystems and sub-subsystems with different responsibilities and minimal interdependencies, we have good candidates for separate pieces of work which can be given to different individuals. This division of work between different people could be based on "horizontal slicing" – one person develops the entire GUI, another develops the database, etc., or "vertical slicing" – one person develops the GUI, functional core and database interface for one part of the system (e.g. the waiters use cases in the restaurant system), another person does the same for another part (e.g. the stock managers use cases). The latter is probably more interesting for the people involved, and produces prototypes which are more informative as guides to how the complete system will behave, but requires greater co-operation in the team to ensure consistency and integratability of their work, and a wider range of skills in each individual.
- The design also identifies units of work in the development whose development time can be estimated and whose (time) dependencies are well-

known: if subsystem **A** depends on subsystem **B** then they can nonetheless usually be developed and partly tested in parallel, but for integration testing of **A** to take place, **B** must already be developed and unit tested.

2.7.1   General Project Activities

The following activities are necessary in most software projects:

Requirements Elicitation: Extract the actual requirements from the customer and other "stakeholders" in the system, such as end users, to determine what the real expectations and scope of the system are. Techniques such as *task analysis* [18] can help in this activity. For some student projects this stage can be reduced to questioning the person who set the problem, to clear up any lack of clarity in the requirements. More substantial systems will actually be intended for some real users so it is important to get the views of these potential users in identifying necessary capabilities and properties of the system. The case of the London ambulance service dispatch software [44] shows what can happen if the needs of users are not considered.

   Use cases are one means of documenting requirements – or the analysts understanding of what the requirements are supposed to be – and a means by which stakeholders can check that this understanding is actually correct.

Background Research: Identification of relevant theoretical and technical knowledge that is or could be needed to develop the system, such as information on the capabilities of different web servers that could be used in the application, or space and time requirements of alternative data structures and algorithms.

Planning: Allocating tasks and roles to people within the project team; estimating time required for tasks, identifying intermediate deliverables, milestones and integration and review points; setting up project infrastructure such as a code repository, definitive documentation file, standards and conventions (e.g. common coding or naming styles to be used in the project, common makefile structures, etc.). A project timeline diagram such as a Gantt chart[2] should be produced.

Analysis: Formalising the problem as it is understood so far: express the requirements in use cases and natural language, classifying them as "mandatory" (must be in the developed system), "desirable" and "possible". Write use cases for all the system scenarios, and define an analysis class diagram of entities and relationships to describe the problem.

Design: Identifying the system architecture, subsystems, modules, communication and coordination structures, etc., writing pseudocode for methods.

---

[2]Gantt charts were invented in 1917 and have become a very common project planning notation. Different tasks are shown down the vertical axis, and time is shown on the horizontal axis. However they do not show task dependencies, unlike PERT charts.

Implementation: Coding of modules in a specific programming language.

Testing: Module, unit and integration testing of the parts of the system, validation of the completed system.

Review: Evaluation of the progress of the project and identification of problems and risks, both technical (e.g. failure of a prototype GUI to satisfy the customers requirements) and other (e.g. a programmer being much less productive than expected).

In a waterfall development life-cycle, these activities would be performed in a specific order, once in the history of the project. In an iterative model such as the Rational Unified Process [47], parts of each of these activities could be performed in separate iterations, usually with a review and (re)planning phase at the end of each cycle.

The Rational Unified Process defines four phases in the development process:

1. *Inception*: definition of project scope, evaluation of feasibility and general estimates of project cost and time. A prototype may be built to assist in checking if the project is viable.
2. *Elaboration*: requirements analysis and definition of architectural design.
3. *Construction*: design and implementation through the development of prototypes, culminating in the delivery of a beta version of the system to user sites.
4. *Transition*: correction of defects detected by users, rollout of new versions until a production version is reached.

The major milestones in development are the progression from one phase to another: the decision to commit to the project in the **Inception → Elaboration** progression, an accepted first revision of the requirements document in the **Elaboration → Construction** progression, and a beta release in the **Construction → Transition** progression.

The activities defined above can be directly mapped into the RUP phases, and more generally into most development lifecycles from the classical waterfall model [46] to Boehm's spiral model [10].

A development method which takes the opposite approach to RUP, in the sense that it tries to minimise the complexity of following a particular development process, is the *Extreme Programming (XP)* method of [8]. Instead of prescribing a rigid set of development steps and milestones, it emphasises a number of *practices*:

- *Realistic planning*: customers make the business decisions about a system, the developers make the technical decisions. Review and revise plans as necessary.
- *Small releases*: release a useful system quickly, and release updates at frequent intervals.
- *Metaphor*: all programmers should share an understanding of the purpose and global strategy of the system being developed.

- *Simplicity*: design everything to be as simple as possible instead of preparing for future complexity.
- *Testing*: both customers and programmers write tests. The system should be frequently tested.
- *Refactoring*: the system should be restructured whenever necessary to improve the code and eliminate duplication.
- *Pair programming*: put programmers together in pairs, each pair writes code on the same computer.
- *Collective ownership*: all programmers have permission to change any code as necessary.
- *Continuous integration*: whenever a task is completed, build a complete system containing this part and test it.
- *40-hour week*: don't work extreme hours to try to compensate for planning errors.
- *On-site customer*: an actual customer of the system should be available at all times.
- *Coding standards*: follow standards for self-documenting code.

XP seems to be very popular with students doing projects, since it is a lightweight development approach avoiding the time-consuming documentation and structures of other methods. However, while many of the above practices are clearly desirable, others, such as collective ownership, could be a recipe for chaos. A more disciplined version is to make a single programmer responsible for modifications to a given module, but to have this module reviewed by other programmers, particularly those whose modules depend on or are depended on by this module (the "one writer, many readers" protocol).

We illustrate several of the XP practices in the design case study of Appendix B. In our design approach, refactoring is triggered by design reviews of each design decision and in particular by the need to minimise the interfaces of modules and to minimise their dependencies.

2.7.2   Example Student Individual Project: Restaurant System

A typical development process for a 24 week individual project could be as follows:

Requirements Elicitation: involved interviews with restaurant staff to identify what tasks needed computer assistance, in addition to discussion with supervisor. (Duration: 1 week.)

Background Research and Planning: identifying existing systems and their functionality, and what technology could be used in the final system. Planning the project using a Gantt chart. (1 week.)

Analysis: development of class diagram and use cases. (1 week.)

Design: architectural design of complete system, and subsystem, module and detailed design of the stock operations subsystem. Implementation and testing of this subsystem. (6 weeks.)

Using this subsystem as a template, subsystem, module and detailed design and implementation of the other parts of the restaurant system were carried out. (12 weeks.)

Documentation: writing a final report and user manual. (3 weeks.)

This is a two iteration development life-cycle, with the first iteration being used to test out GUI, core processing and database design ideas on the stock operations subsystem, the second being used to "roll out" the templates devised for this subsystem for the others.

2.7.3   Example Student Group Project: Noughts and Crosses

This system is an example of a simple software project, probably suitable for a three-person team taking a few weeks to develop, part-time, as coursework for a Java design or programming course. The task is to develop an interactive system which plays noughts and crosses (tic tac toe) against the user, with a choice of strategies and with replay of previous games. This can be seen as a trial of a software architecture for much more sophisticated game-playing systems, e.g. for Diplomacy or chess.

The project activities for this system, assuming a programming team of three people, **A**, **B** and **C**, and a completion deadline of 4 weeks, might work out as follows:

Requirements Elicitation: Involves obtaining more detail on the problem and the allowed flexibility in devising a solution: any GUI was considered acceptable provided it is easy to use for people with limited computer experience, clearly represents the state of the game at all times, and is simple. Several strategies were required for the software game player: including at least (i) random guessing of a move in response to the users move; (ii) "optimal" positioning of a piece to block a successful completion by the user of a line of three squares whenever possible.

Background Research: Consists of internet and library searches for information on solutions to similar "artificial intelligence" problems. For example, a search for "chess playing programs" under yahoo.com yields a set of links to papers and course material on techniques such as the *minimax* and *alpha-beta* board game strategies [13].

Analysis: Use case diagrams are constructed (Figure 2.5) as is an abstract class diagram (Figure 2.6). For the **make move** use case we have the textual description:

1. *Starting event* – user selects place they wish to occupy.

2. *Ending event* – system displays its response move, or indicates that the user move was invalid, and if the game has been won or drawn.

3. *Interaction* – the system changes the screen display of the board to show the users move if it was a valid move, then computes and displays the response move if there is a possible move, and identifies

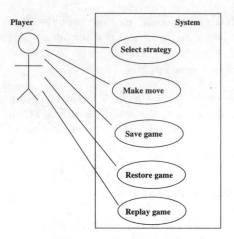

Figure 2.5: Use Cases of Noughts and Crosses Game

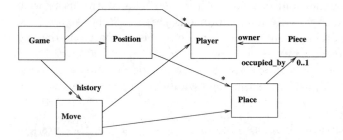

Figure 2.6: Class Diagram of Noughts and Crosses Game

if the game has been won or drawn, and displays a message to this effect if this is the case.

4. *Exchanges of information* – the user enters the place for their move by clicking the mouse on the representation of this place on the board display. The system shows message dialogs to communicate that the move was invalid or that the game has been won/drawn, and for valid moves it shows the user and response moves by updating the board display.

Design: The architectural design of this system is shown in Figure 2.7. The subsystems are: (i) GUI; (ii) algorithms for responding to user moves and determining the computers move and when a game is stalemated or won; (iii) storing and restoring of games from files.

Notice that to support decomposition of the system into tasks for separate programmers, it is only necessary to pursue design to this architectural level, at which point the interfaces which a programmer has to implement (for their own subsystems) or which they can rely on (for the subsystems which their own subsystems use) have been made pre-

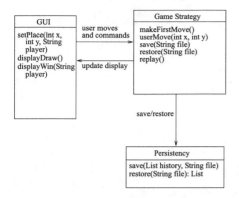

Figure 2.7: Architectural Design of Noughts and Crosses Game

cise. Further design progression within subsystems could be made the responsibility of the developers of those subsystems, although this carries a risk in divergent approaches being used and other incompatibilities and wasteful redundancies arising.

In this case the GUI subsystem must supply methods **displayWin (String player)** and **displayDraw()** to display suitable messages depending on the outcome of the game, and **setPlace(int x, int y, String player)** to put a cross or circle in the (x, y) coordinate of the board.

The game strategy subsystem must provide methods **makeFirstMove()** (to ask the software to make the first move), **userMove(int x, int y)** to record and respond to the user player attempting to move to location (x, y), **save(String file)** and **restore(String file)** to save and restore the history and current state of the game from a given file, and **setStrategy(int n)**, where $n = 0$ is the default random strategy and $n = 1$ the optimal one. **replay()** instructs the system to play back, with one move per second, the moves of the current game in the order they occurred. (The subsystem will also need internal methods to change player, to select a response move and to determine if the game has been won or drawn, but these methods are private to it and don't need to be part of its visible interface.)

The persistency subsystem needs to provide methods **save(List l, String file)** to save the history l of moves (individual **Place/Player** objects, not entire **Position/Board** objects) and **List restore(String file)** to reconstruct these.

The decision was made to do all programming in Java.

Planning: Programmer A was seen as the strongest programmer and also volunteered to be the project leader and to take on tasks (ii)a – random strategy and (ii)b – optimal strategy. Programmer B was given the task (i) of GUI development, since they had some experience of this. Programmer C was given task (iii) and was also made responsible for writing the project documentation and managing the project code repository, where

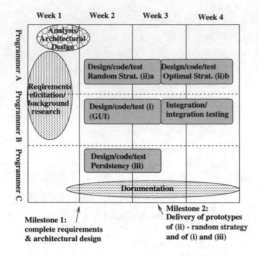

Figure 2.8: Gantt Chart of Project

stable versions of the subsystems would be held during development. The Gantt chart of Figure 2.8 was produced.

Implementation: This proceeded according to plan for tasks (i) and (iii), but (ii) proved too difficult for programmer A, and only the "random guess" strategy for the system was completed in time. There were also integration problems between (ii) and (iii) due to misunderstandings about the form in which the history of a game was to be recorded (a history of individual moves, versus a sequence of complete layouts of the 3×3 board).

Testing: There was insufficient time for integration testing, or for unit testing of task (ii). As a result incorrect behaviour occurred in the project demonstration: it was possible for a user to select a square to move into that was already occupied, and the system would respond as if the user had moved into an unoccupied square.

2.7.4 Problems and Pitfalls

Some of the most common reasons that projects fail are:

Teamwork – or rather, lack of it! Individuals or subgroups within a project may have a different understanding of what their tasks/roles are than the rest of the team, resulting in a failure to produce some parts of the system. A team may split into mutually hostile subgroups, and if one group is in control of resources, it may "constructively dismiss" the other group from the project by starving it of work. These issues should be resolved by the project leader, who should be non-partisan in such conflicts. If no solution is found at this level, higher levels of line management (in industry) or the projects academic supervisors (in college) will have to become involved. People within a team may agree to carry out a task and then fail to do this, or simply disappear and never turn up to team meetings. Problems in co-operation can also be caused by the team leader themselves, if they are also (or think they are) the strongest programmer, and insist on taking over as much as the programming as possible, with the result of a loss of productivity for the team as a whole, and increased risks of overruns/failure to complete the project. Mistaken allocations of tasks to people without the necessary knowledge or skills is also a problem that should be resolved within the project but often requires external intervention. In a student project, avoid allocating all the documentation and administration duties to the person who is seen as the weakest programmer: this person should also be given some programming tasks otherwise they will not get any practise in programming.

Chaotic Planning – no serious attempt to estimate the time of tasks, to take account of their dependencies and scheduling, or failure to identify and manage risks to the project such as unavailability of essential technology or expertise.

Lack of Control – inadequate reviews of work at intermediate stages of the project, resulting in divergence of the system from the requirements and from good design techniques, failure to recognise or respond to other problems during the development.

Lack of Resources – unavailability of tools or personnel needed for the project, because of secondment of key people to other projects, internal company politics, priority of other more immediately commercial projects over the current project, etc.

Warning signs of a bad design

It's a good indication that things are going wrong with the way a program is structured if any of the following start to happen:

- **Convoluted control structures**: For example, methods with deeply nested sets of conditionals (two is the limit of easy comprehension) with complicated conditions. This is a sign of inadequate factoring of methods and lack of rationalisation of cases.

- **Complex interconnections and dependencies between objects**: where an object **a** has a link to an object **b** which has a link back to **a**, or more complicated "spider's web" structures of objects, etc. This suggests inadequate partitioning of responsibilities between objects.

- **Method engorgement**: huge methods spanning several pages of printout (50 lines is a reasonable maximum limit for most methods). This indicates inadequate factoring of methods and possibly incomplete partitioning into subsystems and modules.

> - **Large numbers of parameters in methods**: more than 5 or 6 parameters indicates the method combines too many functionalities or is located in the wrong class (some parameters should be attributes instead).
>
> - **Excessive class sizes**: classes with more than 20 to 30 methods indicate insufficient partitioning of the system into modules, or inappropriate factoring of methods. There may be several methods which are very similar in their functionality, these should be replaced by a more general method possibly with extra parameters. For example, searching for a line of three "X" characters in a noughts and crosses game, and searching for a line of three "O" characters are both special cases of searching for a line of a given character.
>
> - **Unstable code**: having to search through many classes and methods to see if a proposed change to one class will be "safe" and not affect existing functionality in unexpected ways.

Summary

In this chapter we have defined the different stages in the design process which can be useful to apply to systems: module and detailed design may be sufficient for the simplest programs, consisting of a few classes and methods, but for substantial systems all stages will typically be applied. Techniques for organising and reorganising code between and within modules have also been described, and we have given examples of the use of design techniques and project planning within software development projects.

Exercises

1   Give a subsystem description for the **Stock Operations** subsystem of the restaurant management system.

2   Give a module specification for the accounts system defined in Chapter 1, assuming that **Customer** is the main class of this module and **Account** is auxiliary.

3   Apply factoring of methods to the following problem:

Write a program which prints out the truth tables of the && and || operators, i.e. given two boolean variables

```
boolean a;
boolean b;
```

print out each of the four possible combinations of values of **a** and

b, followed on the same line by the values of **a** && **b** and **a** || **b**. For example, the header and one line would be:

```
a     b    a && b    a || b
-------------------------------
....
false true  false     true
....
....
```

4 Apply factoring of methods to the following problem:

Write a program which plots the distribution of marks in an exam (marks are between 0 and 100). The program should print 21 vertical columns: 1 column for the marks between 0 and 4, another for the marks from 5 to 9, etc. The height of each column is the number of students who have a mark in the range. Use X characters to draw the columns. Marks are entered by the user one after another, entry is terminated by a mark outside the range 0..100. For example user input

```
33
15
0
7
6
10
-1
```

would produce the histogram:

```
 X
XXXX  X
```

Chapter 3

Software Architectures

This chapter describes different kinds of software architecture which may be used during architectural design. It also covers detailed design techniques for two common architectural layers: GUIs and databases, using Java Swing and JDBC.

3.1 Architectures

The *architecture* of a piece of software is the overall organisation of the program code into separate subparts, responsible for different aspects of functionality. For example, many traditional application programs can be separated into a "Front end" responsible for dealing with interaction with users (i.e. the GUI), and a "Back end" responsible for storing data and performing calculations in response to user requests (relayed via the GUI). Many web-based applications can similarly be separated into a client-side GUI (HTML pages and forms) and server-side processing (data access/computations and generation of web pages).

The benefit of such separation is that these separate parts can be developed, tested and modified relatively independently, and may be deployed on separate hardware.

3.1.1 Front End/Back End Architectures

These are also called "two tier" or client/server architectures and define separate subsystems/tiers for the GUI and the rest of the application. To illustrate this architecture we will use a simple example of an address book application supporting storage of (name, address, phone no.) records, which has a menu-based Java Swing interface providing options to enter records and search for records with particular values for the name and other fields.

The back end of this system consists of classes **DataItem** representing individual records as objects, and **Database** which contains a list of all of these records. The front end consists of a Swing **JFrame** with menus for

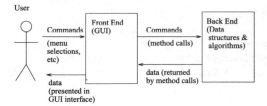

Figure 3.1: Typical Front End/Back End Architecture

commands such as **Add** and **Search**, and listener methods to detect and act on user selections of these menus. It also presents the results of commands (e.g. in a **JTextArea** or **JList**); see Figure 3.1.

DataItem could be defined by:

```
public class DataItem    /* Holds individual entries */
{ private String name = "";
  private String address = "";
  private String phone = "";

  public DataItem(String nme, String addr, String ph)
  { name = nme;
    address = addr;
    phone = ph;
  }

  public String getName()
  { return name; }

  public String getAddress()
  { return address; }

  public String getPhone()
  { return phone; }

  public String toString()
  { return name + " @ " + address + " Ph: " + phone; }
}
```

The **Database** class which encapsulates the stored data is:

```
import java.util.ArrayList;
import java.util.List;

public class Database
{ private List entries = new ArrayList();  /* of DataItem */

  public void addEntry(String nme, String addr, String ph)
  { DataItem di = new DataItem(nme,addr,ph);
    entries.add(di);
  }
```

```
public List searchByName(String nme)
{ List res = new ArrayList();
  for (int i = 0; i < entries.size(); i++)
  { DataItem di = (DataItem) entries.get(i);
    if (di.getName().equals(nme))  /* Exact match */
    { res.add(di); }
  }
  return res;
}


/* Similarly for searchByAddress, etc. */
}
```

The structure of this subsystem is given in Figure 3.2.

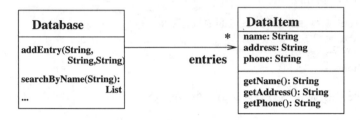

Figure 3.2: UML Diagram of Back End

This is the complete back end. It can be tested before a GUI is written, by putting test scenarios in the **main** method of **Database**:

```
public static void main(String[] args)
{ Database db = new Database();
  db.addEntry("Alex Ferguson",
      "MUFC, Old Trafford, Manchester",
      "+44 (0)161 000 2343");
  db.addEntry("Ann Widdecombe",
      "House of Commons, Westminster", "");
  List res = db.searchByName("Alex Ferguson");
  System.out.println(res);
}
```

The **Database** class is the only interface between the front and back ends: the GUI calls **database.searchByName(n)** with the string parameter **n** entered by the user, and gets back a list of matching data items. Therefore the GUI and back end can be modified relatively independently: we could change the back end to use **Map** or **Vector** data structures instead of **ArrayList**, or to interface to an Access database, etc., without any change to the GUI. Likewise we can change the GUI to use a "direct manipulation" style of interaction where the user flicks through a visual simulation of the address book instead of using menus. (In this case we may need to extend the interface of the back end, e.g. to provide a **getNext** method, but 90% of the code change will be in the GUI).

3.1.2 Three Tier Architectures

Many commercial applications use a *Three Tier Architecture*, in which the separate levels are: (1) GUI; (2) Business logic; (3) Data repository (Figure 3.3). This separates the subparts of the program into separate areas of responsibility: the GUI deals with user interaction, the business logic performs computations, and the data repository stores persistent data (i.e. the data is stored permanently from one execution of the program to another). Any of the tiers may use pre-existing code or external applications, commercial off-the-shelf products (COTS), etc. to carry out all or part of their functionality, this will be the usual case with the database tier in particular.

In the following sections we will describe some techniques for design of the GUI and database elements of such three tier architectures.

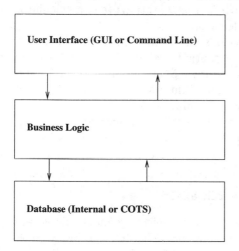

Figure 3.3: Three Tier Architecture

3.2 User Interface Design

A quality user interface can make the difference between an application being useful and being commercially successful, or being used only with great difficulty and reluctance, and commercially failing. Some general principles for user interface design were formulated by Mandel [37]:

- place the user in control;
- reduce the users memory load;
- make the interface consistent.

Corollaries of these principles include that we should reduce complexity in interaction; use conventional layouts and interaction styles in preference to experimental styles, e.g. use standard icons for standard functions; take account of how the system will be actually used, etc. Some examples where one or more of these principles are violated for actual systems are given in [49].

The interface and interaction between a user and a system should enable the user to carry out all the required functions of the system. The interaction should be as simple as possible and should support the "natural" sequence of actions a user performs to carry out a required function: to find out what this sequence should be, the developer needs to look at the required use case scenarios described in analysis models, and design the menus and command/display layout of the interface so that users can go easily from one action to another which follows it in a scenario.

The interface should also be easy to use in the general sense of being "ergonomically sound", i.e. not requiring greater mental/physical effort to use than necessary, and it should be consistent with user expectations (e.g. a calculator interface should usually "look like" a calculator).

We will introduce GUI design using the address book program, then consider more complex interfaces from the restaurant system. The address book has operations for the creation of name/address/phone number records, and searching of entries: in principle we could do all interaction with the program using strings on the command line. This is certainly simple, but it is far from being a natural interface for people to use with such an application.

A typical scenario for this application is:

```
Select the search by name option;
Enter name to search for;
If unsuccessful, amend name and search again.
```

This is much easier for the user to carry out by selecting menu items and entering text into dialogs than with the command line. It is probably more familiar as well, because it is similar to filling out HTML forms on a web page.

3.2.1   Why User Interface Design Matters

The quality of the GUI of a system has a major impact on how usable it is, and hence for commercial applications, on its success. If the user interface of an application is poor, the system will not get used (unless the developer has a monopoly of the market and can set de-facto standards that everyone has to follow). It may be difficult for the programmer to spot problems with an interface (since they are probably not a typical user, and they know how the application works), so there may need to be a GUI design review by a user interface expert and/or consultation with users to check that the interface is usable. Prototyping is a useful way to test out possible GUI designs, and in practice there may be many iterations before the interface looks and behaves in a satisfactory way. Sometimes a poor interface for a system has contributed to loss of life or high risk: for example the Therac 25 radiation therapy system [35], the London Ambulance Service despatch software [44], the A300 autopilot which was involved in the 1994 Nagoya crash [31], and the Three Mile Island incident [35] are all cases where lives could have been or were lost due to misleading information provided by the system, or mismatches between the information and interaction that the users needed or expected and that which the system provided.

3.2.2   Menu-based Interfaces

GUI design in Java 2 is carried out using the Swing classes **JFrame**, **JPanel**, **JMenu**, **JDialog**, **JList**, **Icon**, etc., contained in the `javax.swing` package and subpackages. One standard style of interface which is simple to construct is the "MS Office" style, where frames have pull-down menus and pop-up dialogs. This can be used for many different kinds of application, e.g. text editors, diagram editors, database search/display, graph plotting, etc. It may seem a bit dull but 90% of your users will be familiar with it! Figure 3.4 shows the typical structure of this type of GUI.

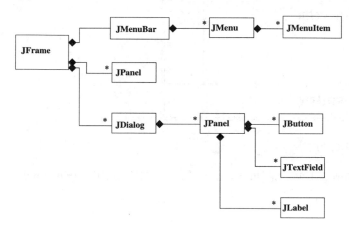

Figure 3.4: Standard Menu-based GUI Architecture using Java Swing

The building blocks of this are:

- **JFrame** – the main window of the application, other GUI elements are directly or indirectly components of this. By default a **JFrame** has a *border* layout with five subareas in which GUI elements can be placed: **NORTH**, **SOUTH**, **EAST**, **CENTER** and **WEST** regions (Figure 3.5). A border layout is used for a container such as a **JFrame** whenever the container holds heterogeneous (mixed) parts which should have fixed positions relative to each other. This is typically the case for the top level GUI of an application, and also for dialogs;
- **JPanel** – the area where the main visual information of the application is presented (e.g. graphs, charts, text files) or edited (e.g. diagram elements, text editing). By default a **JPanel** has a *flow* layout in which subelements

are displayed in successive rows in left-to-right order like text in a line-wrapping editor. Flow layouts are useful when we want to display several items of the same kind, such as a row of buttons;

- **JMenuBar** – this houses menus and menu items to select a particular system operation/function;
- **JDialog** – these may be needed to enter/edit detailed information as part of a system operation. They have a border layout and typically consist of subelements such as **JLabel**s to name fields, **JTextField**s for entry of string or numeric data, and **JButton**s to select options.

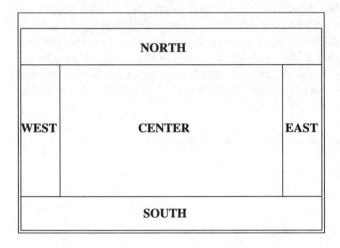

Figure 3.5: Border Layout

In the case of the address book application, a simple GUI in this style can be defined as:

```
import javax.swing.*;
import javax.swing.event.*;
import java.awt.*;
import java.awt.event.*;

public class AddressBook extends JFrame
implements ActionListener
{ // the area for text output:
  private JTextArea abPanel;

  public AddressBook()
  { addWindowListener(      /* Kills application when */
    new WindowAdapter()  /* window is closed.      */
    { public void windowClosing(WindowEvent e)
      { System.exit(0); }
    });

  // Add regular components to the window,
```

```
// using default BorderLayout of JFrame:
  Container contentPane = getContentPane();

// Create the text area:
  abPanel = new JTextArea();
// Put the text area in a scroll pane:
  JScrollPane scroller =
    new JScrollPane(abPanel,
          JScrollPane.VERTICAL_SCROLLBAR_ALWAYS,
          JScrollPane.HORIZONTAL_SCROLLBAR_ALWAYS);
  scroller.setPreferredSize(new Dimension(600,600));
  contentPane.add(scroller, BorderLayout.CENTER);


// Construct the menu system:
  JMenuBar menuBar = new JMenuBar();
  setJMenuBar(menuBar);   /* Adds menu bar to frame */

// Build the first menu:
  JMenu fileMenu = new JMenu("File");
  menuBar.add(fileMenu);

// A group of JMenuItems under the "File" option:
  addMenuItem("Open",fileMenu);
  addMenuItem("Save",fileMenu);
  addMenuItem("Close",fileMenu);
// A separator:
  fileMenu.addSeparator();
  addMenuItem("Exit",fileMenu);

// Build second menu in the menu bar:
  JMenu createMenu = new JMenu("Create");
  menuBar.add(createMenu);

// A group of JMenuItems for Create:
  addMenuItem("Entry",createMenu);

/* Search menu: */
  JMenu searchMenu = new JMenu("Search");
  menuBar.add(searchMenu);

  addMenuItem("Search by Name",searchMenu);
  addMenuItem("Search by Address",searchMenu);
  addMenuItem("Search by Phone no.",searchMenu);
}   /* End of constructor */

private void addMenuItem(String label, JMenu m)
/* Convenience method to create and add new
   menu item to menu m. */
{ JMenuItem mi = new JMenuItem(label);
  mi.addActionListener(this);
```

```
      m.add(mi);
    }

    public void actionPerformed(ActionEvent e)
    /* Respond to menu item selections by user: */
    { Object eventSource = e.getSource();
      if (eventSource instanceof JMenuItem)
      { String label = (String) e.getActionCommand();
        if (label.equals("Exit"))
        { System.out.println("Exit Address Book Tool");
          dispose();
          System.exit(0);
        }
        else if (label.equals("Open"))
        { System.out.println("Opening a database"); }
        else if (label.equals("Save"))
        { System.out.println("Saving database"); }
        else if (label.equals("Close"))
        { System.out.println("Closing database"); }
        else if (label.equals("Entry"))
        { System.out.println("Creating a new database entry"); }
        else if (label.equals("Search by Name"))
        { System.out.println("Searching for item by name"); }
        else if (label.equals("Search by Address"))
        { System.out.println("Searching for item by address"); }
        else if (label.equals("Search by Phone no."))
        { System.out.println("Searching for item by phone no."); }
      }
    }

    public static void main(String[] args)
    { AddressBook window = new AddressBook();
      window.setTitle("Address Book Tool");
      window.setSize(500, 400);
      window.setVisible(true);
    }
}
```

This gives an interface as shown in Figure 3.6.

The corresponding structure of GUI Java Swing objects is shown in Figure 3.7.

This is a bare interface with no functionality behind it: selecting the menu options leads to stub code executing. This enables us to test it independently of the back end. Design review includes checking that the most popular operations (e.g. create, search by name) are easily accessible menu items, not buried deep in the menu structure; that operations often done successively are easily reached from each other, etc. The interface code given above is a standard template, it can simply be copied and adapted for a new application.

The **extends JFrame implements ActionListener** in the **Address-**

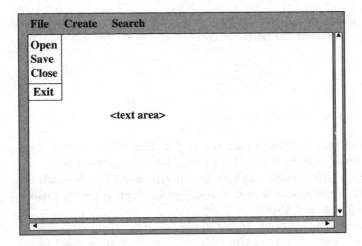

Figure 3.6: Prototype GUI of Address Book

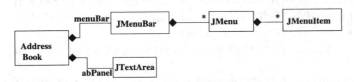

Figure 3.7: Structure of Address Book GUI

Book header indicates that the application main window is a **JFrame** and it is an **ActionListener**, i.e. it can respond to events such as menu items being selected by the user. These menu items must register **this** as a listener to their events by the command **mi.addActionListener(this)**. Then, whenever the user selects a menu item, the method **actionPerformed(e)** is invoked on **this**, i.e. the **AddressBook** object, with **e** representing the selection event. Figure 3.8 shows the pattern of communication in such an interface.

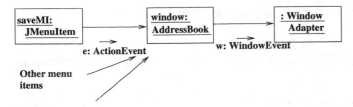

Figure 3.8: Event Sources and Targets

    public void actionPerformed(ActionEvent e) is the **ActionListener** method. The **ActionEvent e** carries information about the component that has been clicked on: **Object eventSource = e.getSource();** and the command that was selected: **label = (String) e.getActionCommand();**

Having got this information, we can then call appropriate methods of the back end to actually carry out the selected command.

3.2.3   Menu Design

Some general guidelines for menu design are:

- Each menu item should relate to a required function of the system (e.g. **Search by name**), ideally there should be a 1-1 correspondence.
- Group related menu items into a single pull-down menu, e.g. **Search by name**, **Search by address** as items in a general **Search** menu, **Open**, **Save** as menu items in a **File** menu, etc.
- Group by "level" of operations, for example the **File** menu contains all operations that concern/act on the database as a whole instead of on individual entries.
- Group items which are frequently done one after another, e.g. **Search** may often be followed by **Edit**, so put these on the same menu if they are at the same level (entry versus file operation).
- If there is a natural order of operations in each group, list menu items in this order.
- If operation **op** *must not* be performed until a preceding operation **f** has been executed, we can invoke **opMI.setEnabled(false)** to initially disable this menu item. It can be enabled again in **f**'s code by **opMI.setEnabled(true)**.
- Physically separate the menu items for operations with drastically different effects (e.g. **Create** and **Delete**) to avoid user errors in selection having major consequences.

In the GUI the menus are created as follows. Creation of an empty menubar is done by:

```
JMenuBar menuBar = new JMenuBar();
```

Attachment of the menu bar to the frame is carried out by the call:

```
setJMenuBar(menuBar);
```

The following statements create the first (leftmost) menu, and add it to the menubar:

```
JMenu fileMenu = new JMenu("File");
menuBar.add(fileMenu);
```

The menu items for the "File" menu are then created, for each we register the frame as being a listener for their events (i.e. the action of being pressed) and add the menu item to **fileMenu**. This is done by calling the **addMenuItem** method, which has the same effect as the expanded code:

```
JMenuItem openMI = new JMenuItem("Open");
openMI.addActionListener(this);
fileMenu.add(openMI);

JMenuItem saveMI = new JMenuItem("Save");
saveMI.addActionListener(this);
fileMenu.add(saveMI);

JMenuItem closeMI = new JMenuItem("Close");
closeMI.addActionListener(this);
fileMenu.add(closeMI);
```

After these we put a separator in, because the "Exit" option is a different kind of operation to the Open/Save/Close group:

```
fileMenu.addSeparator();

JMenuItem exitMI = new JMenuItem("Exit");
exitMI.addActionListener(this);
fileMenu.add(exitMI);
```

Many other kinds of menu item are possible, e.g. **JCheckBoxMenuItem**, **JRadioButtonMenuItem** and menu items containing submenus. Figure 3.9 shows the layout of the menus in this system.

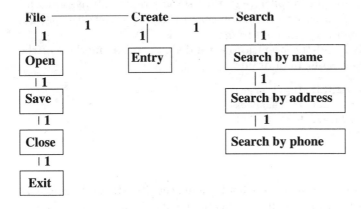

Figure 3.9: Address Book GUI Menu Structure

Putting the **Create** options second makes sense from the viewpoint of the history of actions we will perform on entries (we must first open a database before creating entries for it), but **Search** may be used more frequently than **Create** so could be considered in the second position instead. We could add up the cost of edges from the top left hand corner to get a rough estimate of the time/cognitive steps required to select a command. We can group a subset of related menu items within a menu by using separators (e.g. print commands in MS Word).

Notice that menus themselves are not registered with the frame as sources of events, only the listed menu items are, since only these correspond to user commands.

Some extra (optional) bits in the **AddressBook** constructor are:

```
addWindowListener(new WindowAdapter()
  { public void windowClosing(WindowEvent e)
    { System.exit(0); }
  });
```

This defines an anonymous *inner class* and an anonymous object of it to be an action listener for events (window events) that the frame itself generates, in particular the **windowClosing** event.

To define a scrollbar around the text area we write:

```
abPanel = new JTextArea();

JScrollPane scroller =
  new JScrollPane(abPanel,
    JScrollPane.VERTICAL_SCROLLBAR_ALWAYS,
    JScrollPane.HORIZONTAL_SCROLLBAR_ALWAYS);
scroller.setPreferredSize(new Dimension(600,600));
contentPane.add(scroller, BorderLayout.CENTER);
```

This defines options for the scroller (e.g. that scrollbars are always present, etc.) and adds the text area into the scroller and the scroller into the central area of the border layout of the main frame.

To create the GUI and the application, we define a **main** method of the **JFrame** subclass that is our main frame:

```
public static void main(String[] args)
{ AddressBook window = new AddressBook();
  window.setTitle("Address Book Tool");
  window.setSize(500, 400);
  window.setVisible(true);
}
```

This creates an instance of the address book frame, sets its title and initial size and makes it visible (and makes all its subcomponents visible as well). Notice that its size is smaller than that of the scrollpane.

3.2.4   Toolbars, Mnemonics and Accelerators

Menu Mnemonics

A **Mnemonic** is a means to navigate through a menu hierarchy using the keyboard. On Java menus and menu items mnemonics can be defined by:

```
JMenu fileMenu = new JMenu("File");
fileMenu.setMnemonic(KeyEvent.VK_F);  // set F key as mnemonic
                                      // for File menu
```

```
JMenuItem newMI = new JMenuItem("New");
newMI.setMnemonic(KeyEvent.VK_N);
...
```

Pressing `Alt-F` when the application is running makes the **<u>F</u>ile** menu appear. Pressing `N` then chooses the **<u>N</u>ew** option from this menu.

The presence of a mnemonic for a menu or menu item is shown by underlining the first occurrence of the mnemonic character in the name of the menu/menu items (so mnemonics are not much use for icon-only menu items!). This visibility helps a user to learn and use it.

Keyboard Accelerators

An **Accelerator** is a means to select a command using the keyboard, *without* going through the menus. On menu items an accelerator can be defined by:

```
newMI.setAccelerator(KeyStroke.getKeyStroke(
                KeyEvent.VK_N, ActionEvent.ALT_MASK));
...
```

Pressing `Alt-N` when the application is running then chooses the **New** option. Accelerators are shown by text after the label of a menu item: `Alt+N` in the above case. Only leaf menu items, without submenus, can have accelerators: because only these correspond to application commands.

Mnemonics and accelerators:

- Can enhance usability: mnemonics speed up navigation (but the user has to become familiar with which keys to use, so these should be chosen to be as obvious and memorable as possible: "S" for save, "C" for close, "X" or "Q" for exit/quit, etc.).
- Accelerators speed up selection even further, but require greater familiarity with the correspondence of keys to commands, since the user won't be able to see what menu item they are selecting. Again we should make the accelerator keys as obvious as possible, but these must not clash with menu mnemonics.

Toolbars

Like keyboard accelerators, toolbars provide a way of invoking a command without going through the menu structure. The toolbar of an application sits below the menubar and contains buttons (with icons or with icons and a textual name) which correspond to the most frequently used menu items from the menus. The following guidelines should be followed if possible:

- Place the commands from the menus onto the toolbar in the same order (but horizontally) that these options occurred in the menus. Use separators to separate option groups from different menus.
- We may just use icons (e.g. standard "Open" or "Save" icons) instead of names for commands.

- Put the most frequently used commands onto the toolbar, e.g. New, Open, Save, Print, Entry and Search in the Address Book.

Figure 3.10 shows a possible layout for the address book toolbar, where **New** and **Print** options have been added to the file menu.

Figure 3.10: Toolbar Design for Address Book

Swing provides the **JToolBar** class to allow toolbars to be created. The main methods of **JToolBar** are:

- **JToolBar()** – creates a new tool bar. It has **Box** layout by default.
- **Component add(Component comp)** – adds **comp** to the end of the toolbar.
- **void addSeparator()** – adds a vertical separator at the end of the toolbar.
- **JButton add(Action act)** – adds an action to the toolbar, generates a **JButton** for it and adds this.
- **void setFloatable(boolean b)** – floatability means that the toolbar can be dragged out to a separate window or an unused region of the **BorderLayout** of the enclosing frame. This is true by default.

Here is the code to add a toolbar to the address book:

```
public class AddressBook extends JFrame
implements ActionListener
{ ...
  private Icon openIcon = new ImageIcon("open.gif");
  private Icon newIcon = new ImageIcon("new.gif");
  private Icon saveIcon = new ImageIcon("save.gif");
  private JToolBar toolBar;

  public AddressBook()
  { ...
    toolBar = new JToolBar();
    Action newAct =
      new AbstractAction("New",newIcon)
      { public void actionPerformed(ActionEvent e)
        { System.out.println("New selected"); }
      };

    Action openAct =
      new AbstractAction("Open",openIcon)
      { public void actionPerformed(ActionEvent e)
        { System.out.println("Open selected"); }
      };
```

```
Action saveAct =
  new AbstractAction("Save",saveIcon)
  { public void actionPerformed(ActionEvent e)
    { System.out.println("Save selected"); }
  };

toolBar.add(newAct);
toolBar.add(openAct);
toolBar.add(saveAct);

contentPane.add(toolBar, BorderLayout.NORTH);
```

An **Action** represents the single command which may be selected either by clicking on the toolbar button, or selecting the menu item. A name and an icon can be provided, in the above example we have used standard "open", "save" and "new" icons.

3.2.5   Dialog Design

Swing provides a number of simple dialog types via the **JOptionPane** and related classes. However for more complex data entry involving several fields of different kinds, we need to define our own custom dialogs. The following guidelines can be used to ensure consistency across the dialogs of an application and enhance their usability:

- Use a single dialog per group of related data items which are entered together (e.g. fields of the same class). Don't have unrelated data items on the same dialog, or split related data items across several dialogs (exceptions are wizard specifications, successive installation steps, very large classes, etc.).
- Explain each entry field with an attached label or title with a concise description of the field.
- List key/more significant attributes above others.
- Un-modifiable fields should have **setEditable(false)** invoked on them.

The Swing classes used for dialog fields should correspond to the type of data they are being used to create/edit:

- String/integer data – entered via a **JTextField** component;
- boolean data – single **JCheckBox** or paired **JRadioButtons**;
- element of a fixed, small, enumerated set – multiple **JRadioButtons** defined as elements of the same **ButtonGroup** (so that they are mutually exclusive) or a **JComboBox** (for a large enumerated set) or a **JList** (for large or dynamic sets of choices);
- multiple selection from a small and fixed enumerated set – multiple **JCheckBox**es, one for each element of the set;

- multiple selection from large or dynamic sets – **JList**;
- tabular data – **JTable**.

Entry fields of the same kind can be placed in the same panel within a dialog.

For example, consider an entry creation dialog for the address book application. In this case we have three string fields: name, address and phone. A layout where we have a single panel containing three entry fields of the form **JLabel: JTextField** arranged in a single column would seem to make sense. The fields should be ordered vertically with **name** first, then **address**, etc., and aligned with each other. A separate panel at the bottom of the dialog can contain the **Ok** and **Cancel** buttons.

Here is the main class of the creation dialog, as a subclass of **JDialog**:

```java
import java.awt.*;
import java.awt.event.*;
import javax.swing.*;
import javax.swing.event.*;

import javax.swing.border.*;
import java.util.EventObject;
import java.io.*;

public class EntryCreateDialog extends JDialog
{ private JPanel bottom; /* Contains buttons: */
  private JButton okButton, cancelButton;

/* The panel with the entry fields: */
  private CreateDialogPanel dialogPanel;

  private String defaultName = "";    // Data set by main
  private String defaultAddress = ""; // application GUI
  private String defaultPhone = "";

  private String newName;    // Data retrieved from the
  private String newAddress; // text fields.
  private String newPhone;

  public EntryCreateDialog(JFrame owner)
  { /* Create modal JDialog with owner the main frame,
       and title "Create entry": */
    super(owner, "Create entry", true);

  /* Create the subcomponents: */
    okButton = new JButton("Ok");
    cancelButton = new JButton("Cancel");
  /* Instance of nested class for event handling: */
    ButtonHandler bHandler = new ButtonHandler();
    okButton.addActionListener(bHandler);
    cancelButton.addActionListener(bHandler);
```

```
bottom = new JPanel();
bottom.add(okButton);      // Uses the implicit flow
bottom.add(cancelButton);  // layout of JPanel.

bottom.setBorder(
    BorderFactory.createEtchedBorder());  // a fancy border
dialogPanel = new CreateDialogPanel();
/* Dialog is given a Border Layout: */
getContentPane().setLayout(new BorderLayout());
/* Put button panel at base of dialog, field
   panel in center: */
getContentPane().add(bottom,
                    BorderLayout.SOUTH);
getContentPane().add(dialogPanel,
                    BorderLayout.CENTER);
}
```

This sets up the structure of the main dialog panel, consisting of a bottom (button) panel with the buttons and a top (field entry) panel (Figure 3.11). This structure follows the normal order of viewing:

- Top of dialog – contains the dialog title. We could also put a menubar here if different variants or pages of the dialog need to be selected;
- main body of dialog – contains a panel with the fields to fill in;
- bottom – contains confirmation, cancellation, etc. buttons.

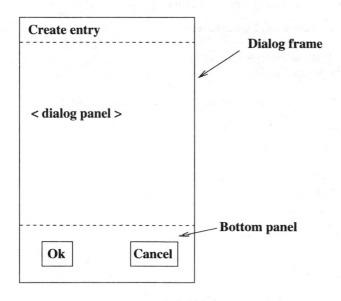

Figure 3.11: Structure of Entry Creation Dialog

A collection of operations for transfer of data between the dialog and the main program are defined in **EntryCreateDialog**:

```
public void setOldFields(String nme, String addr, String ph)
{ defaultName = nme;
  defaultAddress = addr;
  defaultPhone = ph;
  dialogPanel.setOldFields(nme,addr,ph);
}

public void setFields(String nme, String addr, String ph)
{ newName = nme;
  newAddress = addr;
  newPhone = ph;
}

public String getName()
{ return newName; }

public String getAddress()
{ return newAddress; }

public String getPhone()
{ return newPhone; }
```

setOldFields() is used by the GUI to enter initial values into the dialog fields
(this is not used for the create entry operation, but could be used if we were
editing a selected entry). **getName()** is used by the GUI to read new entered
values from the dialog. **setFields()** is used by the nested button event handler
to record what the user has written in the text fields:

```
class ButtonHandler implements ActionListener
{ public void actionPerformed(ActionEvent ev)
  { JButton button = (JButton) ev.getSource();
    String label = button.getText();

    if ("Ok".equals(label))  // Transfer data to EntryCreateDialog
    { setFields(dialogPanel.getName(),
                dialogPanel.getAddress(),
                dialogPanel.getPhone());
    }
    else /* Cancel pressed */
    { setFields(null,null,null); }

    dialogPanel.reset();
    setVisible(false);  // close dialog.
  }
 } /* End of nested class */
} /* End of EntryCreateDialog */
```

The field entry panel is:

```
public class CreateDialogPanel extends JPanel
{ private JLabel nameLabel;
  private JTextField nameField;
```

```
private JLabel addressLabel;
private JTextField addressField;
private JLabel phoneLabel;
private JTextField phoneField;

public CreateDialogPanel()
{ /* Create subcomponents: */
  nameLabel = new JLabel("Name:");
  nameField = new JTextField();
  addressLabel = new JLabel("Address:");
  addressField = new JTextField();
  phoneLabel = new JLabel("Phone:");
  phoneField = new JTextField();
  setBorder(
    BorderFactory.createTitledBorder("Create fields"));

  add(nameLabel);        // Add the subcomponents in
  add(nameField);        // the order they should appear
  add(addressLabel);     // in the dialog.
  add(addressField);
  add(phoneLabel);
  add(phoneField);
}

public void setOldFields(String nme, String addr,
                         String ph)
{ nameField.setText(nme);
  addressField.setText(addr);
  phoneField.setText(ph);
}

public Dimension getPreferredSize()
{ return new Dimension(400,120); }

public Dimension getMinimumSize()
{ return new Dimension(400,120); }

/* Customised layout method, fixed positions
   (xstart,ystart,width,height) for components: */
public void doLayout()
{ nameLabel.setBounds(10,10,90,30);
  nameField.setBounds(100,15,270,20);
  addressLabel.setBounds(10,40,90,30);
  addressField.setBounds(100,45,270,20);
  phoneLabel.setBounds(10,70,90,30);
  phoneField.setBounds(100,75,270,20);
}

public void reset()
{ nameField.setText("");
```

```
    addressField.setText("");
    phoneField.setText("");
}

public String getName()
{ return nameField.getText(); }

public String getAddress()
{ return addressField.getText(); }

public String getPhone()
{ return phoneField.getText(); }
}
```

Each attribute entry label and field is laid out as shown in Figure 3.12. This layout ensures that successive labels and text fields are exactly the same width and therefore that they are vertically aligned. The completed dialog is shown in Figure 3.13.

Figure 3.12: Custom Layout of Dialog Fields

Create entry

┌─ **Create fields** ─────────────────┐

Name: [   ]

Address: [   ]

Phone: [   ]

Ok   **Cancel**

Figure 3.13: Completed Entry Dialog

The steps in the dialog entry processing are:

1. User presses "OK" after filling in the fields.

2. The **ButtonHandler** instance in **bHandler** calls **setFields** to get the entered data from the text fields of the field panel and transfers them to the **newName** etc. attributes of the main dialog class.
3. The GUI can then call **getName** etc. to retrieve these values.
4. Because this is a *modal* dialog the rest of the application is suspended once the dialog is opened, until the dialog is hidden by **setVisible(false)** (the last action of the button handler). So there is no danger of the application trying to retrieve data which has not been fully transferred. Non-modal dialogs are generally only used for information presentation, not user data entry/responses.

This dialog is used by the main application as follows:

```
else if (label.equals("Entry"))     // in actionPerformed(...)
{ System.out.println("Creating a new database entry");
  createEntry();
}
```

where:

```
private void createEntry()
{ if (createDialog == null)
  { createDialog = new EntryCreateDialog(this);
    createDialog.pack();
    createDialog.setLocationRelativeTo(this);
  }
  createDialog.setOldFields("","","");
  createDialog.setVisible(true);
  /* User enters data and closes dialog. Main program
     waits here. Then gets fields: */

  String name = createDialog.getName();
  String addr = createDialog.getAddress();
  String ph = createDialog.getPhone();
 /* Finally, the new entry is added: */
  if (name != null && addr != null && ph != null)
  { database.addEntry(name,addr,ph); }
  repaint(); /* Redraw frame */
}
```

The system can now be tested by creating new entries and searching for them.

This set of classes may appear very complex but it is a template that can be reused with few changes for many applications: just rename the dialog attributes and the label text corresponding to entry fields, etc. The above structure will work for any dialog that deals with three text data items and is simple to adapt for 2, 4, 5 or more items.

3.2.6   Button-based Interfaces

A button-based interface uses rows or columns of buttons instead of menus to communicate commands to a system. Such an interface is generally faster to use than menus, but only if there are relatively few options, e.g. the controls of an MP3 player, shape selection options in a palette, etc.

A layout manager which is useful for these interfaces is the *Grid Layout*. This arranges components in a regular grid (i.e. all the buttons have the same size), with components stretched if necessary so that the grid fills the entire container.

The constructors of a grid layout are:

- **GridLayout(r, c, hGap, vGap)** – creates grid layout manager with **r** rows and **c** columns and specified horizontal and vertical gaps between rows and columns.
- **GridLayout(r,c)** – creates grid layout manager with **r** rows and **c** columns. Gaps are set to 0.
- **GridLayout()** – creates grid layout manager with 1 row. Gaps are set to 0.

If **r** or **c** are 0, this indicates that the number of rows or columns are unconstrained.

A simple example of a button-based GUI is a calculator. This should:

- have a simple calculator-style keyboard interface with keys for 0, 1, ..., 9, and +, =;
- display the running total of values summed by +, and a final total when = is pressed.

This could be used as a data-entry subsystem within a larger subsystem, e.g. to enter the number of an order item in the restaurant system. The completed interface is shown in Figure 3.14.

Figure 3.14: Calculator Interface

The **Calculator** class (combining the GUI and back end in this case because the back end is minimal) is:

```java
import javax.swing.*;
import javax.swing.event.*;
import java.awt.*;
import java.awt.event.*;

public class Calculator extends JFrame
implements ActionListener
{ private Container pane;
  private int accumulator = 0;
  private int currentVal = 0;

  public Calculator()
  { addWindowListener(
      new WindowAdapter()
      { public void windowClosing(WindowEvent e)
        { System.exit(0); }
      });  /* Kills application if main frame is closed */

    // Add components to the window, using GridLayout.
    pane = getContentPane();
    setTitle("Calculator");
    pane.setLayout(new GridLayout(3,4));

    addButton("1");
    addButton("2");
    addButton("3");
    addButton("+");
    addButton("4");
    addButton("5");
    addButton("6");
    addButton("=");
    addButton("7");
    addButton("8");
    addButton("9");
    addButton("0");
  }

  /** Convenience method to add a button */
  private void addButton(String label)
  { JButton b = new JButton(label);
    b.addActionListener(this);
    pane.add(b);
  }

  public void actionPerformed(ActionEvent ev)
  { JButton button = (JButton) ev.getSource();
    String label = button.getText();

    if ("+".equals(label)) // add current value to total
    { accumulator += currentVal;
```

```
        System.out.println("Sum is: " + accumulator);
        currentVal = 0;
    }
    else if ("=".equals(label)) // display and clear total
    { accumulator += currentVal;
        System.out.println("Total is: " + accumulator);
        currentVal = 0;
        accumulator = 0;
    }
    else  // build up the current number
    { int digit = Integer.parseInt(label);
        currentVal *= 10;
        currentVal += digit;
        System.out.println(currentVal);
    }
}

public static void main(String[] args)
{ Calculator calc = new Calculator();
    calc.setSize(300,200);
    calc.show();
}
}
```

This GUI has a very similar program structure to **AddressBook**, but it uses **JButton**s as sources of events instead of menu items.

An example execution of this system is:

```
1       /* pressed 1 */
10      /* pressed 0 */
100     /* pressed 0 */
1003    /* pressed 3 */
Sum is: 1003 /* pressed + */
6       /* pressed 6 */
66      /* pressed 6 */
666     /* pressed 6 */
Total is: 1669  /* pressed = */
```

3.2.7   Restaurant System Interface

Some of the restaurant system interfaces are very simple, for example the kitchen and bar staff interfaces could consist of a **JFrame** containing a scrollable **JList**. Selection of an item from the list indicates it has been prepared and is ready for collection. The waiters interface and billing interface are more complex. If we adopted an "MS Office" style for the former, we might come up with something like that shown in Figure 3.15. We put **Add** above **Remove**, **Cancel** and **Delivered** as this corresponds to the temporal sequence in which these events can occur. Similarly for the "global" operations, **New**, **Open**, etc., on an order. Selecting **Add** will bring up a dialog which contains a list of

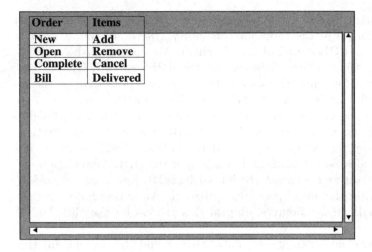

Order	Items
New	Add
Open	Remove
Complete	Cancel
Bill	Delivered

Figure 3.15: Waiters Interface

all the starters, main course, etc., items available for selection, and the waiter clicks on one of these to add it to the order. In contrast **Remove, Cancel** and **Delivered** bring up a list of the items already in a particular order: the order must be selected from a list of those the waiter is dealing with. The main frame of the interface could show a layout of the restaurant, with the tables the waiter is dealing with marked in red, with the names of the orders at these tables shown. Clicking on an order could bring up its details. There could be icons for the bar and kitchen which could flash if there were items to collect from them. Alternatively a purely button-driven interface might be preferred, since selecting items from menus is a relatively slow process. An MS Office style interface would be more suitable for the stock controller and manager.

3.3   Design of Databases using JDBC

JDBC (Java database connectivity) provides a means to connect Java programs to databases in Access, PostgreSQL, Oracle, and many other database formats. It allows programs to make queries on and modify database tables using standard SQL (Structured Query Language) statements. This is an example of the need to interface between different applications and languages (in this case Java, SQL and Access) which is typical of professional applications.

3.3.1   Example: Turning Address Book into Three-Tier Application

We show how to turn the address book application of the previous section into a three-tier application using JDBC. The first step is to design database tables for the entities to be stored: in this case there is just one entity,

AddressBookEntry. We identify the primary key[1] (**AddressBookEntryID**) and the other columns of the table for this entity (these are the attributes **Name**, **Address** and **Phone** all of type **String**). We construct the table in a blank database, using Access, then register the database with ODBC (the Windows mechanism for connecting databases with applications that use them) and select a suitable database driver, the Access driver in this case.

Once the database has been created within Access, select (32 bit) ODBC from the Control Panel in Windows. Open the ODBC icon, and in the "System DSN" menu, choose the Access driver, and the option "Add" to select the physical database file and the name and location for the ODBC interface to it: this name is the "data source name" (DSN) **AddressDb** which will be used in the database URL in the Java application program. An appropriate location for the DSN is ODBC/Data Sources. Repeat this process for the "File DSN" menu.

Table 3.1 gives an example of data that could be stored in the **AddressBookEntry** table.

AddressBookEntryID	Name	Address	Phone
1	J. Fox	123 Houndsditch	0787 909 112
2	A. Widdecombe	Smith Square	
3	A. Ferguson	Old Trafford	club call 909
4	A. Ferguson	1087 Salford Quays	

Table 3.1: Example of **AddressBookEntry**

As far as Java is concerned, the primary key is an integer, and the other attributes are string values. In the Java program, we need to load the JDBC-ODBC bridge class:

```
import java.sql.*;

public class AddressBookDb
{ public static void main(String args[])
  { try
    { Class.forName("sun.jdbc.odbc.JdbcOdbcDriver"); }
    catch(Exception e)
    { System.out.println(e.toString());
      System.exit(1);
    }
    ...
```

There are also direct JDBC drivers for many databases, which do not need to use an ODBC bridge. An example is given in Chapter 8.

Once the driver class is loaded, the program can attempt to connect to the database:

---

[1]A primary key for a table is a column which uniquely identifies the rows of the table, i.e. two different rows will have different values in the primary key column.

```
try
{ String s = "jdbc:odbc:AddressDb";  /* URL of database */
  Connection con = DriverManager.getConnection(s);
  System.out.println("Connection established");
  ... <process database> ...
}
catch(SQLException sqle)
{ while (sqle != null)
  { System.out.println("SQLState: " + sqle.getSQLState());
    System.out.println("Message: " + sqle.getMessage());
    System.out.println("ErrorCode: " + sqle.getErrorCode());
    sqle = sqle.getNextException();
    System.out.println(" ");
  }
}
```

There are four basic operations on a database, expressed in SQL:

1. Adding a new item to a database table: `INSERT INTO table VALUES (keyval,val1,val2,...,valn)`
2. Searching for a database item: `SELECT * FROM table WHERE att = val`
3. Deleting a database item: `DELETE * FROM table WHERE att = val`
4. Updating a database item: `UPDATE table SET att = val WHERE P`

Adding an Item to a Table

Let **con** be an established database **Connection** object. We create an **INSERT** statement and execute it by:

```
Statement stat = con.createStatement();
String insert = "INSERT INTO AddressBookEntry " +
                "VALUES (" + entryID + ",'" + name + "','" +
                        address + "','" + phone + "')";
stat.executeUpdate(insert);
con.commit();
```

inside a `try` with a `catch(SQLException sqle)`, where **entryID** is an integer variable and **name**, **address** and **phone** are strings. The table name and the number and types of attribute values must be specified correctly, otherwise an obscure exception may be returned. Any statement which modifies the database needs a **commit** following it to confirm the changes, otherwise the database will remain unchanged.

Java String values need to be enclosed in single quotes for correct translation to database string values (in some implementation environments).

Searching for an Item in a Table

Let **con** be an established database **Connection** object, and **nameval** a string variable holding the name we are searching for. We create a **SELECT** statement and execute it by:

```
Statement stat = con.createStatement();
String find = "SELECT * FROM AddressBookEntry " +
               "WHERE Name + " = '" + nameval + "'";
ResultSet res = stat.executeQuery(find);
```

To get all items in the table, we do:

```
public void displayAll()
{ String sQuery = "SELECT * FROM AddressBookEntry";
  ResultSet res;
  try
  { Statement stat = con.createStatement();
    res = stat.executeQuery(sQuery);
    ...
  }
}
```

Processing Query Results

A list **res** is returned from such enquiry statements. We need to iterate through it to obtain all the individual results (the table rows that satisfy the query):

```
while (res.next())
{ int sId = res.getInt("AddressBookEntryID");
  String sName = res.getString("Name");
  String sAddress = res.getString("Address");
  String sPhone = res.getString("Phone");
  System.out.println("Entry number " + sId + " Name: " + sName +
                     " Address: " + sAddress + " Phone: " + sPhone);
}
```

```
res.close();
```

All results from a query are accessed by the **res** iterator. Individual fields of a result row are accessed by the **getType** operators: Type can be Int, Float, Double, String, Boolean, etc.

Deleting Items

Let **con** be an established database **Connection** object. We create a **DELETE** statement and execute it by:

```
Statement stat = con.createStatement();
String del = "DELETE * FROM AddressBookEntry " +
   "WHERE name + " = '" + nameVal + "'";
stat.executeUpdate(del);
con.commit();
```

with these statements inside a **try** with a **catch(SQLException sqle)**.

The Sun documentation for JDBC is at http://java.sun.com/jdbc/ including information on prepared statements and stored procedures, which have improved efficiency over the basic techniques given above.

Complete Address Book Database Interface
The rewritten database interface for the address book application, replacing
the **Database** class, is then:

```java
import java.sql.*;
import java.util.Vector;
import java.util.List;

public class AddressBookDb
{ private Connection con;  // Connection to address book database
  private int entryId = 0; // Max. id of entries

  public AddressBookDb(String dbName)
  { try
    { String s = "jdbc:odbc:" + dbName;
      con = DriverManager.getConnection(s);
      System.out.println("Connection established");
      entryId = getMaxId();
    }
    catch(SQLException sqle)
    { System.err.println("Unable to connect to " + dbName);
      handleException(sqle);
    }
  }

  private void handleException(SQLException e)
  { e.printStackTrace();
    while (e != null)
    { System.out.println("SQLState: " + e.getSQLState());
      System.out.println("Message: " + e.getMessage());
      System.out.println("Code: " + e.getErrorCode());
      e.getNextException();
    }
  }

  private int getMaxId()  // Returns max primary key
  { int maxId = 0;        // value used in database.
    try
    { Statement stat = con.createStatement();
      String sQuery = "SELECT MAX(AddressBookEntryID) " +
                      "AS MaxId FROM AddressBookEntry";
      ResultSet res = stat.executeQuery(sQuery);
      while (res.next())
      { maxId = res.getInt("MaxId"); }
    }
    catch(SQLException e)
    { System.err.println("Error in getting max id");
      handleException(e);
    }
    return maxId;
  }
```

```
public void addEntry(String nme, String addr,
                     String ph)
{ Statement stat;
  entryId = getMaxId(); // To ensure unique id's are used
  String insert = "INSERT INTO AddressBookEntry " +
    "VALUES (" + (entryId+1) + ",'" + nme + "','" +
              addr + "','" + ph + "')";
  try
  { stat = con.createStatement();
    stat.executeUpdate(insert);
    entryId++;
    con.commit();
  }
  catch(SQLException sqle)
  { System.err.println("Adding an entry failed");
    handleException(sqle);
  }
}

public void displayAll()
{ String sQuery = "SELECT * FROM AddressBookEntry";
  ResultSet res;
  try
  { Statement stat = con.createStatement();
    res = stat.executeQuery(sQuery);
    while (res.next())
    { int sId = res.getInt("AddressBookEntryID");
      String sName = res.getString("Name");
      String sAddress = res.getString("Address");
      String sPhone = res.getString("Phone");
      System.out.println("Entry number " + sId +
                         "\t Name: " + sName +
                         "\t Address: " + sAddress +
                         "\t Phone: " + sPhone);
    }
    res.close();
  }
  catch(SQLException e)
  { System.err.println("Display-all failed");
    handleException(e);
  }
}


public List searchByName(String nameval)
{ Statement stat;
  ResultSet res;
  Vector items = new Vector();
  String find = "SELECT * FROM AddressBookEntry " +
```

```
                        "WHERE Name = '" + nameval + "'";
  try
  { stat = con.createStatement();
    res = stat.executeQuery(find);

    while (res.next())
    { int sId = res.getInt("AddressBookEntryID");
      String sName = res.getString("Name");
      String sAddress = res.getString("Address");
      String sPhone = res.getString("Phone");
      System.out.println("Entry number " + sId +
                         "\t Name: " + sName +
                         "\t Address: " + sAddress +
                         "\t Phone: " + sPhone);
      DataItem item = new DataItem(sName,sAddress,sPhone);
      items.add(item);
    }
    res.close();
  }
  catch(SQLException e)
  { System.err.println("Search by name failed");
    handleException(e);
    return items;
  }
  return items;
}

public void remove(String nameVal)
{ Statement stat;
  String del = "DELETE * FROM AddressBookEntry " +
               "WHERE Name = '" + nameVal + "'";
  try
  { stat = con.createStatement();
    stat.executeUpdate(del);
    con.commit();
  }
  catch(SQLException e)
  { System.err.println("Deletion failed");
    handleException(e);
  }
}

public static void main(String args[])
{ try
  { Class.forName("sun.jdbc.odbc.JdbcOdbcDriver"); }
  catch(Exception e)
  { System.out.println(e.toString());
    System.exit(1);
  }
  AddressBookDb dbInterface =
```

```
        new AddressBookDb("AddressDb");
    dbInterface.addEntry("T. Fox", "123 Houndsditch",
                         "0787 909 112");
    dbInterface.displayAll();
    dbInterface.addEntry("A. Widdecombe", "Smith Square", " ");
    dbInterface.addEntry("A. Ferguson", "Old Trafford",
                         "club call 909");
    dbInterface.addEntry("A. Ferguson", "1087 Salford Quays", " ");
    dbInterface.searchByName("A. Ferguson");
    dbInterface.remove("A. Ferguson");
    dbInterface.displayAll();
  }
}
```

The result of executing the above test in **main** is:

```
WIN J:\teaching\cs2sap\Code2>java AddressBookDb
Connection established
Entry number 1 Name: A Jennings
               Address: 123 Houndsditch
               Phone: 33445 44-55
Entry number 2 Name: T. Fox
               Address: 123 Houndsditch
               Phone: 0787 909 112
Entry number 4 Name: A. Ferguson
               Address: Old Trafford
               Phone: club call 909
Entry number 5 Name: A. Ferguson
               Address: 1087 Salford Quays
               Phone:
Entry number 1 Name: A Jennings
               Address: 123 Houndsditch
               Phone: 33445 44-55
Entry number 2 Name: T. Fox
               Address: 123 Houndsditch
               Phone: 0787 909 112
Entry number 3 Name: A. Widdecombe
               Address: Smith Square
               Phone:
```

where the database already contained the entry for **A Jennings**.

Notice that the **DataItem** class is still used to transfer query results from the database interface to the GUI, but that the **Database** class has been entirely replaced by **AddressBookDb**.

3.3.2   Database Design for the Restaurant System

For the restaurant system there are a large number of entities and relationships between them which must be stored in the database. First we need to define a *relational database schema* which defines these entities and relationships in terms of database tables and many-one mappings between them, based on *foreign keys*: a foreign key is an attribute of one table whose values correspond to values of a primary key of another table. This means that for every row of the first table we can identify a row of the referenced table: this serves the same purpose as directed associations in a UML class diagram (from the source entity/table to the target) and object-valued attributes of a class. That is, they provide a means to navigate from an instance of one entity to a corresponding instance of another, such as from a person to their employer, or from an **Order** to the **Waiter** dealing with it.

To turn an analysis data model expressed in UML, such as Figure 1.2, into a relational schema we can carry out the following transformations:

- If a class **C** has no super- or sub-classes, convert it to a table **T** with a new primary key **CId** and attributes those of **C,** except that many-one relationships **att** from **C** to **C′** become foreign keys in **T** to the table **T′** representing **C′**.

  For example, **Payment** could become the table **PaymentTable** with attributes **PaymentId: int, method: String, amount: int** and **BillId: int**.

- For other classes, gather together all classes within the same "tree" of super and subclasses, e.g. **OrderItem**, **Drink** and **Dish**, and define a table **T** to represent the class **C** at the top of this tree (the class with no superclass). **T** has a new primary key, plus all the attributes of **C** and all the attributes of any of its subclasses, plus a flag **CSubclass: String**, whose value ranges over the *names* of all the possible subclasses that an instance of **C** may actually belong to – i.e. the *concrete*, non-abstract, subclasses of **C**. **T** has foreign keys for each of the many-one relationships that originate from **C** or any of its subclasses.

  For example, we get a table **OrderItemTable** with primary key **OrderItemId**, attributes **name: String, isVegetarian: yes/no, price: int, alcoholic: yes/no, dishType: String** and **orderItemSubclass: String** (possible values being "Drink" and "Dish"), and foreign key **OrderId: int**.

- Many-many relationships **r** between classes **C** and **C′** are represented as tables **rT** with a new primary key, and two attributes which are foreign keys to **C** and **C′**. If rolenames are given then the foreign keys can be named after these roles, otherwise after the classes (if the two classes are the same we will have to make the key names different, however).

  For example, the **OrderItem–Ingredient** relationship becomes a table **OrderItemIngredientTable** with a new primary key, and attributes **OrderItemId: int** and **IngredientId: int**.

The result of this process for the restaurant is shown in Figure 3.16. A "crow's foot" indicates the many end of a many-one relationship, i.e. the table containing the foreign key. This is a general translation, which may not be optimal in particular cases. Alternative translations could instead:

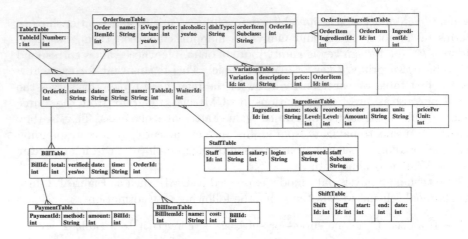

Figure 3.16: Relational Database Schema for Restaurant System

- Represent subclasses of a class in separate tables to their superclass, each table for a subclass has columns for each additional attribute of the subclass, and a foreign key to the superclass table;
- Represent *all* relationships as tables, in order to increase flexibility – if the cardinality of a relationship is changed to become more general, e.g. an order being associated to several tables or several staff members instead of one, the database design would not have to change.

Whatever translation is chosen should satisfy the property that all necessary data and data access/update capabilities that are required for the system are supported by the resulting database schema.

Next we have to write SQL statements to carry out the accesses/updates we need to perform the operations of the system. In the restaurant case, for example, we need to be able to extract all the order items connected to a given order with id **X**:

```
SELECT * FROM OrderItemTable
WHERE OrderId = X
```

This is then coded up in a suitable database interface class similar to **AddressBookDb** above. In this case the class is **OrdersData**, corresponding to the module of that name in Figure 2.3.

OrdersData returns Java objects that satisfy the structures shown in the analysis class diagram (Figure 1.2): it therefore has to convert the JDBC **ResultSet** iterators into this form, which the rest of the application works with. The above SQL would therefore be used in an operation

```
public List getOrderItems(Order x)
// REQUIRES: x is non-null
// EFFECTS: returns the list of OrderItem objects
//          connected to x.
```

of **OrdersData**. Such conversion from result sets to Java objects can become a substantial task. Environments such as J2EE [25] manage this conversion automatically, enabling applications to use *entity enterprise Java beans* which correspond to each database table, the instances of these beans correspond to rows in the table, and foreign keys are expressed by object to object navigations.

The database also needs to include tables to hold the lists of possible starters, main courses, desserts and drinks that may be selected for an order. Only the manager should be able to modify these tables.

Summary

We have introduced two and three-tier architectures and the detailed design techniques of GUI and database design. Chapter 8 will give further examples of three tier architectures and GUI design for internet systems.

Exercises

1 Explain the advantages of a three tier architecture over a two tier architecture, if an application involves a GUI, significant computations and a persistent data store.

2 Give a **REQUIRES/EFFECTS** specification of the **addEntry** method in **AddressBookDb** above.

3 Convert the Person–Company class diagram given in Chapter 1, Figure 1.8, into a relational database schema.

4 Most SQL implementations support the **COUNT**(*) pseudo-attribute, similar to the **MAX**(**Att**) pseudo-attribute used in the **getMaxId**() method of the address book above. **COUNT**(*) returns the number of distinct rows in the table which satisfy the given SELECT statement condition. Use this to define a method **int numberWithName(String n)** of **AddressBookDb** which returns the number of distinct address book entries with name attribute equal to **n**.

5 In an application that holds information about students, there is a dialog for entering student exam performance for a year, and decisions about student progression. The data to be entered is: number of units taken so far; number of units passed; whether they have passed the year (boolean choice); whether they are allowed to take resits (boolean choice); student name; student number; year (i.e. 1st, 2nd, 3rd, etc.). The last three fields should already be filled in by the software when the dialog is opened.

Design a layout for this dialog, explaining what **Swing** classes would be used in which parts of the layout.

6 Identify and explain the flaws in the set of menus shown in Figure 3.17, which is the proposed interface for a statechart editor tool. The tool is intended to allow the user to draw states (represented as rounded rectangles) and transitions between states (represented as arrowed lines), to print such diagrams, save and restore them from files, and to move, edit and delete states and transitions. Conversion to Java and C++ class skeletons is also supported. Draw an improved structure for the menus of the system.

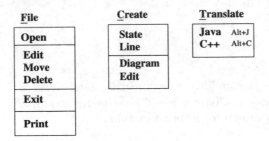

Figure 3.17: Proposed Menus for Statechart Editor

Which menu items would be candidates for a toolbar? Draw a diagram of such a toolbar.

Chapter 4

Design Patterns

Design patterns are standard design structures which have been found to be useful in many different applications. They therefore provide a set of ready-made solutions to design problems which are encountered in software development, and a repertoire of building blocks for software design. This chapter gives a brief history of software design patterns and their role and purpose. Java examples of the most frequently used patterns: the State, Template Method, Observer, Visitor, Iterator, Mediator and Proxy patterns are defined, and a list of all widely used design patterns, with a brief description of each, is also included.

Design patterns are an important technique for organising the structure of components (modules or subsystems) in a clear and systematic fashion. They usually require that the elements they organise adhere to a strict protocol (that they subclass a particular class, or provide or call specific methods) however, so they are not so useful in organising the interaction between components, especially when this interaction is likely to evolve as requirements for the system change. To solve this problem, we use coordination contracts, as described in Chapter 5.

4.1 The History of Design Patterns

The concept of *design patterns* for software was inspired by similar ideas in the field of architecture in particular. In contrast to software engineering, the discipline of architecture and systematic techniques for creating buildings have existed for 6000 years or more. Christopher Alexander's work on architecture patterns considered how such techniques have been used through history in characteristic ways to achieve certain goals, and he attempted to make explicit what makes a good building good, i.e. what are the good techniques and patterns to use in their construction. His books include *The Timeless Way of Building* [1] and *A Pattern Language: Towns, Buildings, Construction* [2].

Alexander's ideas can be summarised as stating that function affects form and form affects function. Alexander argues that the nature of the physics of the world and behaviours, sociology and psychology of people leads to a necessary pattern of architecture, use of buildings and use of space some of which is cultural, most of which is because we are human.

Similar concepts arise in engineering fields such as bridge design, where there are a number of standard patterns or stereotypical structures:

- arch;
- box girder;
- suspension.

According to Alexander (Page x of [1]):

> *"A pattern describes a problem which occurs over and over again in our environment, and then describes the core of the solution to that problem, in such a way that you can use this solution a million times over, without ever doing it the same way twice."*

The same principle applies to software patterns: the core concept of what the purpose and structure of the pattern is remain unchanged, but there are an endless number of variations on the pattern which occur as we apply the pattern to individual systems.

A pattern is a generalised solution to a problem in a context. A pattern formalises and documents design experience and knowledge generically. Since patterns are available and are used in many branches of design and engineering, it seemed reasonable that they must also have application in software development.

The key developments which led to the current concepts of software patterns were:

- Alexander's work on patterns of architecture;
- Anderson's "Architecture Handbook" [4], and Coplien's work on idioms [15];
- the "Gang of Four" book defining the core software design patterns [21].

Bruce Anderson, inspired by Alexander's creation of a pattern handbook for architecture, tried to create an equivalent for software systems: The Architecture Handbook. This was presented at OOPSLA workshops in 1991 and 1992 and was a principal part of the genesis of the patterns phenomenon in the object-oriented systems community. James Coplien on the other hand focussed on the small-scale patterns called *idioms of use*. His book "Advanced C++ – Programming Styles and Idioms", introduced the concept of idiom explicitly. In Java a common idiom is the use of a **for** loop to iterate through the members of a collection **coll** of **Element** objects:

```
for (int i = 0; i < coll.size(); i++)
{ Element e = (Element) coll.get(i);
  ... do something with e ...
}
```

An idiom is a characteristic way of using a particular programming language, at the level of individual statements. Design patterns on the other hand are mainly independent of programming language, and are at the level of classes and groups of classes and objects.

Bruce Anderson's attempt to construct an architecture handbook for software and Coplien's introduction of C++ idioms led to the "Gang of Four" (aka GoF) book, which introduced the idea of a design pattern in object-oriented software. According to GoF, a pattern can only be a pattern if it can be shown to exist in many different and distinct items of software. A pattern in this sense is a codification of uses found phenomenologically. GoF divided patterns into three general categories: creational, structural and behavioural, depending on their primary aim (i.e. organising object creation, the structure of classes and relationships, or the distribution of behaviour amongst objects).

Subsequently, there has been a considerable amount of research into recognising and cataloguing patterns [24], with many books and papers being published, and a dedicated conference "Pattern languages of programs" on the issue.

The role of design patterns is to capture descriptions of good solutions to recurring design problems, and to show how collections of classes and objects can be customised to solve a general design problem in a particular context. Figure 4.1 gives a classification of some of the most popular patterns. Patterns are a means of organising the structure of a module or subsystem, they can be distinguished from related concepts such as *frameworks* by the scale of their application:

- **Frameworks**: template architectures which can be used to organise a complete application, such as J2EE for internet applications in Java [25]. The event broadcast/listener mechanism used in Java Swing, Java Beans and Jini could also be regarded as a framework.
- **Design patterns**: apply at medium scale, to define a collaborating group of classes, objects and methods as part of an application. Many variations

		Purpose		
		Creational	**Structural**	**Behavioural**
Scope	Class	Factory Method	Adapter (Class)	Template Method Interpreter
	Object	Abstract Factory Singleton Builder Prototype	Adapter (Object) Facade Proxy Bridge Composite Decorator Flyweight	State Observer Iterator Visitor Mediator Chain of Responsibility Command Strategy

Figure 4.1: Classification of Design Patterns

are possible on how a pattern is applied, and they are mainly independent of particular programming languages.

- **Idioms**: characteristic way of using the constructs of a specific programming language. For example, using **public static final int** constants in Java to define enumerated types. Unlike patterns, idioms are local in scope, applying at the statement level, and limited in variation, e.g. different variable names being used in different cases.

In the following sections, we give examples of some patterns and their implementation in Java. The structural patterns described here have in common that they introduce an indirection between client and supplier classes: an intermediary class or classes which adapt the supplier operations to those needed by the client (in the case of Adapter), or simplify the dependencies between client and supplier (in the case of Facade), or provide a surrogate for a supplier (in the case of Proxy). The behavioural patterns have in common the idea of separating out some kinds of processing into separate classes or objects from other processing. For example the observer pattern separates presentation processing from data processing; the state pattern separates processing carried out in different modes into separate classes, Visitor separates traversal of a data structure from the processing carried out on its elements, and Mediator separates individual component behaviour from the processing that co-ordinates these components.

4.2   The State Pattern

Objects often have internal modes or states, with different behaviour – responses to messages – in each mode. For example a lift will respond to a request to move to a floor differently depending on whether it is idle or busy, and on whether it is at the requested floor or not. The state pattern introduces explicit subclasses of a class, to represent each different mode that objects of the class may be in. In this pattern, the choice between different responses to methods is handled by polymorphism of **State** subclasses, not by the programmer (so the program decisions are not hard-coded in one class, but depend on what subclass an object belongs to at runtime: this is potentially more efficient and maintainable). Figure 4.2 shows the general structure of the state pattern. Each **Context** has a reference to some **State** object, which may be a member of the **State1** or **State2** subclass at particular points in time.

State could be introduced to replace some original pseudocode:

```
public class Context
{
  public static final int MODE1 = 0;
  public static final int MODE2 = 1;
  private int mode;
  ....
```

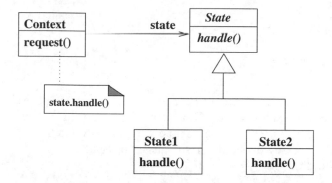

Figure 4.2: General Structure of State Pattern

```
public void request()
{
    if (mode == MODE1)
    { Code1 }
    else if (mode == MODE2)
    { Code2 }
}
    ....
} // Context
```

The problem with this version is that it is difficult to maintain, since any change to the set of modes in the system will require a change to every method that depends on the mode.

Applying the state pattern we would instead obtain:

```
public class Context1
{
  private State state;
  ...
  public void request() { state.handle(); }


  ...
} // Context1

abstract class State
{
  ...
  public abstract void handle();
} // State
```

There are two subclasses of **State**:

```
class State1 extends State
{
  public void handle() { Code1 }
} // State1
```

```
class State2 extends State
{
  public void handle() { Code2 }
} // State2
```

Now a change in the behaviour of **State** objects in mode **n** only requires modification of the local class **Staten**, not **Context1**. Introducing a new mode only involves creating a new subclass of **State** and possibly modifying **Context1**, but does not affect any of the other subclasses of **State**.

The state pattern should be used when:

- An objects behaviour depends on its mode, and it must change its behaviour at run-time depending on that mode.
- Operations have large multipart conditional statements depending on the mode.

The involved classes are:

- **Context1** – this defines the interface for clients; and it maintains a **State** instance, corresponding to the original **mode** variable.
- **State** – this is the abstract superclass of classes representing particular modes.
- **State1**, etc. – each subclass of **State** implements the behaviour of a particular mode.

The benefits of the pattern are that:

- The state pattern puts each mode of behaviour into a separate class, *localising* this behaviour. New states and transitions can be added by defining new **State** subclasses.
- It reduces the size and complexity of operations, enhancing code understanding and maintainability.
- It makes state transitions more explicit (they are represented by changes in the class of the **State** object instead of by assignments of constants to **mode**).
- **State** objects can be shared between contexts if they have no instance variables of their own.

4.2.1   State Pattern Example: Drawing Tool

A common use of the state pattern is to reorganise applications such as drawing tools which have different behaviour in different modes (e.g. the modes of a drawing tool could be shape creation, text editing or shape selection) but which respond to the same basic sets of events (such as mouse events). In this example (Figure 4.3) **Context** is a **DrawingController** responding to

mousePressed(), **keyPressed()**, etc., events. The role of **State** is played by the **Tool** class: the drawing controller has a current drawing tool.

Subclasses of **Tool** are **CreationTool**, **DeletionTool**, **SelectionTool** etc., representing the behaviour of the drawing tool when it is in the corresponding mode: each of these subclasses must handle **mousePressed()**, etc. in different ways. For example, pressing the mouse when in the creation tool mode indicates that a shape should be created at the mouse press location, whilst in the selection tool mode it would select any shape under this location. Therefore these methods are shown in Figure 4.3 as being redefined in each of the tool subclasses.

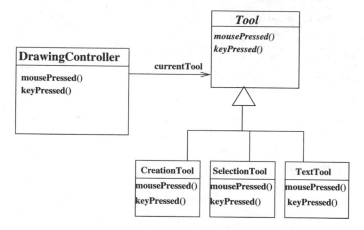

Figure 4.3: State Pattern Applied to Drawing Package

4.3   The Template Method Pattern

This pattern defines the skeleton of an algorithm in a superclass method, deferring some details (defined only as abstract *hook* methods in the superclass) to subclasses, allowing subclasses to redefine certain steps/parts of the algorithm whilst leaving other parts unchanged. This is used to factor out common parts/structure of an algorithm into the superclass, so that subclasses only need to implement the parts of the algorithm that differ between the subclasses, thus avoiding code duplication. Figure 4.4 shows the general structure of this pattern.

The classes involved in this pattern are:

- **GenericClass** – this defines the template method which consists of a skeleton algorithm calling one or more hook methods. It also defines hook methods that subclasses can override.
- **ConcreteClass** – implements the hook methods.

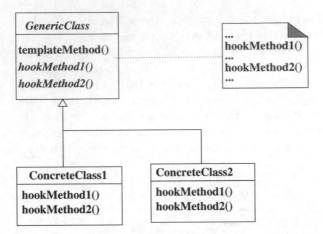

Figure 4.4: Structure of Template Method Pattern

Hook methods may be defined as abstract in **GenericClass,** or given default implementations there. Template Method differs from the state pattern in that the superclass is used to define common algorithms, the template methods, and the subclasses only redefine elements of these algorithms, the hook methods. In the state pattern, the superclass declares the common set of methods which the system may respond to in any mode, all subclasses usually redefine each of these methods.

4.3.1   Template Method Pattern Example: Student Pass Marks

The problem in this example is:

> A student database has to manage two kinds of student, MSc and BSc students, which have common attributes **int studentId** and **int numberPassed**: the latter attribute records the number of courses passed by the student so far. There is a common method **addMark(int m)** which inputs the mark given for a course.
> For MSc students **addMark(m)** increments the number of courses passed, **numberPassed**, only if **m** $\geq$ 50, the pass mark for MSc students. Similarly for BSc students, except that the pass mark is 40 in this case.

Template Method can be applied, with **addMark** defined in a generic way using a hook method **isPass**, which has a different definition in the two subclasses.
    The code of the resulting classes is as follows:

```
abstract class GeneralStudent
{ private int studentId = 0;
  private int numberPassed = 0;
```

```
  public GeneralStudent(int id)
  { studentId = id; }

  abstract protected boolean isPass(int mark);   /* Hook method */

  public void addMark(int m)              /* Template method */
  { if (isPass(m))
    { numberPassed++; }
  }
}

class MScStudent extends GeneralStudent
{ public MScStudent(int id)
  { super(id); }

  protected boolean isPass(int m)
  { return (m >= 50); }
}

class BScStudent extends GeneralStudent
{ public BScStudent(int id)
  { super(id); }

  protected boolean isPass(int m)
  { return (m >= 40); }
}
```

Notice that **MScStudent** and **BScStudent** *only* redefine the hook method
isPass, since the template method **addMark** is unchanged from the superclass
definition. Figure 4.5 shows the structure of this system. If the pattern was
not used, we would have to define **addMark** in both subclasses:

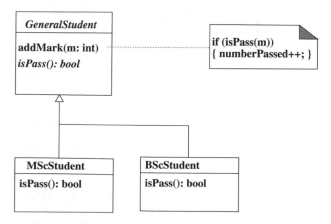

Figure 4.5: Template Method Example

```
public void addMark(int m)
{ if (m >= 50)
  { numberPassed++; }
}
```

in **MScStudent** and

```
public void addMark(int m)
{ if (m >= 40)
  { numberPassed++; }
}
```

in **BScStudent**, even though these definitions are almost identical. **numberPassed** would also have to be made visible to the subclasses, by using **protected** visibility instead of **private**.

4.4   The Visitor Pattern

The visitor pattern aims to separate the algorithms which operate over a data structure from the definition of that structure, so that these may independently vary. An example of this pattern is shown in Figure 4.6. The involved classes are:

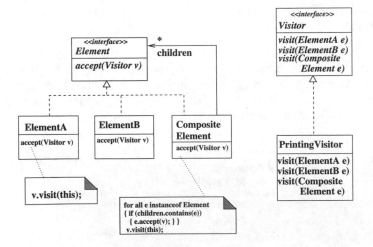

Figure 4.6: Example Structure of Visitor Pattern

- **Element** – superclass of all classes of objects found in the structure to be iterated over. It has an abstract **accept** method to process general visitors.
- **ConcreteElement** – specific classes of elements in the structure, such as **ElementA** and **CompositeElement** in Figure 4.6. Each class must give a concrete definition of **accept** for a general **Visitor** object, specifying in

what order the visitor should traverse any subelements and the concrete element itself.

- **Visitor** – defines abstract **visit(ConcreteElement ce)** methods for each concrete element class.
- **ConcreteVisitor** – encapsulates a particular processing algorithm for the data structure, and defines the **visit** methods giving the actions to be taken when visiting each type of element in the structure.

4.4.1 Visitor Pattern Example: Parse-Tree Processing

A parse tree for a simple programming language is represented in the following classes (Figure 4.7):

1. **BasicExpression**s, representing numbers or string values. These have a **String value** attribute to hold the value, and **int type** to hold the type (0 for numbers, 1 for strings).
2. **Variable**s, representing variables, with a single **String name** attribute to hold the variable name.
3. **BinaryExpression**s, representing expressions **e** = **f**, **e** < **f**, **e** > **f**, etc. The operator is held in the **String operator** attribute, and the arguments in the **Expression left** and **Expression right** attributes.

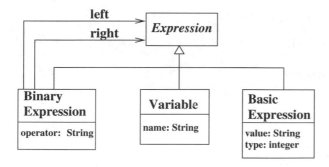

Figure 4.7: Classes for Parse Tree Representation

Several functions are to be implemented to extract properties of and locally modify elements of such trees:

- An operation to compute the list of all variable names (without duplicates) used in a parse tree of the above form.
- An operation to perform a simultaneous renaming of all variables in a parse tree of the above form, i.e. given a **Map replacement** from **String** to **String**, if **s** is the name of variable **v**, given by **v.getName()**, and **s** occurs in the domain of **replacement**, execute **v.setName((String) replacement.get(s))**.

A suitable visitor framework over parse trees can be defined as:

```
abstract class Visitor
{ public abstract void visit(Variable v);

  public abstract void visit(BasicExpression be);

  public abstract void visit(BinaryExpression be);
}

abstract class Expression
{ public abstract void accept(Visitor v); }

class BinaryExpression extends Expression
{ private Expression left;
  private Expression right;
  private String operator;

  public void accept(Visitor v) // Visit left subtree,
  { left.accept(v);             // then right, then
    right.accept(v);            // myself.
    v.visit(this);
  }
  ...
}

class BasicExpression extends Expression
{ private String value;
  private int type;

  public void accept(Visitor v)
  { v.visit(this); }
}

class Variable extends Expression
{ private String name;

  public void setName(String nme)
  { name = nme; }

  public String getName()
  { return name; }

  public void accept(Visitor v)
  { v.visit(this); }
}
```

This definition specifies a post-order traversal over the expression tree structures, i.e. visitor processing is carried out on the left argument of a binary expression first, then on the right argument, and then on the expression itself.

The first required function can be achieved by a **GetUsesVisitor**:

```
import java.util.Vector;

public class GetUsesVisitor extends Visitor
{ private Vector vars = new Vector();

  public void visit(Variable v)
  { if (vars.contains(v.getName())) {}
    else
    { vars.add(v.getName()); }
  }

  public void visit(BasicExpression be) {}

  public void visit(BinaryExpression be) {}
}
```

This accumulates all the variable names in a list as it traverses the expression tree, carrying out a skip action when visiting any other kind of expression.

The renaming operation can be achieved by a **RenamesVisitor**:

```
import java.util.Map;
import java.util.HashMap;

public class RenamesVisitor extends Visitor
{ private Map replacements = new HashMap();

  public void setReplacement(String old, String rep)
  { replacements.put(old,rep); }

  public void visit(Variable v)
  { String s = (String) replacements.get(v.getName());
    if (s != null)
    { v.setName(s); }
  }

  public void visit(BasicExpression be) {}

  public void visit(BinaryExpression be) {}
}
```

4.5   The Observer Pattern

This pattern is intended for situations where there are multiple views or presentations of a set of data, such as alternative graphical views (pie charts and bar charts of sales figures, for example). In general it defines a one-to-many dependency between objects so that when one object (the data) changes state, all its dependants (the views) are notified and update themselves automatically.

It is applicable whenever there are two entities being represented in software, one dependent on the other, so that a change to one object requires changes to

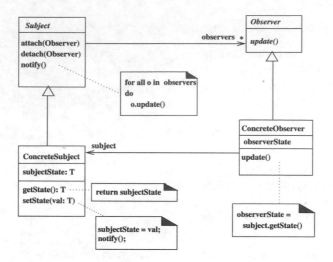

Figure 4.8: Structure of Observer Pattern

others (its dependants). Figure 4.8 shows the structure of this pattern.

The classes in this structure have the following roles:

- **Subject** – abstract superclass of all classes containing observed data. Provides methods **attach** and **detach** to add and remove observers of a subject, and **notify** to inform all observers that a significant state change has occurred in the observable and that they may need to update their presentation of it.
- **ConcreteSubject** – specific observable data, any method of this class which modifies its state may need to call **notify** on completion.
- **Observer** – abstract superclass of observers of subjects. Declares an **update** method whose function is to adjust the observer's presentation on any subject state change.
- **ConcreteObserver** – class defining a specific view, such as a bar chart.

It is important to maintain *referential integrity* when using this pattern, this means that for a subject object **s**, its set **s.observers** of attached observers has the property that

$$o \in s.observers \equiv o.subject == s$$

That is, these observers are exactly the observer objects whose subject is **s**. This implies that whenever we execute **s.attach(o)** we must also set **o.subject = s**, and whenever we execute **s.detach(o)**, we must also set **o.subject = null**.

The positive consequences of using the pattern are:

- Modularity: subject and observers may vary independently.
- Extensibility: we can define and add any number of observers to a given subject.

- Customisability: different observers provide different views of a subject.

This pattern is widely used in commercial languages and libraries, for example, in the Smalltalk Model-View-Controller (MVC) paradigm. In Java the Swing event model is directly related to Observer, with **Listener** objects playing the role of **Observer** for the event source (**Subject**) objects. Java Beans and Jini also use a similar event notification model.

4.6 The Iterator Pattern

The purpose of this behavioural pattern is to support access to elements of an aggregate data structure (such as a tree or array) sequentially. It is applicable whenever we:

- require multiple traversal algorithms over an aggregate;
- require a uniform traversal interface over different aggregates;
- or when aggregate classes and traversal algorithm must vary independently.

The general structure of this pattern is shown in Figure 4.9.

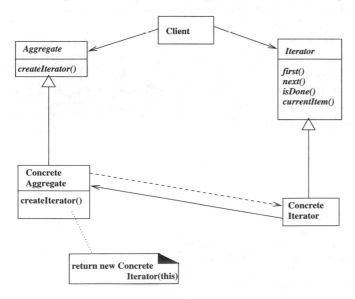

Figure 4.9: Structure of Iterator Pattern

An iterator object acts like a cursor or pointer into a structure, indicating a current location within this structure and providing operations to move this cursor forwards or backwards in the structure.

The classes involved are:

- **Aggregate** – the class defining a general composite data structure such as a list or tree.
- **ConcreteAggregate** – specific subclass defining a particular data structure such as a linked list or binary search tree.
- **Iterator** – interface for general iteration operations such as accessing the first element in the collection, stepping through the collection, etc.
- **ConcreteIterator** – iterator subclass specific to a particular data structure. The **createIterator()** method of the data structure returns a **ConcreteIterator** instance for the structure.

The consequences of the pattern are an increase in flexibility, because the aggregate and the traversal mechanism are independent. It is possible to have multiple iterators acting on the same aggregate object simultaneously, possibly with different traversal algorithms. Compared to an approach using navigation methods within the aggregate however there is an additional communication overhead between the iterator and the aggregate.

If the iterator pattern was not used, we would require direct access to the private parts of the data structures being iterated over. For a list, for example:

```
for (LinkedList.Node cur = list.head; cur != null; cur = cur.next)
{ System.out.println(cur.element); }
```

This requires that the fields of **LinkedList** and its inner class **Node** are accessible to clients of **LinkedList**.

Providing iteration methods for the data structure objects: **reset()**, **next()**, **hasNext()** for **LinkedList** is a preferable alternative, however it only supports one iteration at a time (no nested iterations). Thus we need the full flexibility of the iterator pattern in general, which allows the creation of as many independent iterator objects as are needed for each complex data object.

Some examples of iterators in Java are:

- Simple integer indexing into an array:

  ```
  for (int i = 0; i < a.length; ++i)
  { x += a[i]; }
  ```

- Java Collections iteration over an **ArrayList**:

  ```
  for (Iterator i = a.iterator(); i.hasNext(); )
  { x += ((Integer) i.next()).intValue(); }
  ```

- Java JGL iteration over an **Array**:

  ```
  for (ForwardIterator i = a.start(); !i.atEnd(); i.advance())
  { x += ((Integer) i.get()).intValue(); }
  ```

The Java Collections library of data structures, distributed with the JDK, has a single **Iterator** interface with operations **hasNext()** and **next()**. The first of these returns **false** once the iterator has reached the end of its iteration, the second returns the current element that the iterator points to, and moves forward one position. Each container class has a method **iterator()** which returns an **Iterator** object positioned at the start of the container data.

In the JGL library (http://www.objectspace.com) in contrast there are several kinds of iterator:

- **InputIterator**: reads items in forward direction.
- **OutputIterator**: writes items in forward direction.
- **ForwardIterator**: reads/writes in forward direction.
- **BidirectionalIterator**: a **ForwardIterator** that can also read/write items in the backwards direction.
- **RandomAccessIterator**: a **BidirectionalIterator** that supports relative position comparisons within the container (between two **RandomAccessIterator** objects).

In JGL the creation of an iterator for a container is carried out by the **start** method of the container class. The test for the end of an iteration is the **atEnd()** method (the inverse of **hasNext()**). Access to the current element is by the **get()** method, which is separate to the movement operations **advance()**, **retreat()**, etc.

The typical implementation of iterators in Java uses concrete iterator classes defined as inner classes of the container class they are for, which implement the **Iterator** interface of Collections:

```
import java.util.Iterator;

public class MyLinkedList
{ protected Node head;

  protected class Node
  { Object element;
    Node next;
    .... }

  public Iterator iterator()
  { return new LinkedListIterator(); }

  private class LinkedListIterator implements Iterator
  { private MyLinkedList.Node cur;

    LinkedListIterator() { cur = head; }

    public boolean hasNext()
    { return cur != null; }

    public Object next()
    { Object obj = null;
      if (cur != null)
      { obj = cur.element;
        cur = cur.next;
```

```
      }
      return obj;
    }

    public void remove()
    { throw new UnsupportedOperationException(); }
  }
}
```

The iterator and visitor patterns are related in that they both provide frameworks for navigating through data structures, however their scope and purpose differ: Iterator is concerned with providing mechanisms for accessing individual objects of a collection and navigating over the structure. It does not define what processing is performed on these elements, this is an issue outside the pattern. With Visitor the navigation strategy is built-in to the collection classes and cannot be varied: all visitor algorithms for that structure must use this strategy. With Iterator, the navigation strategy is defined within the different iterator classes, and there can be several of these for the same structure. With Visitor what may vary is the function applied to each collection element, with Iterator what may vary is the navigation strategy to traverse a structure and access its elements.

4.7   The Mediator Pattern

The mediator pattern centralises dependencies between objects. Instead of code being written in one (dependent) object to update the state of that object when another object that it depends on changes state, there is a separate mediator object which links them and performs the necessary logic to compute the change needed in the dependent object. This reduces the complexity of the objects and increases flexibility (e.g. if the rules connecting the objects need to change without the objects themselves changing).

- *Aim*: to simplify complex connections and dependencies between a set of objects by defining **Mediator** objects which centralise information about these dependencies.
- *Implementation*: based on the idea of event sources (objects for which a change of state/method invocation needs to be communicated to other objects so that an overall required relationship can be maintained) and event targets (objects that depend on/receive information from the event sources).
- The mediator object is registered as an *event listener* with each event source object, and has a link to each target object.

Figure 4.10 shows the general structure of the pattern.

If objects of class **EventTarget** are dependent on objects of **EventSource**, we can define the mediator pattern structure as follows:

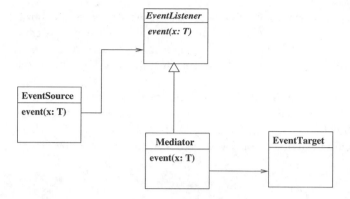

Figure 4.10: Structure of Mediator Pattern

```
class EventSource
{ private Vector eventListeners = new Vector();

  public void addEventListener(EventListener el)
  { eventListeners.add(el); }

  public void event(T x)
  { /* Do local changes in response to event */
    ...
    /* Inform all listeners of the event: */
    for (int i = 0; i < eventListeners.size(); i++)
    { EventListener el = (EventListener) eventListeners.get(i);
      el.event(x);
    }
  }
}

interface EventListener
{ void event(T x); }

class Mediator implements EventListener
{ private EventTarget eventTarget;

  public void registerEventTarget(EventTarget et)
  { eventTarget = et; }

  public void event(T x)
  { /* Update eventTarget as required to maintain
       invariant/dependency with event source */
  }
}
```

Issues to note regarding the mediator pattern include:

- Mediator is more general than Observer in that objects may be both event sources and event targets, and the code for updating event targets on a notification of an event is separated out from these target objects.
- The communication approach is similar to the Java Swing GUI event/event listener model.
- The pattern enhances maintainability/flexibility because it removes knowledge of dependencies/the detail of dependency management code from collaborating objects and puts it in the mediator object instead. When the rules of dependency change, only the mediator object needs rewriting.

4.7.1   Mediator Pattern Example: Accounts System

This system (described in Chapter 1) can be implemented using the mediator pattern, as follows. The **Customer** class is a source of **withdraw** events:

```
import java.util.Vector;

public class Customer
{ private String name;
  private Vector withdrawListeners = new Vector();

  public Customer(String nme)
  { name = nme; }

  public void addWithdrawListener(WithdrawListener w)
  { withdrawListeners.add(w); }

  public void withdraw(int amount)
  { for (int i = 0; i < withdrawListeners.size(); i++)
    { WithdrawListener wl =
        (WithdrawListener) withdrawListeners.get(i);
      wl.withdraw(amount);
    }
  }
}
```

The listener interfaces for **withdraw** and **credit** events are:

```
interface WithdrawListener
{ void withdraw(int amount); }


interface CreditListener
{ void credit(int amount); }
```

The **Mediator** class co-ordinates the response to the **withdraw** and **credit** events:

```
class Mediator // reacts to withdraw and credit events
implements WithdrawListener, CreditListener
```

```
{ private CurrentAccount caccount;
  private DepositAccount daccount;

  public void registerCurrentAccount(CurrentAccount ac)
  { caccount = ac; }

  public void registerDepositAccount(DepositAccount ad)
  { daccount = ad; }

  /* Implements business rule that money is taken from current
     account, and then from deposit, if current insufficient: */
  public void withdraw(int amount)
  { int caBal = caccount.getBalance();
    int daBal = daccount.getBalance();
    if (caBal >= amount)
    { caccount.debit(amount); }
    else if (caBal + daBal >= amount)
    { caccount.debit(caBal);
      daccount.debit(amount-caBal);
    }
  }

  /* Implements business rule that excess balance over 500
     in current account is transferred to deposit: */
  public void credit(int amount)
  { int caBal = caccount.getBalance();
    if (caBal > 500)
    { caccount.debit(caBal - 500);
      daccount.credit(caBal - 500);
    }
  }
}
```

An **Account** is both a source of **credit** events and the target of **debit** actions in response to **withdraw** and **credit** events[1]:

```
class Account
{ private int balance = 0;
  private int accountNo;
  private Vector creditListeners = new Vector();

  public Account(int ac)
  { accountNo = ac; }

  public void addCreditListener(CreditListener cl)
  { creditListeners.add(cl); }

  public int getBalance()
  { return balance; }
```

---

[1] Care is needed in such situations to avoid infinite loops of messages.

```
  public void credit(int amount)
  { balance += amount;
    for (int i = 0; i < creditListeners.size(); i++)
    { CreditListener cl =
        (CreditListener) creditListeners.get(i);
      cl.credit(amount);
    }
  }

  public void debit(int amount)
  { balance -= amount; }
}

class CurrentAccount extends Account
{ public CurrentAccount(int ac)
  { super(ac); }
}

class DepositAccount extends Account
{ public DepositAccount(int ac)
  { super(ac); }
}


public class AccountTest
{ public static void main(String[] args)
  { Mediator med = new Mediator();
    CurrentAccount ca = new CurrentAccount(1022);
    DepositAccount da = new DepositAccount(7565);
    Customer cust = new Customer("Felix");
    cust.addWithdrawListener(med);
    ca.addCreditListener(med);
    med.registerCurrentAccount(ca);
    med.registerDepositAccount(da);

    /* Test: */
    ca.credit(600);
    System.out.println(ca.getBalance()); /* 500 */
    System.out.println(da.getBalance()); /* 100 */
    cust.withdraw(550);
    System.out.println(ca.getBalance()); /*   0 */
    System.out.println(da.getBalance()); /*  50 */
  }
}
```

In the above test a credit of 600 is added to the current account, resulting in
ca's credit listener being activated, and this then trims 100 from the current
account balance and adds this to the deposit account. In the second action,
withdraw(550), the withdraw listener of the customer is activated and removes 500 units from the current account and 50 from the deposit.

4.8   The Proxy Pattern

This is a structural design pattern, which provides a surrogate or placeholder (the "proxy" object) that represents another ("real") object. It is applied when there is a need for a more versatile or sophisticated interface to an object than a simple direct reference. Examples include:

- *remote proxy*: e.g. the stub in Java RMI, providing a local representative for a server object residing on a remote host;
- *virtual proxy*: creating space/time consuming objects only on demand (e.g. database connections);
- *protection proxy*: controlling access to the real object to provide different levels of access rights.

Figure 4.11 shows the general structure of this pattern.

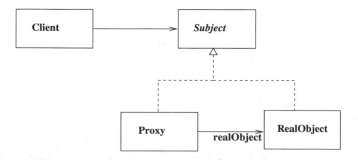

Figure 4.11: Structure of Proxy Design Pattern

The classes involved in the pattern are:

- *Proxy*: implements the **Subject** interface, so that a proxy can be substituted for the real object. It has a reference to the real object, or other means for forwarding commands to it.
- *Subject*: defines the common interface of **Proxy** and **RealObject** so that a **Proxy** can be used anywhere that a **RealObject** is expected.
- *RealObject*: defines the real object that the proxy represents.

4.8.1   Proxy Pattern Example: Java RMI

RMI (remote method invocation) is a mechanism for distributed processing allowing method invocations to be made on remote objects (i.e. objects running on a different host machine to the caller). It involves:

- **Server**: an object providing services to other objects, possibly on different hosts.

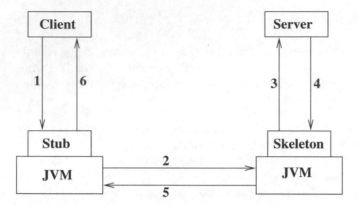

Figure 4.12: Steps of RMI

- **Service contract**: an interface declaring the services provided by server objects.
- **Client**: an object using services of remote servers.
- **Stub**: an object on the same host as the client (i.e. a *local* object), serving as a proxy for a remote server object.
- **Skeleton**: an object on the same host as the server, which receives requests from stubs and dispatches requests to the server.

The steps of RMI are shown in Figure 4.12. These steps are:

1. a remote invocation **server.m(p)** by the client is carried out as an invocation of a method of the stub: **stub.m(p)**;
2. the stub marshals the arguments **p** (i.e. puts them into a form that can be transmitted over the network), then sends the arguments and call information to the skeleton on the server host;
3. the skeleton unmarshals the arguments and the call information, then invokes the server method **server.m(p)** with these arguments;
4. the server object executes the method, and returns its result to the skeleton;
5. the skeleton marshals the result, and sends this back to the stub;
6. the stub unmarshals the result, and returns this to the client.

Using Java RMI

The *RMI registry* maps server program names to actual programs on the server host. If **name** is registered, then the URL **rmi://host:port/name** identifies the server program, where **host** is the name/IP address of the host running the registry, **port** is the registry port number. The **java.rmi** package provides support for RMI classes: the **Naming** class in this package encapsulates the RMI registry operations, and provides the following static methods (Table 4.1).

To use RMI to manage communication between a local and remote program, we:

bind(name,ob)	binds object **ob** to **name**
rebind(namc,ob)	binds **ob** to **name**: replaces the old binding of **name**
unbind(name,ob)	removes the binding of **ob** to **name**
lookup(url)	returns the object **ob** named by **url**
list(url)	lists the registered bindings of the RMI registry running on **url**

Table 4.1: Methods of the **Naming** class

1. Define the interface of the remote object, e.g.

```
public interface Contract extends Remote
{
  public void aService(...) throws RemoteException;
  /* other services */ ...
}
```

The types of service arguments and return types must be serialisable, so that they can be marshalled and transmitted over a network.

2. Define a server implementing **Contract**:

```
public class ServiceProvider extends UnicastRemoteObject
       implements Contract
{
  public void aService(...) throws RemoteException
  { /* implementation */  }
  /* implementation of other services */ ...
}
```

3. Create an instance of this server class and register it:

```
Contract server = new ServiceProvider(...);
Naming.rebind(name,server);
```

4. Generate the stub **ServiceProvider_Stub** and skeleton **ServiceProvider_Skel** classes by calling **javac ServiceProvider.java** then running the RMI compiler **rmic** on **ServiceProvider**. The stub implements **Contract**.

5. Each client object must locate the remote server object, then invoke methods on it:

```
class AClient
{ ...
  Remote remoteObj = Naming.lookup("rmi://host:port/name");
  Contract serverObj = (Contract) remoteObj;
  ...
  serverObj.aService(...);   // remote invocation
  ...
}
```

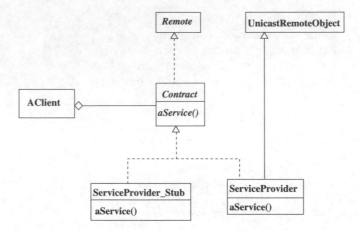

Figure 4.13: Typical RMI Application Structure

remoteObj is an instance of the stub.

Figure 4.13 shows the typical structure of an RMI-based system. The correspondence with the proxy pattern is:

- **Contract** corresponds to **Subject**.
- **AClient** corresponds to **Client**.
- **ServiceProvider_Stub** corresponds to **Proxy**.
- **ServiceProvider** corresponds to **RealObject**.

The RMI mechanism is a good candidate for the communication subsystem in the restaurant management system: notification of new dishes and drinks for preparation can be sent to the kitchen and bar interfaces by invoking operations on the remote objects that manage these interfaces.

4.9   Creational Patterns

These patterns provide some ways of managing object creation. In general they try to abstract away from creation of specific instances of classes, to avoid dependence by one part of a system on the exact classes provided by another.

Some examples are:

- Abstract Factory.
- Builder.
- Factory Method.
- Prototype.
- Singleton.

We will look in detail at Abstract Factory and Singleton.

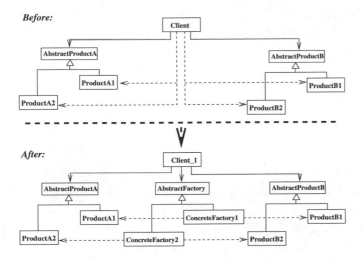

Figure 4.14: Application of Abstract Factory

4.9.1   The Abstract Factory Pattern

This pattern:

- Provides an interface for creating families of related objects without the need to specify their concrete classes (e.g. to create a window and an attached scrollbar, in a consistent visual style such as X/Motif or Presentation Manager, without individually specifying their style).
- Different subclasses of an **AbstractFactory** class are responsible for creating objects appropriate to particular families.

Figure 4.14 shows how the pattern avoids dependence on specific classes. The **Client** class in the version without the pattern needs to know details of all product hierarchies, which is not good for flexibility or maintainability. In the revised version, **Client_1** has no knowledge of the concrete products being created, it only has reference to the abstract product and abstract factory classes.

Before application of the abstract factory pattern we could have the following code structure:

```
public class Client
{ private AbstractProductA productA;
  private AbstractProductB productB;
  public static final int TYPE1 = 0;
  public static final int TYPE2 = 1;
  private int implementation_kind;  /*  { TYPE1, TYPE2 }  */

  public Client()
  { implementation_kind = TYPE1; }
```

```
  public void settup()
  { if (implementation_kind == TYPE1)
    { productA = new ProductA1();
      productB = new ProductB1();
    }
    else
    { productA = new ProductA2();
      productB = new ProductB2();
    }
  }
}
```

After application of the abstract factory pattern the code could be:

```
public class Client_1
{ private AbstractFactory factory;
  private AbstractProductA productA;
  private AbstractProductB productB;

  public Client_1()
  { factory = new ConcreteFactory1(); }

  public void settup()
  { productA = factory.createProductA();
    productB = factory.createProductB();
  }
}
```

An **AbstractFactory** object can create products (e.g. products A or B) of either implementation kind 1 or 2:

```
abstract class AbstractFactory
{ public abstract AbstractProductA createProductA();

  public abstract AbstractProductB createProductB();
}
```

Each **AbstractFactory** subclass creates products for a particular implementation kind/family:

```
class ConcreteFactory1 extends AbstractFactory
{ public AbstractProductA createProductA()
  { ProductA1 prod = new ProductA1();
    return prod;
  }

  public AbstractProductB createProductB()
  { ProductB1 prod = new ProductB1();
    return prod;
  }
}
```

Similarly for **ConcreteFactory2**.

Abstract Factory is used when:

- A system should be independent of how its products are created, composed and represented;
- a system needs to be configured with one of a number of families of products;
- a family of related objects is designed to be used together, and this constraint needs to be enforced.

The pattern involves the classes:

- **AbstractFactory** – this declares operations which create abstract product objects.
- **ConcreteFactory** subclasses – these implement creation operations for concrete products belonging to a particular implementation kind/family.
- **AbstractProduct** – this declares an interface for one type of products.
- **ConcreteProduct** – implements the **AbstractProduct** interface, and defines a product type to be created by the corresponding concrete factory.
- **Client_1** – uses only **AbstractProduct** and **AbstractFactory** interfaces, so it is independent of the particular family in use.

The benefits of this pattern are that it:

- Reduces the dependence of clients on specific concrete products – so these can be changed without affecting clients provided the abstract product interface and semantics are satisfied.
- Promotes consistency among products – the pattern enforces that applications only use products from one family at a time.

4.9.2   The Singleton Pattern

This pattern is used to define classes which must have only a single instance (e.g. mathematical utility classes, a printer spooler, etc.), in a way that is more elegant than using a global non-object variable. Figure 4.15 shows the structure of this pattern.

Singleton is used when:

- There must be a unique instance of a class, and it must be accessible to clients from a well-known access point;
- when the sole instance should be extensible by subclassing, and clients should be able to use an extended instance without modifying their code.

The involved classes are:

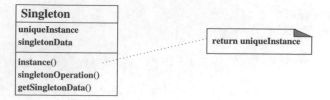

Figure 4.15: Structure of Singleton Pattern

- **Singleton** – defines an operation **instance** that lets clients access its unique instance. **instance** is a class level operation: a class method in Smalltalk, static method in Java, or static member function in C++.
- **Singleton** may also be responsible for creating its own unique instance.

The benefits of this pattern are that it:

- provides controlled access to the **Singleton** instance – this can only be accessed via the **instance** method;
- reduces the name space of the program – a class instead of a global variable;
- permits subclassing of **Singleton**;
- it can be adapted easily to give a fixed number **N** > 1 of instances.

Example Java code of a **Singleton** class could be:

```java
class Singleton
{ private static Singleton uniqueInstance = null;
  private int singletonData = 42;

  private Singleton() { }

  public static Singleton instance()
  { if (uniqueInstance == null)
    { uniqueInstance = new Singleton(); }
    return uniqueInstance;
  }

  public int getData()
  { return singletonData; }
}

public class Test
{ public static void main(String args[])
  { Singleton d = Singleton.instance();
    System.out.println(d.getData());          /* 42 */
    System.out.println(d.instance() == d);    /* true */
  }
}
```

4.10   Structural Patterns

These patterns are concerned with the composition of classes or objects into larger structures. Examples include:

- Adapter.
- Bridge.
- Decorator.
- Facade.
- Flyweight.
- Proxy.

In the following we will describe Adapter, Bridge and Facade. Adapter and Facade, like Proxy, involve the definition of an intermediary class between a client and supplier, in order to adapt the services provided by the supplier to those required by the client, in the case of Adapter, and to reduce the dependencies between the client and its suppliers, in the case of Facade.

4.10.1   The Adapter Pattern

This pattern can be used to convert the interface of a class (the Adaptee) into another interface suitable for use by particular clients. For example, the pattern can be used to define a wrapper around legacy or library code to enable its use in a new application. It is somewhat analogous to the use of plug converters: when you go to Australia, you can't modify the wall socket (the Adaptee), but instead need to bring a converter (an Adapter) for your UK equipment. Figure 4.16 shows the class version of this pattern, which uses inheritance to form the wrapper layer. Figure 4.17 shows the object version, which uses clientship instead.

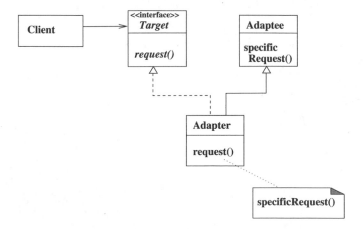

Figure 4.16: Class Adapter Structure

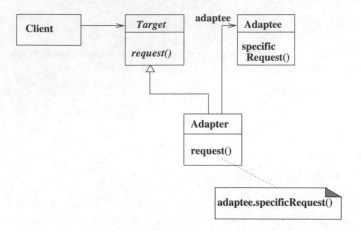

Figure 4.17: Object Adapter Structure

The original design of a client, without using the pattern, could be:

```
public class Client
{ private Adaptee adaptee;

  public void m(X x)
  { C1;
    adaptee.specificRequest(f(x));
    C2
  }
  ...
}


class Adaptee
{ public void specificRequest(S s) { ... }
}
```

Here the client has to do the adaption itself. If instead we use Object Adapter, we get:

```
public class Client_1
{ private Target target;
  ...
  public void m(X x)
  { C1;
    target.request(g(x));
    C2
  }
  ...
}


abstract class Target
{ ...
```

```
   public abstract void request(T t);
   ...
}

class Adapter extends Target
{ private Adaptee adaptee;
   ...
  public void request(T t)
  { adaptee.specificRequest(h(t)); }
}
```

where $\mathbf{h(g(x))} = \mathbf{f(x)}$ for $\mathbf{x} : \mathbf{X}$.

For example, **h** could convert strings in one format (used by the client) to a format expected by the adaptee. The **target** object should be in the **Adapter** subtype of **Target** when **target.request(g(x))** is executed.

This pattern is applied when:

- An existing class needs to be reused, and its interface does not match one required by a new application.
- We want to create a reusable class which co-operates with unrelated or unforeseen classes, classes which do not necessarily have compatible interfaces.

The classes involved are:

- **Target** – this defines a domain-specific interface used by **Client_1**.
- **Client_1** – this collaborates with objects conforming to the **Target** interface.
- **Adaptee** – this defines an existing interface that needs adapting.
- **Adapter** – adapts interface of **Adaptee** to that of **Target**.

The benefits of the class adapter pattern are:

- It lets the **Adapter** override some of the **Adaptee**s methods, because it is a subclass of **Adaptee**.
- It introduces only one extra object, and no pointer indirection is needed to get to the adaptee.

However, **Adapter** is specific to **Adaptee**, it won't work for subclasses of **Adaptee**. In Java, multiple inheritance is not allowed, so the class adapter pattern is only possible if we use a Java interface instead of a class for **Target**.

Object Adapter solves these problems, but then the **Adapter** cannot override methods of **Adaptee**.

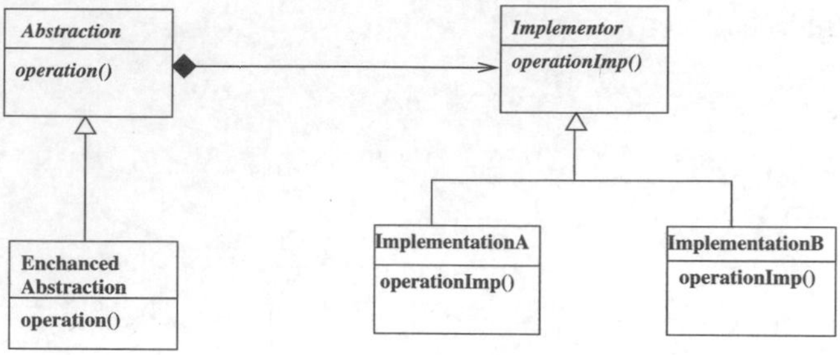

Figure 4.18: Structure of Bridge Pattern

4.10.2   The Bridge Pattern

The intent of this pattern is to separate an abstraction from its implementation by moving these aspects into separate classes, connected by a reference. It can be applied when an interface and its implementation should vary independently, or when we require a uniform interface to interchangeable class hierarchies.

Figure 4.18 shows the typical structure of the pattern.

The benefits of this pattern are that:

- The abstraction and implementation are independent.
- It removes the "subclass explosion" problem, where explicit classes have to be defined for each enhancement/concrete implementation variety combination.
- Implementations may vary dynamically.

A disadvantage, common to many patterns, is that an added level of indirection is introduced.

An example of the simplification of class hierarchies which Bridge can produce is shown in Figure 4.19. On the left hand side each combination of a model element and its possible visual representation is given a specific class in which these aspects are integrated. On the right hand side the visual and conceptual classes are separated, which not only reduces the number and complexity of the classes, but gives a cleaner separation of concerns in the system.

4.10.3   The Facade Pattern

This pattern is used to provide a single interface to a set of classes in a subsystem: it defines an interface for clients which makes the subsystem easier to use (Figure 4.20). Effectively it acts as an interface for a module containing the classes.

An example would be a report writing system, where access to a set of low-level report generation classes may be needed by some clients, but most just want to run standard operations **produceReport** and **printReport**: these operations can be placed in the facade class.

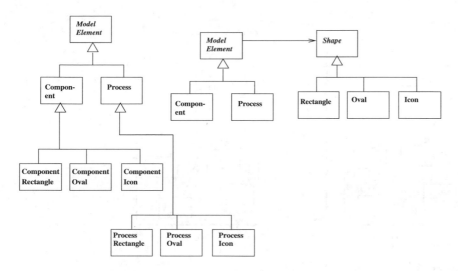

Figure 4.19: Example of Bridge Pattern

The pattern is applied if:

- A simple interface is needed for a complex subsystem – a default view that is adequate for most clients;
- there are many dependencies between clients and a set of classes. The facade can decouple the details of this set from clients and other modules, promoting subsystem independence and reuse;
- layering of subsystems is needed – the facade provides a "specification" interface of a layer/module so that other layers do not need to depend on the internal classes of the module.

The classes involved are:

- **Facade** – this knows which subsystem classes are responsible for particular requests; it delegates client requests to appropriate subsystem objects and may combine functionalities from several objects in a single module operation;
- subsystem classes – these carry out work assigned by the facade, but have no knowledge of it (reference to it).

The benefits of this pattern include:

- It shields clients from internal module details, making it easier to modify the module without affecting clients;
- it reduces compilation dependencies and hence time;
- some clients can still access internal classes (or preferably, interfaces for them) if they really need to.

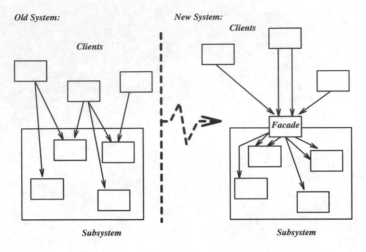

Figure 4.20: Application of Facade pattern

4.11   Behavioural Patterns

These patterns are concerned with organising patterns of communication between objects, algorithms and functional responsibilities of objects. Some examples of behavioural patterns are:

- Chain of Responsibility.
- Command.
- Observer.
- State.
- Mediator.
- Template Method.
- Visitor.

4.11.1   The Chain of Responsibility Pattern

This is an object-oriented analogue of the procedural programming pattern "filter" or cascade of conditional tests: the chain of responsibility pattern enables a request to be passed down a chain of objects until one is able to respond to it.

Examples could include exception handling routines, utility cost calculation routines, etc. Figure 4.21 shows the typical structure of this pattern.

It is used:

- When more than one object may handle a request, and the handler isn't known *a priori* to a client.

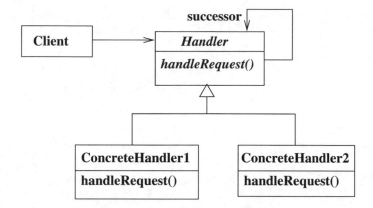

Figure 4.21: Chain of Responsibility Class Structure

- When a request should be issued to several objects, but you need to avoid explicitly specifying which ones (e.g. in a dynamic network, a node may not be aware of what are all existing nodes).
- The set of objects that can handle a request is specified dynamically.

The classes involved are:

- **Handler** this defines the interface for handling requests, and a successor link.
- **ConcreteHandler** – this handles those requests that it is responsible for, otherwise it forwards the request to its successor object.
- **Client** – initiates request to a **ConcreteHandler** object in the chain.

The benefits include:

- Reduced coupling – a client doesn't have to know what object will actually respond to its request.
- Flexibility in assigning responsibilities to objects – the chain can be dynamically modified, unlike a static conditional cascade approach.

But we need to ensure that always *some* object will eventually be reached that can handle each request.

The following is a small example of applying the pattern. Before the pattern is used, we could have a hard-coded structure of tests:

```
void Op()
{ if (C1)
  { Code1 }
  else if (C2)
  { Code2 }
  else
  { Code3 }
}
```

This code is directly written in the **Client**.

Using the chain of responsibility pattern we could replace this by:

```
abstract class Handler
{ protected Handler successor;

  public abstract void handleRequest();
}

class C1Handler extends Handler
{
  public void handleRequest()
  { if (C1) { Code1 }
    else
    { successor.handleRequest(); }
  }
}
```

and similarly for **C2Handler** and **C3Handler**, and we set up a chain of objects
o1: C1Handler, **o2: C2Handler** and **o3: C3Handler** with:

$$o1.\text{successor} = o2$$

and

$$o2.\text{successor} = o3$$

(Figure 4.22). The client operation is:

```
void  Op() { handler.handleRequest(); }
```

where **handler: C1Handler**.

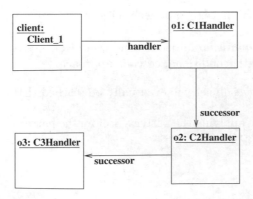

Figure 4.22: Object Structure of Chain of Responsibility

4.12   Selection of Design Patterns

Recognising which pattern to use when is a difficult problem, which depends on experience and understanding. Some general guidelines can be given, however:

- Given the constraints of a specific application area and problem, consider the key requirements of the problem, for example, a need to support multiple visual formats (Motif style windows, etc.) in an extensible way, or a need to repeatedly access all the elements of a collection (e.g. potential winning lines in a noughts and crosses game).
- Select a pattern (or combination of patterns) which best fits these requirements, such as the abstract factory pattern to consistently and abstractly create different styles of windows, etc., Singleton to generate a unique copy of each concrete factory, Iterator to access all elements of a collection.
- Check that the design goals are met.

For example, for the structural patterns we have the properties:

- Structural class patterns compose interfaces or implementations using inheritance.
- Structural object patterns compose objects using clientship, their advantage over the class pattern approach is that configurations can be changed at runtime.

Summary

Design patterns provide a useful catalogue of design solutions for common design problems, at the level of individual modules or subsystems.

We have shown how design patterns can be used to organise the structure of a program in a way which makes this structure more systematic, and improves the maintainability and flexibility of the code.

Exercises

1 An application manages the set of current students registered in a university department. This information is stored in a class

```
class StudentData
{ private Map students;   /* Map from String to Student */
  private Vector studentIds;
      /* List of valid student id's, as Strings */
  ...
}
```

Given a student id, **ss**, if **studentIds.contains(ss)** then it is a valid id, and **students.get(ss)** is non-null.

Define a Java implementation for the **StudentData** class of a bi-directional iterator **LinearIterator** which is defined by the interface:

```
interface LinearIterator
{ public boolean hasNext();
  public boolean hasPrev();
  public Object getNext();
  public Object getPrev();
}
```

This iterator should return **Student** objects from **students** according to the order defined by **studentIds**.

2   Identify a suitable design pattern to implement the following system:

> An estate agents database has to manage two kinds of property, Houses and Flats, which have common attributes **int price** and **String vendor**.   **House** has an additional attribute **int numberOfFloors** and **Flat** has an additional attribute **String position** describing its location in a larger property.
> There is a common method **display()** which lists the attributes and values of the properties.

Implement the system using the selected design pattern.

3   Assume we have a list **list** of integers, and we want to detect all pairs **x** and **y** of elements in the list which satisfy **x < y ∗ y**. If the class of lists has built-in traversal methods **reset**, **next** and **hasNext**, what is wrong with the following attempt at a solution?

```
for (list.reset(); list.hasNext();)
{ Integer i1 = (Integer) list.next();
  int x1 = i1.intValue();
  for (list.reset(); list.hasNext();)
  { Integer i2 = (Integer) list.next();
    int x2 = i2.intValue();
    if (x1 < x2*x2)
    { System.out.println(x1 + " is less than " + x2 + " squared"); }
  }
}
```

4   Apply the observer pattern to the following problem:

> In a simplified version of the restaurant order system, the waiter enters orders for food and drink items into a terminal, all the food items are presented in sequence on the "to prepare" display in the kitchen, and all the drink items are presented on a similar display in the bar.

The relevant classes are:

```
public class Order
{ private Vector orderItems = new Vector();
  /* List of OrderItem objects */

  public void add(OrderItem oi)
  { orderItems.add(oi); }
}

abstract class OrderItem
{ private String name;

  public OrderItem(String nme)
  { name = nme; }

  public String toString()
  { return name; }
}

class Food extends OrderItem
{ public Food(String nme)
  { super(name); }
}

class Drink extends OrderItem
{ public Drink(String nme)
  { super(nme); }
}

public class KitchenDisplay extends JFrame
{ public void add(Food fd)
  { ... adds fd to list in display ... }
}

public class BarDisplay extends JFrame
{ public void add(Drink dk)
  { ... adds dk to list in display ... }
}
```

Hint: the bar and kitchen only need to know about the most recent order item, not the whole list **orderItems**, so modify the observer pattern so that **update** communicates this item to each observer.

5   Apply the state pattern to the following problem:

> An aircraft goes through several modes in its lifetime (Figure 4.23): **Parked** at a stand, **Taxiing** at the airport, **ManualFlight** and **AutopilotFlight**. A plane is initially in the parked mode, then starts taxiing, etc. Build a software representation of an aircraft,

supporting two operations: **raiseWheels()** and **turnLeft()**. These operations should just print out their actions, e.g. a plane on the ground will do

```
public void turnLeft()
{ System.out.println("Turning wheels left"); }
```

whereas a plane in the air will do

```
public void turnLeft()
{ System.out.println("Turning rudder left"); }
```

Also define methods to move an aircraft from one mode to another, i.e. the methods **park**, **startTaxiing**, etc.

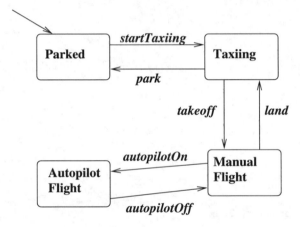

Figure 4.23: Aircraft Modes

6 Imagine that we have an application which outputs VRML files [3] (these produce 3-D VR images when viewed through a suitable web browser or browser pluggin). It has Java classes **VRMLGroup**, **VRMLShape** which represent the corresponding VRML items:

```
class VRMLGroup
{ private Vector items = new Vector();

  public void addItem(VRMLShape s)
  { items.add(s); }
}

class VRMLShape
{ private String geometry; /* Name of the shape */
  private int depth;  /* z extent */
  private int width;  /* x extent */
```

```
  private int height; /* y extent */
  private String colour; /* R G B fractions */

  public VRMLShape(String s, int x, int y, int z,
                   String col)
  { geometry = s;
    depth = z;
    width = x;
    height = y;
    colour = col;
  }
}
```

Use the visitor pattern to define a class which prints out a **VRMLGroup** object and its contained objects in the usual VRML format. For example if we had a **VRMLGroup** object **g** with **g.items** = [b] and **b.geometry** = "Box", **b.depth** = 15, **b.width** = 6, **b.height** = 5 and **b.colour** = "0.99 0.9 0.9", then the class should print:

```
Group
{ children
  [
    Shape
    { geometry Box { size 6 5 15 }
      appearance Appearance
      { material Material
        { diffuseColor 0.99 0.9 0.9 }
      }
    }
  ]
}
```

You will need to add query methods to the VRML classes so the visitor can access their attributes, and define a **postVisit** method of the printing visitor to print the closing] and } brackets of a group.

Chapter 5

Coordination Contracts

This chapter defines the concept of *coordination contract* as a means of organising applications in terms of business rules or other required invariants which constrain the joint behaviour of the components they apply to. This approach to organisation of an application supports its adaption to changing requirements. We also show that some design patterns can be alternatively expressed in terms of contracts.

5.1   Beyond Object-oriented Design

According to [38], "There are only two ways to use a class ... One is to inherit from it; [...]. The other one is to become a client of [it]." Indeed, it is generally accepted that, in object-oriented software construction, these are the two basic techniques for structuring systems. Inheritance allows us to reuse the behaviour of a class in the definition of new classes. Clientship, i.e. the ability to establish client/supplier relations between objects, provides, through feature calling, the basic mechanism of object-oriented computation.

By the use of inheritance and clientship, object-orientation has made software construction more scalable. Inheritance provides a powerful organisation mechanism via which we can better control the complexity of the process of software construction. On the other hand, building on what we could call a "societal metaphor" according to which the envisaged system is conceived as a "society" of objects that interact by drawing on the services that each provides, clientship allows us to decompose the global behaviour of the system in a way that mimics typical ways in which people organise themselves in society, which helps in taming the complexity of establishing the interconnections that are necessary to make the global properties required of the system emerge from more basic and controllable behaviours. Such forms of "programming by emergence" fit well with the General System approach to behavioural modelling that can be found in many other disciplines, including Economic and Social Sciences [19].

However, clientship leads to systems of components that are too tightly coupled and rigid to support the levels of agility that are required to operate in environments that are "business time critical", namely those that make use of web services, business-to-business (B2B), peer-to-peer (P2P), or otherwise operate in what is known as "internet-time" [53]. More and more, organisations require systems that can evolve together with the business domain, in response to external changes coming from new legislation or the competition, or as an instrument of their own business strategies, namely when it is important to have an aggressive presence in the market.

As a result, building applications is becoming a dynamic process that consists of locating services that provide required basic functionalities, and "orchestrating" them, i.e. establishing collaborations between them, so that the global properties required of the application, at that time, can emerge from their joint behaviour. This translates directly to the familiar characterisation of web services as "late binding" or, better, "just-in-time binding", showing that flexible architectures are required to make the resulting systems amenable to a continuous process of reconfiguration. For this purpose, interactions cannot be hardwired into the code that implements the services. If collaborations are not modelled explicitly as first-class entities that can be manipulated by a process of dynamic reconfiguration, the overhead that just-in-time integration and other operational aspects of this new architecture represent will not lead to the levels of agility that are required for the paradigm to succeed.

Because interactions in object-oriented approaches are based on *identities*, in the sense that, through clientship, objects interact by invoking specific methods of specific objects (instances) to get something specific done, the resulting systems are too rigid to support the identified levels of agility. Any change on the collaborations that an object maintains with other objects needs to be performed at the level of the code that implements that object and, possibly, of the objects with which the new collaborations are established. On the contrary, interactions in a service-oriented approach should be based on the description of what is required, thus decoupling "what one wants to be done" from "who does it". In the context of the "societal metaphor" that we mentioned above, it is interesting to note that this shift from "object" to "service"-oriented interactions mirrors what has been happening already in human society: more and more, business relationships are established in terms of acquisition of services (e.g. 1000 Watts of lighting for your office) instead of products (10 lamps of 100 Watts each for the office).

Naturally, object-oriented technology does not prevent such flexible modes of interconnections to be implemented. Design mechanisms, making use of event publishing/subscription through brokers and other well-known patterns [21], have already found their way into commercially available products that support implicit invocation [41], instead of feature calling (explicit invocation). However, solutions based on the use of design patterns are not at the level of abstraction in which the need for change arises and needs to be managed. Being mechanisms that operate at the design level, there is a wide gap that separates them from the business modelling levels at which change is better perceived and managed. This conceptual gap is not easily bridged, and the process that leads from the business requirements to the identification and instantiation of the relevant design patterns is not easily documented or made otherwise explicit in a way that facilitates changes to be carried out. Once instantiated, design patterns code up interactions in ways that, typically, requires evolution to be intrusive because they were not conceived to be evolvable. Hence, most of the time, the pattern will dissolve as the system evolves. Therefore, we need semantic primitives through which interconnections can be externalised, modelled explicitly, and evolved directly as representations of business rules.

In this chapter we show that support for "service-oriented" development can be found in "coordination technologies": a set of analysis techniques, modelling primitives, design principles and patterns that has been developed to externalise interactions into explicit, first-class entities that can be dynamically superposed over system components to co-ordinate their joint behaviour. The key to the move from "identity" to "service"-based interaction is in the separation between "computation" and "coordination" [22], i.e. the ability to separately address the local computations of components that implement the functionalities they advertise through their interfaces, from the coordination mechanisms that need to be superposed on these computations to achieve the required properties of the global system behaviour. It is clear that this separation is not supported by clientship: "In the execution of an object-oriented software system, all computation is achieved by calling certain features on certain objects" [38].

5.2   Why Object-Orientation is not Evolutionary

As an example of the principles and techniques of coordination technologies, and of the differences between these and what is currently available through object-oriented modelling, consider the familiar world of bank accounts and customers who can make deposits, withdrawals, transfers, and so forth.

In a typical classroom modelling exercise, a class **Account** is defined with, among others, an operation allowing for the current balance to be obtained, and an operation **debit** with parameter **amount**. A customer that owns an account is also part of the business domain and, as such, should figure explicitly, under some representation, in the model with an attribute **account: Account** so that transactions performed by that customer can be modelled through calls **account.debit(amount)**. The condition **balance ≥ amount** is typically declared in **Account** as a precondition on **debit(amount)** to ensure that there are enough funds for the withdrawal to be made. This precondition establishes a contractual relationship between account and customer, both in the technical sense developed by B. Meyer [38] and as one of the business rules that establish the way customers are required to interact with accounts.

The relationship between customers and accounts that is established in this way is based on "identities" in the sense that the customer has an attribute that identifies the account and they know precisely which operation of the account to invoke. This mode of interaction leads to systems in which components are too tightly coupled to let them, and their interactions, evolve independently from each other. Hence, for instance, when the bank comes up with a new account package for VIP-customers that gives them some credit allowance limit for overdrawing their accounts, changes need to be made on a variety of components, depending on the way the VIP-package is modelled. Let us analyse a few of them.

A naïve solution to the problem of adapting the existing system to the new business rule would be to enrich **Account** with a new operation, **VIPdebit**, for the more flexible withdrawals (Figure 5.1). **balance′** denotes the value of

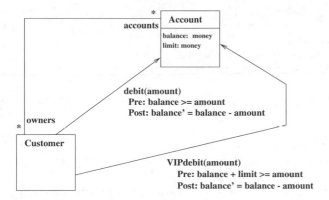

Figure 5.1: Adding VIPdebit operation to Account

balance after the operation.

Besides requiring obvious and direct changes to the class **Account**, this solution is also intrusive on the client side because customers now have to decide which operation to call. A further disadvantage of this solution is in the fact that the "business rule", i.e. the VIP status of the relationship between a customer and an account, is completely coded in the way the customer calls the account and, thus, cannot be "managed" explicitly as a business notion.

The typical OO-solution to this new situation is different: it consists in defining a subclass **VIPAccount** of **Account** with a new attribute **limit** and a weaker precondition on the operation **debit(amount)**, that **balance+limit** $\geq$ **amount** (Figure 5.2).

In this way, the more flexible contractual relationships can be established directly between the client (customer) and the specialisation of the supplier (the **VIPAccount**s). Nevertheless, there are two main drawbacks in this solution. On the one hand, it introduces, in the conceptual model, classes that have no counterpart in the real problem domain. It is the customers who are VIPs, not the accounts. However, having placed the contractual relationship between customers and accounts in **Account**, one is forced to model the revised collaboration through a specialisation of the previous one, which implies the definition of the artificial subclass of **Account**. The second disadvantage is not a methodological but a technical one. The new solution is still intrusive because the other classes in the system need to be made aware of the

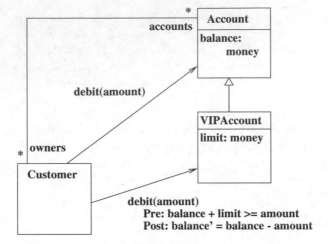

Figure 5.2: Adding VIPAccount subclass to Account

existence of the new specialised class so that links between instances can be established through the new class. More generally, references to accounts need to be reclassified between "regular" and VIP-accounts[1].

The main disadvantages in both solutions result from two important factors. On the one hand, the fact that the business rule that dictates the interaction that is required between customers and accounts is being coded on the side of the supplier (the account), which is what is favoured by Meyer's notion of contract [38]. This makes it difficult to accommodate new forms of the interaction that depend on the client side of it. On the other hand, relationships are established through "identities", i.e. through explicit naming of client/supplier objects and by operation invocation. This requires that any change be intrusive on the code that implements the objects involved.

A more sensible alternative is to place the interaction at the level of the relationship that exists between customers and accounts by promoting it to what in the UML [11] is known as an *Association Class*, i.e. an association that can also have class properties and features. In the account package example, the promotion could be achieved by introducing an association class **ownership** in which the details that pertain to coordination of the joint behaviour of customers and accounts, including the preconditions that apply to the interactions, can be placed (Figure 5.3).

Changes to the ownership, such as the addition of an attribute **limit** and the weaker precondition on the interaction, can now be put on specialisations of the new class without having to change the role classes. Indeed, resorting to association classes keeps the model faithful to the application domain by representing explicitly the business rules that co-ordinate the interaction between the entities involved.

---

[1]In order for a customer to know that a **debit** call should be acceptable, it needs to know which kind of account it is calling the operation on.

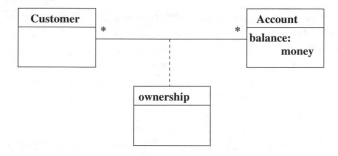

Figure 5.3: Using an Association Class

However, association classes still present severe drawbacks as a solution to our problem because the way they address relationships is still "identity"-based. From the discussion held above about the disadvantages of the attribute-based representation of the relationship between accounts and customers, it seems clear that the typical implementation of associations through attributes would take us one step back. The best way of implementing the interaction through the association class would seem to be for a new operation to be declared for **ownership** that can act as a mediator. Upon a call from the client, the mediator would have the responsibility of determining whether the contractual relationship between the partners is valid and, in case it is, delegate on the supplier to proceed. In this way, it would, indeed, be possible to achieve the required flexibility for accommodating changes in the business rules simply by modifying the contracts as required, e.g. at the level of the preconditions of the mediators, without having to modify the partners in the contract. Notice that the essence of this solution is to put in place a form of implicit invocation [41].

Although the advantage of making relationships first-class citizens in conceptual modelling has been recognised by many authors (e.g. [30]), which has led to the ISO General Relationship Model (ISO/IEC 10165-7), things are not as clean with this solution as they may seem. On the one hand, the fact that a mediator is used for co-ordinating the interaction between two given objects does not prevent direct relationships from being established that may side-step it and violate the business rule. In the case of the account package, nothing prevents a designer from connecting directly a customer to an account through attributes and direct invocation, possibly breaching the contract because the precondition has now been moved from the account to the mediator.

On the other hand, the solution is still intrusive in the sense that the calls to the mediator must be explicitly programmed in the implementation of the classes involved in the association. Moreover, it is not incremental in the sense that the addition of new business rules cannot be achieved by simply introducing new association classes and mediators. The other classes in the system need to be made aware that new association classes have become available so that the right mediators are used for establishing the required interactions. That is, the burden of deciding which mediator to interact with is put again on the side of clients. On the other hand, different rules may interact with each other thus requiring an additional level of coordination among the mediators themselves to be programmed. This leads to models that are not as abstract as they ought to be due to the need to make explicit (even program) the relationships that may exist between the original classes and the mediators, and among the different mediators themselves. In summary, we end up facing the problems that, in the introduction, we identified for the use of design patterns in general.

The primitive that we have developed for modelling this kind of contractual relationship between components circumvents these problems by abandoning the "identity"-based mechanism on which the object-oriented paradigm relies for interactions, and adopting instead a mechanism of *superposition* that allows for collaborations to be modelled outside the components as connectors (coordination contracts) that can be applied, at runtime, to co-ordinate their behaviour. From a methodological point of view, this alternative approach encourages developers to identify dependencies between components in terms of services rather than identities. From the implementation point of view, superposition of coordination contracts has the advantage of being non-intrusive on the implementation of the components. That is, it does not require the code that implements the components to be changed or adapted, precisely because there is no information on the interactions that is coded inside the components. As a result, systems can evolve through the addition, deletion or substitution of coordination contracts without requiring any change in the way the core entities have been deployed.

This is the approach that we are going to present in the rest of the chapter. We start by presenting it as an extension of object-oriented software construction with a new primitive: coordination contracts. We then show how some widely-used design patterns can be alternatively implemented using coordination contracts. Finally we discuss appropriate development methods which are supported by coordination contracts.

5.3   Coordination Contracts

The method that we are advocating for promoting agility in software systems relies on the separation between what can be considered the core business entities and the rules according to which they collaborate in order to provide the services required from the system. It also models dependencies between components in terms of services rather than identities. In the context of object-oriented software construction techniques, this can be achieved through a new semantic primitive called *coordination contract* [6] and on the notion of *superposition* as developed for parallel program design [29].

The main idea is that, through coordination contracts, explicit invocations of the form **a.debit(n)** are decoupled from the execution of the service itself by letting the contract intercept the call and superpose whatever coordination mechanisms are required by the business rules. These mechanisms are specified as event/reaction rules of the form:

```
when <event>
with <guard>
before <action>
do <action>
after <action>
```

The "when"-clause identifies the trigger which, in the context of object-oriented modelling, is, typically, a method invocation. Under "do" we identify the reactions to be performed, replacing the code of the invoked method, when the trigger occurs. It consists of a set of actions of the partners and the contract's own actions, which constitute what we call the synchronisation set associated with the trigger. Additionally or alternatively, we can specify actions to be performed **before** the service and **after** the service.

Under the "with" clause, we include conditions that should be observed for the reaction to be performed. If any of the conditions fails, the reaction is not performed and the occurrence of the trigger fails. Failure is handled through whatever mechanisms are provided by the language used for deployment, such as exceptions in Java. Notice that the **when** and **with** clause deal with separate aspects of the contract rule: the rule can only be triggered by the event in the **when** clause, and can only execute normally without exception if the **with** clause is also true: the **with** clause is similar to a precondition.

Synchronisation sets are executed atomically. The whole interaction is handled as a single transaction, i.e. it consists of an atomic event in the sense that the trigger reports a success only if all the operations identified in the reaction execute successfully and the conditions identified under the "with" clause are satisfied. The execution of services is performed locally by the components that hold them and, as such, may be subject to further local constraints. Hence, the whole reaction may fail even if the "with"-clause is satisfied because some of the operations involved may not execute successfully.

The "with"-clause plays a fundamental role in the externalisation of business rules in the sense that it allows for the effects of operations (the computations that they perform) to be handled locally, and the conditions under which they are performed to be controlled, totally or partially, at the level of coordination contracts.

For instance, we argued already that it seems best that the VIP package be modelled in terms of a contract that externalises completely the business rule so that changes can be performed that are not intrusive on either party. Deciding what is part of an entity and what pertains to a business rule is not an easy matter and requires a good expertise on the business domain itself. For instance, market evolution has shown that the circumstances under which a withdrawal can be accepted keeps changing as competition forces banks to come up with new ways for customers to interact with their accounts. Therefore, it should not be too difficult to come to the conclusion that the precondition on debits derives more from the specification of a business requirement than an intrinsic constraint on the functionality of a basic business entity like **Account**. Hence, it seems best to shift the precondition to the contract: the corresponding coordination rule includes a "with" clause whose purpose is to specify that the reaction to the trigger will only take place when the condition is true; otherwise, the trigger fails. Figure 5.4 shows the contract version of the basic account system. We use a "scroll" notation to illustrate a contract[2]. The notation $*\text{-}\gg$ **obj.m(e)** indicates that any invocation of **m(e)** on **obj** will trigger the contract.

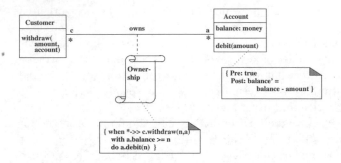

Figure 5.4: Contract for simple Account System

Every coordination rule (trigger-reaction clause) specified in a contract identifies a point of "rendezvous" in which the components are brought together to synchronise their lives. As we have just seen, in execution terms, the rendezvous is an indivisible, atomic action. This paradigm of "joint actions" is present in a number of approaches to parallel program design (e.g. [7] and also in the concurrent composition of UML statecharts), as well as in recent languages for information system modelling like MERODE [50]. Each component has its own "view" of the action and participates in it accordingly, but is unaware of the type of coordination to which it is being subjected.

This decoupling of roles in an interaction is essential for supporting non-intrusive changes by letting the subjects evolve independently. For instance, having moved the precondition to the contract, the VIP package can now be modelled directly as a specialisation of the standard one, which does not intrude with customers nor accounts. The new coordination rule becomes *when* $*\text{-}\gg$ **c.withdraw(n, a)** *with* **a.getBalance() + limit $\geq$ n** *do* **a.debit(n)** (Figure 5.5).

As illustrated by this example, it is possible to declare features that are local to the contract itself. For instance, in the case of VIP-withdrawals, it can make sense to locate the credit-limit that is negotiated between the customer and the bank in the contract itself rather than in the customer or the account. This is because we may want to be able to assign different credit limits to the same customer but for different accounts, or for the same account but for different owners. One could argue for a separate partner of the contract to be defined for **limit** but, being a feature that is local to the contract, it should not be externalised. Indeed, although every contract (instance) has an associated component for implementing these local features, this component should not be

---

[2]In UML terms, this is a new stereotype $\ll$ **contract** $\gg$ of a class.

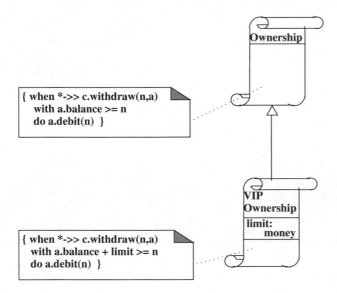

Figure 5.5: VIP Ownership as a Contract

public. For instance, a contract does not define a public class and its instances are not considered as ordinary components of the system.

This is one of the reasons why association classes, as available in the UML, are not expressive enough to model the coordination mechanisms of contracts. Although contracts allow for interactions to be made explicit in conceptual models, they should not be accessed in the same way as the classes that model the core business entities. Contracts do not provide services: they co-ordinate the services made available by the core entities. Another shortcoming of association classes, and the use of mediators as seen in the previous section, is that they do not enforce the synchronisation and atomicity requirements of the coordination mechanisms.

Nevertheless, from a static point of view, a contract defines, implicitly, an association. Restrictions to the population of this association can be defined in order to capture organisational invariants that are independent of current business policies. For instance, it makes sense to restrict withdrawal contracts to customers that own the corresponding accounts.

The general form of a contract is:

```
contract <name>
participants <list-of-objects>
constants <local constants>
attributes <local variables>
operations <local methods>
invariant <properties required>
coordination <coordination rules>
end contract
```

The **invariant** defines those properties that need to be true for the contract to be validly established.

For example, the complete **Ownership** contract can be expressed as:

```
contract Ownership
participants
  c: Customer;
  a: Account;
invariant a.customers.contains(c)
coordination
  allowWithdraw:
    when *->> c.withdraw(amount,a)
    with a.getBalance() >= amount
    do { a.debit(amount); };
end contract
```

and its subclass as:

```
contract VIPOwnership extends Ownership
attributes int limit = 100;
coordination
  allowVIPWithdraw:
    when *->> c.withdraw(amount,a)
    with a.getBalance() + limit >= amount
    do { a.debit(amount); };
end contract
```

In a subclass contract a rule triggered by the same event as a rule in the superclass overrides that rule. As we discuss in Chapter 6, attributes such as **limit** may be modified via the Java API which is automatically associated to a contract.

The semantics of the different contract clauses when the trigger is an operation invocation $*-\gg \mathbf{obj.op(p)}$ is as follows:

- *before* actions: carried out before the execution on **obj** of **op(p)** or its replacement;
- *do* actions: carried out instead of the execution of **op(p)**;
- *after* actions: carried out after the execution on **obj** of **op(p)** or its replacement.

Several contracts with the same trigger may be linked to the same participant object, but in this case there can be at most one **do** clause in the linked contract instances. All the **before** actions are performed, in some order, then the one **do** (or the original operation if there is no **do**), then all the **after** actions, in some order. Figure 5.6 shows the general case.

5.4   Defining Patterns using Contracts

In this section we show that some of the most popular design patterns: Mediator, Chain of Responsibility, Observer and State, can be alternatively and more

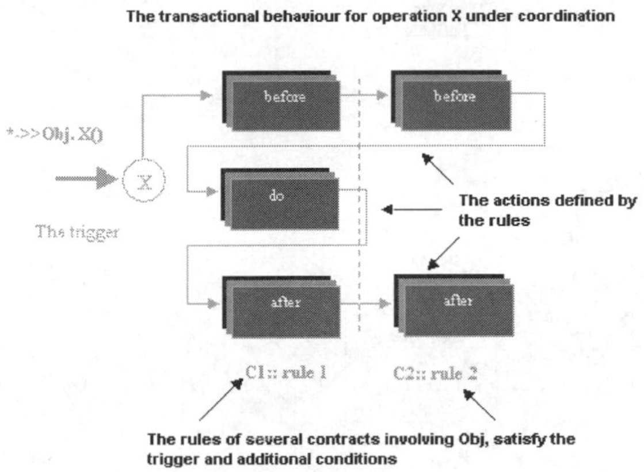

The transactional behaviour for operation X under coordination

Figure 5.6: Contract Execution

flexibly expressed using coordination contracts instead of specific connections and message protocols between objects.

5.4.1   Mediator

The mediator pattern has a similar aim to coordination contracts, in that it regulates the interactions between a set of components whilst avoiding direct communication between them. When an event occurs on a component within the set being mediated, it informs the mediator object, which then delivers information or synchronises actions with selected other components. Figure 5.7 shows a simple example of a mediator application: when the user makes a selection in the list box, the selection should be shown in the text pane. When the button is selected, the dialog should be closed.

Coordination contracts also aim to:

- encapsulate collective behaviour;
- control and co-ordinate the interactions of a group of participant objects;
- use loose coupling and simplify protocols between objects.

But coordination contracts have the advantages that:

- the participants do not know they are being coordinated;
- the behaviour may be simply expressed in several independent contracts with separate responsibilities, not only written in a single mediator.

For example, a coordination contract version of Figure 5.7 is:

```
contract DialogManager
participants
```

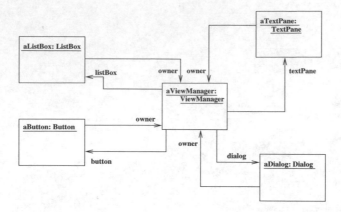

Figure 5.7: Mediator for Dialog Components

```
    lb: ListBox;
    txt: TextPane;
    okBt: Button;
    dlg: Dialog;
coordination
    listBoxChange:
      when *->> lb.changed()
      after
      { txt.setText(lb.getSelection()); };

    okButtonSelected:
      when *->> okBt.select()
      after
      { dlg.close(); };
end contract
```

If we now have additional interaction requirements, such as the need to validate the list box selection, this can be specified and added to the system as a new contract completely independently of any existing contracts:

```
contract DialogDataValidation
participants
    lb: ListBox;
    okBt: Button;
operations
    private boolean validateData(Object obj)
    { ... }  // Definition of validation rule
coordination
    okButtonValidation:
      when *->> okBt.select()
      with (validateData(lb.getSelected()))
end contract
```

In the resulting system (Figure 5.8) the dialog is only closed by pressing the button when **validateData** returns **true** for the list selection.

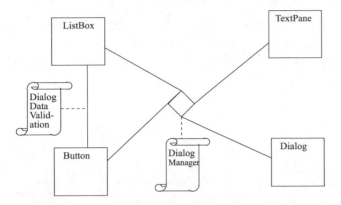

Figure 5.8: Coordination Contracts for Dialog Components

The bank account case study of Chapter 1 can also be specified more simply and flexibly using contracts than by using Mediator. The account classes can be simplified to:

```
public class Account
{ private int balance = 0;

  public int getBalance()
  { return balance; }

  public void credit(int amount)
  { balance += amount; }

  public void debit(int amount)
  { balance -= amount; }
}


class CurrentAccount extends Account {}

class DepositAccount extends Account {}
```

The mediation between these and a **Customer** class which may make invocations of **debit(int x)** and **credit(int x)** on a current account is carried out by two coordination contracts:

```
contract TransferWithdraw
participants
  ca: CurrentAccount;
  da: DepositAccount;
coordination
  transferWithdraw:
    when *->> ca.debit(x)
    do
    { int caBal = ca.getBalance();
      int daBal = da.getBalance();
```

```
      if (caBal >= x)
      { ca._debit(x); }
      else if (caBal + daBal >= x)
      { ca._debit(caBal);
        da._debit(x - caBal);
      }
      else
      { da._debit(daBal);
        ca._debit(x - daBal);
      }
    };
end contract
```

The operations **_debit** and **_credit** are the non-coordinated versions of **debit** and **credit**: their effects are the same as the coordinated versions on the accounts, but they do not trigger any further contracts.

```
contract TransferCredit
participants
  ca: CurrentAccount;
  da: DepositAccount;
coordination
  transferCredit:
    when *->> ca.credit(x)
    after
    { int caBal = ca.getBalance();
      if (caBal > 500)
      { ca._debit(caBal - 500);
        da._credit(caBal - 500);
      }
    };
end contract
```

Figure 5.9 shows the structure of this revised system.

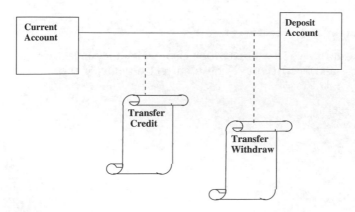

Figure 5.9: Revised Accounts System Using Contracts

In contrast to the mediator pattern version of this case study, shown in Chapter 4, there is no complex code for setting up event listening and broadcast protocols, and the contracts themselves can be separated into different contract classes instead of aggregated into a single mediator class.

Each contract maintains a constraint between the states of the components they connect: **TransferWithdraw** ensures that the current account can only become overdrawn if all possible funds have already been transferred from the deposit account:

```
ca.getBalance() < 0  ->  da.getBalance() <= 0
```

TransferCredit ensures that any surplus funds over 500 pounds are transferred from the current to the deposit account:

```
ca.getBalance() <= 500
```

The combination of both contracts maintains the conjunction of these constraints.

5.4.2   Chain of Responsibility

In the chain of responsibility pattern (Figure 5.10) the operation we want to handle in a distributed manner has to be isolated, and all the possible handlers that may handle the requests of the operation are organised in a specific object structure (usually a chain) attached to the client. In contrast, the coordination

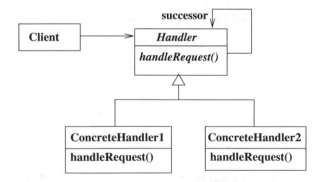

Figure 5.10: Chain of Responsibility Pattern

contract approach defines new handlers as new contracts on top of the handler object (Figure 5.11). Each handler contract has the form:

```
contract Handler_N
participants obj: Handler;
coordination
  myHandling_N:
    when *->> obj.handleRequest() && (handling condition)
    after
```

```
     { /* specific processing */ };
end contract
```

But we could also put such handlers on any object or operation we want, without needing to fit these into a chain of responsibility inheritance structure. The handlers may use the **before, after** and **do** clauses to impose their processing before, after or instead of the original target object's response to the request.

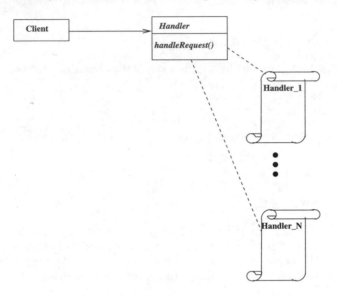

Figure 5.11: Chain of Responsibility Pattern Using Contracts

5.4.3   Observer

In the observer pattern, the classes representing observable data must be grouped as subclasses of a **Subject** class, which has a specific protocol with an abstract **Observer** class. All classes representing views of the data must be defined as subclasses of **Observer** (Figure 5.12). In a coordination contract version, no classes are needed except the specific **ConcreteSubject** and **ConcreteObserver** classes which are the source and target of the change of state notification (Figure 5.13).

The advantages of the contract version are:

- The participants of the notification protocol are not aware of it: there is no need for methods such as **notify** on the subject side or invocations of **getState** from the view side.
- There is no coupling between participants.
- There is easy support of other protocols such as more complex and bi-directional protocols.

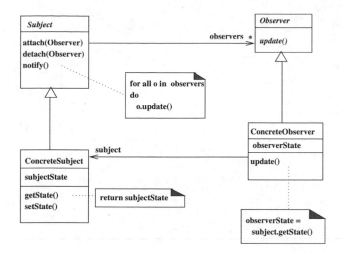

Figure 5.12: Observer Pattern Structure

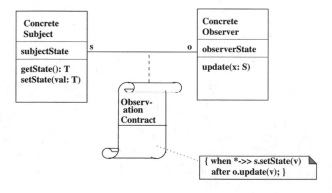

Figure 5.13: Observer Pattern Using Contracts

The attach/detach operations of **Subject** correspond to the creation/destruction of coordination contracts.

5.4.4   State

The state pattern defines the different behaviour carried out in response to a request depending on the current state of an object (Figure 5.14).

In the contracts version of this pattern we define a contract to represent the behaviour of the object in a particular state (Figure 5.15). For example the contract representing the **TCPListen** state could be:

```
contract TCPListen
participants conn: TCPConnection;
coordination
```

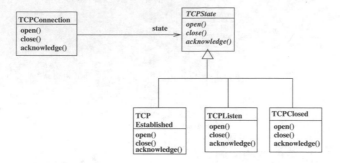

Figure 5.14: State Pattern Example

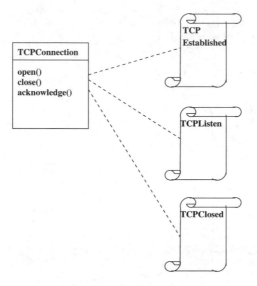

Figure 5.15: State Pattern Using Contracts

```
onClose:
  when *->> conn.close()
  do { /* close action */ };
  after
  { new TCPClosed(conn);
    this.Delete();
  };

onOpen:
  when *->> conn.open()
  ...
end contract
```

The **after** clause carries out the change of state caused by the **close()** event:
a new contract representing the **TCPClosed** state is created and attached to

the object, and the current contract is deleted. Of course if a transition does not cause an exit of a state, then such a clause is not needed.

The contracts version permits multiple contracts representing states to be attached to the same object, in order to represent the cases when the object is in multiple states (e.g. substates of states). This is difficult to achieve using the state pattern: either the pattern structure must be iterated, resulting in a large number of classes, or we must "flatten" the state hierarchy and only define **State** subclasses for the basic states at the leaves of the state hierarchy structure: resulting in complex and difficult to maintain state transition rules.

5.5   Invariant-driven Development

There are many ways that contracts can be used in development, for example they can be used as an analysis tool and then replaced in the later stages of design by specific implementations. On the CD we provide a tool to support the creation of contracts and their translation into Java code: developers only need to work with contracts at a high level, and do not need to inspect or change the generated code that implements them.

How are appropriate contracts and components recognised? Components should represent relatively stable subsystems or modules in an application, such as the core concept of a bank account used in the accounts case study, or the display subsystems (kitchen and bar displays) in the restaurant case study. Contracts represent semantic relationships between components, that is, *constraints* or invariants that define the expected state or response actions of some components given the state or trigger actions of others in the same relationship (Figure 5.16). In a commercial application such constraints are business rules (e.g. that a current account should have a balance no more than 500 pounds). In an industrial control application they are control rules defining actuator behaviour depending on sensor states (Chapter 7).

Contracts are a kind of *active constraint* in UML terms: a dependency between diagram elements which represents a property relating these elements, and which itself acts to maintain this property by invoking operations in response to events that may invalidate it.

The process of writing the code of a contract therefore can be considered as defining sufficient actions in order to ensure preservation of the constraint that the contract is responsible for. If a contract is intended to maintain constraint **I**, then for each component event **e** which could invalidate **I** (in the absence of coordination), it must provide a rule **r** triggered by **e**, such that **r**'s actions ensure **I** is preserved. **I** will be some property defined in terms of local data and operations of the contract, and accessor methods/attributes of its participant objects. Therefore the relevant events **e** will be updater methods of these participants. In the accounts example given above in the discussion of the mediator pattern, for example, it is the **ca.debit(x)** event which may violate the constraint of **TransferWithdraw**, so a rule **transferWithdraw** is needed to respond to this event or a request for it.

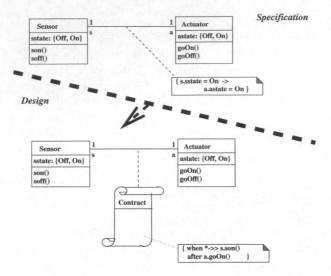

Figure 5.16: Deriving Contracts from Invariants

Where the contract approach differs most dramatically from other approaches is in the *additive* nature of contracts: if there are two separate contracts C_1 and C_2 enforcing constraints I_1 and I_2 on a set E of components, then the resulting system should satisfy *both* constraints, i.e. their conjunction $I_1 \wedge I_2$. This means that the structure of a system can correspond more closely to the system requirements – in that there are explicit elements responsible for enforcing each requirement – than with traditional designs, where the code for satisfying a given requirement may be dispersed into many separate methods and classes and intermixed with code for other requirements.

As an example, consider the restaurant management system case study. An invariant which relates the **WaiterOperations**, **KitchenInterface** and **BarInterface** subsystems in the restaurant is that the current display of the kitchen interface should consist of all the undelivered **Dish** (food) order items held in all the active **Order** objects managed by **WaiterOperations**, grouped into subsets for each order, and put in the same sequence as they occur within each order (Figure 5.17). Similar constraints link the bar interface and active orders. Implementing this invariant using contracts would consist of defining a contract which responds to **completeOrder()** and **confirmDelivery(o: Order, oi: OrderItem)** requests on the **WaiterOperations** subsystem and responds by adding all the food items from the order to the kitchen interface, in sequence, in the first case, and removing the item, in the second. The requirement for the bar interface can be implemented using a completely separate and independent contract.

However for this to work we must ensure that two contracts in our system cannot interfere or conflict with each other, i.e. they are not derived from inconsistent constraints, or do not carry out contradictory actions. The management of contracts to avoid such conflicts is carried out by *coordination contexts*,

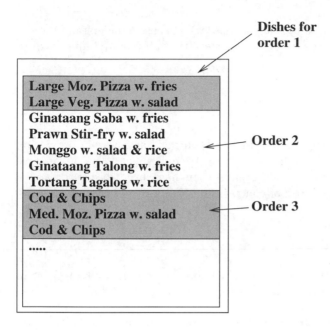

Dishes for order 1

Large Moz. Pizza w. fries
Large Veg. Pizza w. salad
Ginataang Saba w. fries
Prawn Stir-fry w. salad
Monggo w. salad & rice
Ginataang Talong w. fries
Tortang Tagalog w. rice
Cod & Chips
Med. Moz. Pizza w. salad
Cod & Chips
.....

Order 2

Order 3

Figure 5.17: Kitchen Interface

which create and destroy contract instances and connect them to component instances.

The overall design method we have proposed in this book can be summarised as follows:

- Define analysis models of the system, at an abstract level, using notations such as UML class diagrams, statecharts and use cases.
- Identify the system architecture.
- Decompose systems into subsystems and modules.
- Make modules and subsystems as independent of each other as possible: avoid referring to internal classes of one module within another, use specification interfaces to make a client module independent of the implementation of its suppliers, etc.
- Use design patterns to organise module and subsystem structures.
- Use contracts whenever there are system constraints which span subsystems and which need coordination of these subsystems to ensure that the constraints are always true.
- Plan and document designs using notations such as class diagrams, statecharts, interaction diagrams and dependency diagrams.
- Review and refactor designs as necessary to maintain or improve design quality.

It is important to maintain graphical design models such as class diagrams together with the code: these models provide an effective map and overview of the code for the developer and for anyone else who needs to understand the application. They also help the developer to check that all required functionality has been implemented.

Summary

We have introduced the idea of coordination contracts as a way of organising large applications where flexibility is a critical requirement. The advantages of contracts over patterns for such organisation have been discussed, and a development process for the use of contracts has been introduced.

Exercises

1 Define the **transferWithdraw** contract for the account system given in the Mediator example above using an **after** clause instead of **do**.

2 Define classes for the **Sensor** and **Actuator** components in Figure 5.16, and a contract which maintains the two constraints

```
s.sstate = On   ->   a.astate = On
s.sstate = Off  ->   a.astate = Off
```

3 Express the aircraft modes exercise (Chapter 4, Exercise 5) of the state pattern using separate contracts for each mode.

4 Enhance the **DepositAccount** class with a variable **double interestRate** and a method **setRate(double x)** to set this rate. Define a contract which adjusts this rate appropriately on any **credit** or **debit** action on the account: the rates are:

- balance ≤ 2000 – rate is 2.5%
- balance > 2000 and balance ≤ 5000 – rate is 3%
- balance > 5000 – rate is 3.5%

Chapter 6

Business Information Systems

In this chapter we show applications of coordination contracts to software systems in the business and finance domain, using a case study of stock trading. We also describe techniques for the organisation of collections of contracts, and the tool support available for contracts in the Coordination Development Environment (CDE) provided on the CD.

6.1 Case Study: Coordination in Stock Trading

The stock-trading business domain in general, and the area of stock-trading systems in particular, is very complex and volatile. According to the Financial Times, this domain is the place where "the bloodiest financial services battle on the internet will be" [20]. These systems involve a number of different people, possibly different organisations, equipment, material resources and business procedures. Building stock-trading systems normally involves strategic (business), social (human resources) and technological decisions. We will consider a simple stock trading process as an example of such a system, and focus on the variety of accounts and types of trading which are usually offered to a client.

Investors in stock trading are typically offered account types such as Traditional, Margin, Flexible, Discounter, and Upper or Lower Quantity Limit accounts, among others. For each type of account the trading company specifies different business rules that regulate the specific forms of trading that they support. For example, a margin account allows the customer to perform stock trading by borrowing money from the firm on short sales. This allows the trader to increase buying power for a period of time with the obligation that there is enough cash in the account, for instance a minimum balance of an agreed amount, say 60000 currency units.

When trading is performed using a margin account, an order can be committed only if the balance of the account plus the amount awarded by the firm (the margin limit) is greater than, or equal to, the price of the stocks required plus the minimum balance. However, such requirements, which are also specified for all the other types of accounts, can change according to different market situations.

Clearly, the frequent and unpredictable evolution of account types, with types added, changed, or removed according to market rules, as well as the modifications of the legal rules that regulate stock trading based on such accounts, makes evolution a critical concern when designing systems that have to support services such as these.

We will use coordination contracts as defined in the previous chapter to model the rules for different types of stock-trading account. This will also serve as an illustration of further contract features. The trigger of a contract rule in general consists of one event and several trigger conditions, separated by "&&". If any of these conditions is not satisfied when the event occurs, the contract is considered as being "inactive" and, as a result, the participants progress independently of the reaction specified in the rule. This mechanism provides the ability to select which of the contracts imposed on a component will be responsible for coordinating it, thus allowing for dynamic configuration of the component behaviour. In contrast if any condition under the "with" clause is not satisfied, the synchronisation set fails and none of its actions is executed.

6.1.1   Contract-based Solutions for Stock Trading

Our system will have the architecture shown in Figure 6.1, which represents a stock trading subsystem with coordination contracts established between customers and stock orders. In a client-server architecture, Figure 6.1 represents some of the objects that constitute a "customer session" existing on the server side for each customer logged on from the client side. Note that this structure

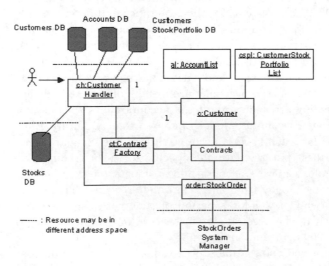

Figure 6.1: Customer Session Server Objects of Stock Trading Subsystem

is only an adaptation of a real-life architecture made in order to illustrate the use of contracts. Therefore, it omits details irrelevant to contracts like support for performance optimisation.

The functionality of the classes of objects involved is straightforward. The **CustomerHandler** is responsible for communicating with the client side and retrieving the required resources from the various databases (DBs). A **Customer** object represents a customer logged onto the trading system, and maintains the list of **Account**s and the list of the **StockPortfolio**s for the customer. A **StockOrder** object is created at the back end to model the order created by the actor at the front end. A typical **StockOrder** object may contain attributes such as **orderNumber**, **stockSymbol**, **desiredPrice**, **quantity** and so on, which model the stock orders taking place in the business domain.

The object can communicate with a **StockOrdersSystemManager** that commits transactions or updates databases according to the system architecture. Notice that it is also possible to use contracts to regulate such communications, as we discuss in Chapter 8.

A **ContractFactory** is an optional object for creating the contracts in place for a particular **Customer** and a particular **StockOrder**.

Consider the scenario in which a client wants to buy a number of stocks using the concept of a margin account. After the **StockOrder** is created (both at the front and back-end) the order is pre-submitted to the system so that the conditions required for the order to be valid can be checked. For instance, as described before, it is necessary to check whether the funds in the customer's account satisfy the conditions for margin trading and act accordingly, either accepting or rejecting the order. The following contract between a **Customer** and a **StockOrder** models the business rules related to a margin account trading.

```
contract MarginAccountTrading
participants
  c: Customer;
  order: StockOrder;
attributes
  int marginLimit = 30000,
      minimumBalance = 60000;
coordination
  marginTrading:
    when *->> order.buyReq(accountNo,stockSymbol,quantity,stockPrice)
    && (c.getAccount(accountNo).getBalance() >= minimumBalance)
    with (c.getAccount(accountNo).getBalance() + marginLimit
            >= (quantity*stockPrice+minimumBalance))
    do
    { order.buy(accountNo,stockSymbol,quantity,stockPrice); };
end contract // MarginAccountTrading
```

The contract models the characteristics of a margin account by including private attributes such as **marginLimit** and **minimumBalance**. In a traditional object-oriented approach, a **MarginAccount** concept would be represented as a subclass of **Account**. However, this account is more related to trading rules than to the usual core business domain entity **Account**. In other words, from the evolution point of view, it makes more sense to model the functionality of the system by considering the business concept of a margin account as a trading type rather than as a core business entity.

The use of coordination contracts dispenses with the use of inheritance for modelling situations like these, thus avoiding the problems that arise when new concepts are added to a business entity. Instead, new attributes or behaviour can be superposed dynamically on the corresponding objects through relevant contracts as illustrated above. At the same time, the contract provides another important advantage: the externalisation of the business rules that regulate margin trading. In other words, the volatile business rules that determine the conditions under which margin trading is allowed, even if they are different for specific customers or orders, can be modelled right from the analysis phases and implemented in a way that can be changed without affecting the functionality of the rest of the system. For instance, if a strategic decision requires new rules to be related to margin trading, a new contract can be inserted into the system in a "plug and play" mode to support this decision without having to "touch" the basic objects that compose the system.

Consider now the case in which the trading firm decides to introduce a new type of trading in order to attract new customers. In fact, this was the case of e-stock trading firms such as Charles Schwab [48] that introduced the notion of Discounter Account trading, a type of trading with a very low fee. In discounter account trading, the customer is required to have an account balance between a minimum and a maximum amount, and the balance must be greater than the sum of the total price of stocks ordered plus the minimum amount plus the trading fee. This new strategic type of trading can be very easily implemented and plugged into the system using a contract such as the one below:

```
contract DiscounterTrading
participants
  c: Customer;
  order: StockOrder;
attributes
  int minimumBalance = 40000,
      maximumBalance = 70000;
  double tradingFee = 20;
operations
  String getMonth();
coordination
  discounterTrading:
  when *->> order.buyReq(accountNo,stockSymbol,quantity,stockPrice)
  &&
  (c.getAccount(accountNo).getBalance() >= minimumBalance
  &&
  getAccount(accountNo).getBalance() <= maximumBalance
  && getMonth().equals("June"))
  with (c.getAccount(accountNo).getBalance()
          >= (quantity*stockPrice + minimumBalance + tradingFee)
```

```
do
  { order.buy(accountNo,stockSymbol,quantity,stockPrice); };
end contract // Discounter Trading
```

Notice that we have configured the contract to be active only when the month is, for instance, June. This kind of configuration allows for implementing short-term or long-term strategies corresponding to decisions occurring at the level of business requirements. Clearly, similar contracts can be specified for **FlexibleTrading**, **UpperQuantityLimitTrading** or any other type of trading the management would like to introduce in order to support the goals of a new business strategy.

Apart from the previous examples, there is another capability of contracts that is useful in this domain: the ability to have state conditions as triggers. Consider, independently of the architecture of Figure 6.1, the following contract that may be part of an "intelligent" stock trading system. The contract performs an automatic buy action for a customer's account when the price decline of a stock is greater than a buying threshold. **getLastPrice()** is the price at the previous sampling point, **getPrice()** is the current price. Naturally, similar "intelligent" contracts may be specified for other business rules such as "Selling High". Such contracts, which may be specified directly by the customer or a trader, may allow companies to implement different management decisions, reduce costs and attract new customers.

```
contract BuyLowContract
participants
  stock: Stock;
  account: Account;
attributes
  double buyMargin;
  int quantity;
coordination
  buyLow:
    when
      ? (stock.getLastPrice() - stock.getPrice() > buyMargin) on stock
    do
    { StockOrder order =
        new StockOrder(ordernumber, stock,
                       quantity, stock.getPrice());
      order.buy(account.number, stock.stockSymbol,
              quantity, order.price);
    };
end contract
```

The nature of the triggers that can be used in coordination rules depends, ultimately, on the languages and platforms in which system components are programmed and deployed. As already mentioned, coordination technologies are essentially language and platform independent in the sense that the underlying principles like coordination and superposition are "universal". However the degree of coordination that can be achieved will always depend on the mechanisms that are offered for components to interact, for error recovery, for transaction management, etc.

6.2   Creating and Deleting Contract Instances

Applications such as the stock-trading system described above rely on the ability to dynamically add or remove contracts. Using the Coordination Development Environment (CDE) tool provided on the CD, each contract class can be implemented as a Java class together with auxiliary classes. Each contract, e.g. **VIPOwnership** defined as:

```
contract VIPOwnership
participants
  c: Customer;
  a: Account;
attributes
  double limit = 100;
coordination
  allowWithdraw:
    when *->> c.withdraw(amount,a)
    with (a.getBalance() + limit >= amount)
    failure
    { throw new AccountException(a, amount, c,
                AccountExceptionTypes.LIMIT_EXCEEDED);
    };
end contract
```

has a corresponding Java class generated for it, with the same name, and with constructor

```
public VIPOwnership(Customer c, Account a)
```

with parameters in the same order and with the same names and types as the participant objects of the contract.

The above contract also illustrates a further feature of contracts: the specification of actions to be taken when the contract fails, in this case, because the **with** condition is violated. In a Java system failure actions will typically involve the creation and propagation of exception objects. The **withdraw** method should declare that it **throws** the **AccountException** because this exception may occur as a result of a contract triggered by **withdraw**.

The class representing a contract will also possess a destructor method **void Delete()** which deactivates a contract instance. For each participant **att** of the contract there is a **getatt** method to return that participant. For example in the case of the above contract there would be methods

```
public Customer getc()
public Account geta()
```

of the **VIPOwnership** generated class. Notice that the names of these methods do not accord with the standard capitalisation of Java method names.

Similarly for each attribute of the contract there are generated accessor and set methods in its corresponding class:

```
public double getlimit()
public void setlimit(double limit)
```

A test program showing how contract instances can be created and connected to components, is:

```
public class Test
{ public static void main(String[] args)
  { Account a1 = new Account();  // initial balance is 1000
    Customer c1 = new Customer();
    a1.addOwner(c1);
    c1.addAccount(a1);
    Ownership con1 = new Ownership(c1,a1);
    c1.withdraw(30,a1);    // Debited amount 30
    System.out.println(a1.getBalance());
    c1.withdraw(1000,a1);  // Exception
    System.out.println(a1.getBalance());

    Account a2 = new Account();   // initial balance is 1000
    c1.addAccount(a2);
    a2.addOwner(c1);
    VIPOwnership con2 = new VIPOwnership(c1,a2);
    c1.withdraw(30,a2);    // Debited amount 30
    System.out.println(a2.getBalance());
    c1.withdraw(1000,a2);  // Ok
    System.out.println(a2.getBalance());
  }
}
```

The result of this test is:

```
Debited amount 30
970
FAILURE:allowWithdraw::allowWithdrawcondition failed
970

Debited amount 30
970
Debited amount 1000
-30
```

showing the expected behaviour: the VIP ownership contract between **c1** and **a2** allows a withdrawal that the basic ownership contract does not.

We illustrated the use of constructors and destructors for contracts in our representation of the state pattern as a contract in Chapter 5. The Java API for contracts enables us to implement the third, configuration, layer in the coordination development approach:

1. The component layer.
2. The coordination layer: contracts coordinating the behaviour of components.
3. The configuration layer: responsible for managing the current configuration of contracts and components, i.e. for determining at each state, which components need to be active and what contracts need to be in place between which components.

There are also language-independent mechanisms for the configuration layer, managing the linking and unlinking of contract instances, the coordination *contexts* of [5]. However these are not currently implemented by the CDE.

Summary

We have described how coordination contracts can be used as part of a design approach for systems in the business and finance domain, and given examples of further features of contracts: conditional triggering of and condition-triggered contracts, failure actions, and dynamic creation, deletion and modification of contracts via the interfaces of generated classes.

Exercises

1 Write a contract class which expresses the concept of a **SellHighContract**, with the same features as the **BuyLowContract** given above, except that it is triggered by an increase in the price of its stock by more than a limit **sellMargin**.

2 Using the CDE, implement suitable outline classes for the stock-trading system given above, and generate code for the **MarginAccountTrading** contract in order that the following test program can be executed:

```
public class TestStockTrading
{ public static void main(String[] args)
  { Customer c = new Customer();
    Account acc = new Account(31324309);
    acc.setBalance(70000);
    c.addAccount(acc);
    StockOrder ord = new StockOrder();
    MarginAccountTrading ma =
      new MarginAccountTrading(c,ord);
    ord.buyReq(31324309,"BTA",100,343);
  }
}
```

3 Define a contract in the stock-trading system which automatically sells 50% of a customers holding of a stock when that stock appreciates in value by 15%

over its purchase price. A stock holding is represented by a **StockPortfolio** object, with methods **getPurchasePrice()** to return the purchase price, **getPrice()** to return the current price, **getQuantity()** to return the amount held, and **getHolder()** to return the **Customer** object holding the stock. There may be several different holdings of stock by the same customer for stocks in the same company: the contract has to apply to the individual holding–customer object pairs.

4 Consider a software engineering CASE tool application which has both a class diagram view of a design and a data flow diagram (DFD) view. These visual presentations must be kept synchronised with each other: the set of small rectangles representing components should be the same in both diagrams, and the set of classes in the class diagram should correspond 1-1 to the processes in the DFD, and be at identical locations in the two panels. If a user makes a change to one diagram to add an element, by clicking with the mouse, the change should be automatically implemented on the other diagram as well. The presentation classes are **CDArea** and **DFDArea**, with the outline forms:

```
public class DFDArea extends JPanel
implements MouseListener
{ public void mousePressed(MouseEvent me)
  { int x = me.getX();
    int y = me.getY();
    if (mode == COMPONENT)
    { // create a basic component:
      createComponent(x,y);
    }
    else if (mode == PROCESS)
    { // create a process oval:
      createProcess(x,y);
    }
  }
}


public class CDArea extends JPanel
implements MouseListener
{ public void mousePressed(MouseEvent me)
  { int x = me.getX();
    int y = me.getY();
    if (mode == COMPONENT)
    { // create a basic component:
      createCDComponent(x,y);
    }
    else if (mode == PROCESS)
    { // create a class rectangle:
      createClass(x,y);
    }
  }
}
```

Define two contracts which connect instances **cda** of **CDArea** and **da** of **DF-DArea** to ensure mutual consistency of these diagrams.

Chapter 7

Reactive System Design

This chapter will consider the design of embedded and real-time control systems. It covers:

- Reactive control system concepts.
- Decomposition of controllers: horizontal, hierarchical (chain of responsibility pattern) and phase (state pattern) decompositions.
- Architectures for fault-tolerance and scheduling.
- Implementation of controllers as input device/output device coordination contracts.

We will use the RSDS (Reactive System Design Support) method and tools as the basis of our approach: this method starts from very abstract UML descriptions of reactive systems in terms of statecharts, class diagrams and invariants, and refines these through design decompositions and controller synthesis to executable programs.

7.1   Reactive Systems

A *reactive system* is any software system which responds to input events (such as someone pressing a lift request button) by issuing commands (such as starting the lift motor moving in a particular direction). The sources of input events are generally termed *sensors*, the destinations of output commands are termed *actuators*. These are usually relatively passive components compared with the reactive system which mediates between them, but may carry out some internal processing. Figure 7.1 shows the overall structure of a typical reactive system.   The EUC ("Equipment under control") is often fixed, and the software the developer writes must be tailored to the specific configuration of the equipment. This results in a need to rewrite the software if the equipment or process changes: in recent years this has become one of the largest sources of costs in the process industry [9]. Greater flexibility and independence from the EUC can be achieved by using structuring strategies such as hierarchical decomposition (Section 7.2) or coordination contracts (Section 7.5).

163

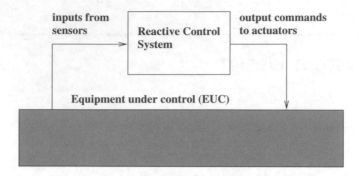

Figure 7.1: Reactive System Structure

7.1.1 Example Reactive System: Gas Burner

A very simple example of a reactive system is a controller for a gas combustion cell, as found for example in domestic central heating boilers (Figure 7.2). This consists of two sensors: a switch **sw** to switch the cell on and off, and a flame detector **fd** which identifies if ignition has occurred yet. There are three actuators: a gas valve **gv** to supply fuel to the cell, an air valve **av** to supply air, and a spark-based igniter **ig**.

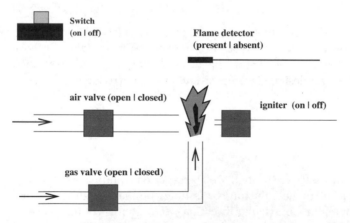

Figure 7.2: Simple Gas Burner

The statemachines defining the possible states and transitions of the valves, igniter and flame detector are given in Figure 7.3. We use dashed lines to indicate transitions for input events, so-called "uncontrolled transitions", because we cannot control when they occur, and solid lines to indicate transitions for output commands, "controlled transitions". The state machine for the switch is similar to that of the flame detector, with event **swtoggle** and states **off** and **on**.

The desired behaviour of the system can be specified by requiring certain invariants to be true. For example:

Gas Burner: Domain Model

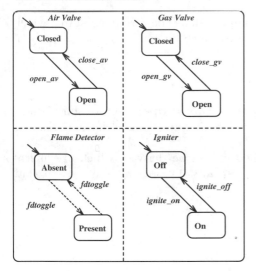

Figure 7.3: Gas Burner Statemachines

- **fd = present ⇒ ig = Off** "The igniter should not be on if the flame is present".
- **sw = on & fd = absent ⇒ ig = On** "if flame if required but is absent, the igniter should be on".
- **sw = off & fd = absent ⇒ av = closed** "if the cell is switched off and flame is absent, the air valve should be closed".
- **fd = present ⇒ av = open** "if flame is present the air valve should be open" (either normal ignition has occurred, and a supply of air is needed, or flame has unintentionally appeared, in which case flushing out the cell with air is usually a safety-enhancing thing to do).
- **sw = on ⇒ gv = open** "if the switch is on then the gas valve should be open" (either the system is trying to ignite the flame, or it is already ignited as intended, in both cases a supply of fuel is needed).
- **sw = off ⇒ gv = closed** "if the cell is off the gas valve should be closed".
- **gv = open ⇒ av = open** "if the gas valve is open, so should the air valve" (this prevents a potentially unsafe buildup of gas).
- **ig = On ⇒ gv = open** "the igniter should not be on unnecessarily", i.e. there is only a need to have the igniter on if there is fuel to ignite.

These invariants, together with the component statemachines, do form a sufficient requirements specification of the system, describing what are the intended states of the system: those states which satisfy all of the invariants, such as the tuple

(**off**, **present**, **open**, **closed**, **Off**)

of states (**sw**, **fd**, **av**, **gv**, **ig**) of the components. The forbidden states which the system must not enter are those states which do not satisfy one or more of the invariants, for example

(**on**, **present**, **closed**, **open**, **Off**)

fails to satisfy the invariant **gv** = **open** $\Rightarrow$ **av** = **open**. As we show below, the invariants also implicitly define how the system should behave, i.e. how it should respond to sensor events.

From the invariants further properties can be derived, which are logical consequences of the requirements and so must be true for any system that satisfies them:

```
av = closed  =>  gv = closed
gv = closed  =>  ig = Off

sw = on & fd = absent  =>  gv = open
sw = off & fd = absent  =>  gv = closed
sw = on  =>  av = open
sw = off  =>  ig = Off
```

For example, **av** = **closed** $\Rightarrow$ **gv** = **closed** is derived as the *contrapositive* of the invariant **gv** = **open** $\Rightarrow$ **av** = **open**. These derived invariants are useful in making explicit dependencies between sensor and actuator states which were only implicit in the original requirements, e.g. that the air valve must be open if the switch is on.

Provided that all of the invariants are considered to be reasonable and are in agreement with our intentions for the system behaviour, we can then proceed to implement a control algorithm to ensure the required behaviour.

Two of the new invariants are redundant, because they simply repeat requirements already in the original set of invariants, so they can be eliminated:

```
sw = on & fd = absent  =>  gv = open
sw = off & fd = absent  =>  gv = closed
```

A reactive system normally deals with just one input event at a time, in the case of this system this means that at most one of the sensor events **swtoggle** and **fdtoggle** will occur in each reaction step of the control system. In response the controller may generate a finite number of actuator commands.

To generate a control algorithm we first derive operational style invariants from the purely declarative requirements listed above. These operational invariants express what the required state of each actuator should be in the next (**AX**) state of the system, once the reaction to the input event has been completed:

```
swtoggle & sw = off  =>  AX(av = open)
swtoggle & sw = on  =>  AX(ig = Off)
swtoggle & sw = off & fd = absent  =>  AX(ig = On)
fdtoggle & sw = on & fd = present  =>  AX(ig = On)
```

```
swtoggle & sw = on & fd = absent  =>  AX(av = closed)
fdtoggle & sw = off & fd = present  =>  AX(av = closed)
fdtoggle & fd = absent  =>  AX(av = open)
swtoggle & sw = off  =>  AX(gv = open)
swtoggle & sw = on  =>  AX(gv = closed)
fdtoggle & fd = absent  =>  AX(ig = Off)
```

These invariants express what the system should do in response to each possible input sensor event, in each possible state of the system. For example the first operational invariant states that if the switch is toggled from off to on, then the air valve should be opened. This requirement was derived from the declarative invariant **sw = on ⇒ av = open** by reasoning that any event which establishes the assumption, such as **swtoggle** occurring in the state where the switch is off, must also, in the state after the event, establish the conclusion.

The statechart of the controller for the system can be derived from these invariants, as shown in Figure 7.4.

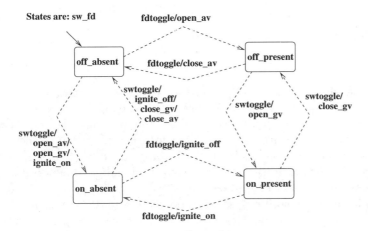

Figure 7.4: Gas Burner Controller Statechart

Having produced an operational description, we can also generate code in a programming language. For example, in Java we could have:

```
class Controller implements SystemTypes
{ public void swtoggle()
  { if (Msw.sw == off)
    { Actuatorav.avSetopen(); // av = open must precede gv = open
      Actuatorgv.gvSetopen();
      if (Mfd.fd == absent)
      { Actuatorig.igSetOn(); }
    }
    else
    if (Msw.sw == on)
    { Actuatorig.igSetOff();
      Actuatorgv.gvSetclosed();
```

```
      if (Mfd.fd == absent)
      { Actuatorav.avSetclosed(); }
    }
  Msw.sw_swtoggle();
}

public void fdtoggle()
{ if (Mfd.fd == absent)
  { Actuatorav.avSetopen();
    Actuatorig.igSetOff();
  }
  else
  if (Mfd.fd == present)
  { if (Msw.sw == on)
    { Actuatorig.igSetOn(); }
    else
    if (Msw.sw == off)
    { Actuatorav.avSetclosed(); }
  }
  Mfd.fd_fdtoggle();
 }
}
```

Mfd encapsulates the **fd** sensor state, and **Actuatorav** the **av** actuator state, etc. Typically in a control system we need to represent, in software, the components being sensed and those being controlled. These representations record the current state (as known by the controller) of these components. Of course the actual physical state of the components in the real world may differ from this software representation, in which case some fault-detection and error-handling processes may be needed, as described in Section 7.3.

Each operation in the **Controller** class corresponds to a sensor event, and the definition of this operation is derived from the collection of action/operational invariants which describe the response to this event. For example the **swtoggle** operation above is derived from the six action invariants for this event, such as

```
swtoggle & sw = off  =>  AX(av = open)
```

We can test the Java code with scenarios based on the use cases of the system:

```
public static void main(String args[])
{ Controller sys = new Controller();
  sys.swtoggle();    /* Switched on */
  sys.fdtoggle();    /* flame appears */
  sys.fdtoggle();    /* flame goes out */
  sys.swtoggle();    /* Switched off */
}
```

The result of this test is:

```
av switched open  // switch goes on
```

```
gv switched open
ig switched on
ig switched off    // flame appears
ig switched on     // flame goes out
ig switched off    // switched off
gv switched closed
av switched closed
```

which is in agreement with the intended behaviour.

7.1.2   Design Process for Reactive Systems

We have just given an example of a simplified design process for reactive systems, which is the process supported by the RSDS tool on the CD. The steps are:

1. Identify the components of the EUC, express their behaviour and states using statemachines.
2. Formalise the required behaviour of the control system as a set of invariants relating the states of the actuators and sensors. These invariants should be *complete*: for every possible combination of sensor states the invariants determine the states of every actuator, and *consistent*: for no combination of sensor states do the invariants require that some actuator is in two different states at the same time.
3. Derive logical consequences from the invariants to provide more information to the developer and to analysis tools on their consequences.
4. Derive operational invariants from the invariants.
5. Generate control code in a particular language (RSDS supports Java, SMV and, via the B language, C).
6. Animate and test the system.

Steps 3, 4 and 5 are automated by the RSDS tool. For more complex systems we need additional steps to break down the system into smaller subparts to which the above process can be applied.

7.2   Structuring of Reactive Systems

Reactive systems may become very large. A typical control system for a chemical or food processing plant may have hundreds of sensors and actuators, for example. So it is essential to find ways of decomposing a large system into smaller subsystems and modules which can be (to a high degree) independently developed and tested. In this section we describe three important ways of splitting a reactive system up into subsystems, based on the physical or temporal divisions in the system under control.

7.2.1　Horizontal Decomposition

The EUC may often be naturally divided into separate physical subsystems, which form coherent and largely independent units of control in their own right. For example, consider a robot manufacturing plant (Figure 7.5) which consists of a feed belt to supply metal "blanks" (e.g. car bodies) into a work cell for processing, and a robot with arms to collect blanks from the feed belt (via an elevating table) and convey them to a press, which stamps them into a particular shape, and then convey them to the deposit belt, which takes the pressed blanks out of the system. In this case the feed belt and the deposit belt, for

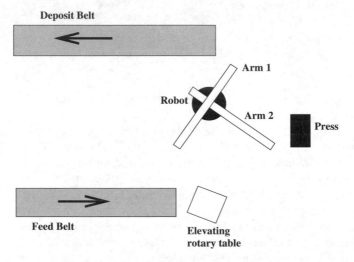

Figure 7.5: Layout of Simple Production Cell

example, are completely independent subsystems (they share no common actuators or sensors) and hence their controllers can be specified and implemented independently. The controllers for these subsystems can therefore be separate software modules without any dependencies between them, this structuring approach is called "horizontal decomposition".

Figure 7.6 shows the typical structure of a horizontal decomposition. This decomposition cannot be applied to the gas burner control system, because the actuators depend on each others states: there are invariants $\mathbf{gv} = \mathbf{open} \Rightarrow \mathbf{av} = \mathbf{open}$, etc., which relate them.

Instead, consider a basic version of the feed belt controller for the production cell, which takes input from two on/off sensors **s1** and **s2**, identical in structure to **sw** in the gas burner, and two actuators, a traffic light **btl** with states **red** and **green**, and a motor **bm** with states on and off (Figure 7.7). This system has invariants:

$$\mathbf{s2} = \mathbf{on} \;\Rightarrow\; \mathbf{btl} = \mathbf{red}$$
$$\mathbf{s2} = \mathbf{on} \;\Rightarrow\; \mathbf{bm} = \mathbf{off}$$

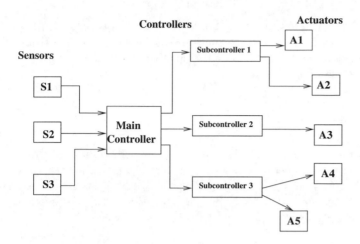

Figure 7.6: Horizontal Decomposition

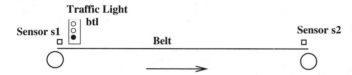

Figure 7.7: Feed belt of Simple Production Cell

"If there is a blank at the end of the belt, the traffic light at its start must be red, and the belt motor must be off".

$$s1 = on \Rightarrow btl = red$$

"If there is already a blank at the start of the belt, the traffic light must be red".

$$s2 = off \Rightarrow bm = on$$
$$s1 = off \ \& \ s2 = off \Rightarrow btl = green$$

"It is safe to move the belt if there is no blank at the end, and safe to put blanks at the start if there is no blank at the end or start".

This system can be horizontally decomposed into two separate controllers for the two actuators. The invariants of the traffic light controller are:

$$s2 = on \Rightarrow btl = red$$
$$s1 = on \Rightarrow btl = red$$
$$s1 = off \ \& \ s2 = off \Rightarrow btl = green$$

and those for the belt motor are:

$$s2 = on \Rightarrow bm = off$$
$$s2 = off \Rightarrow bm = on$$

Controllers for these subsystems can then be developed independently, using their separate sets of invariants. The information from sensor **s2** needs to be copied to both subcontrollers by a "distributor" controller, whilst the sensor **s1** can be local to the traffic light controller.

7.2.2   Mode Decomposition

Systems often go through a number of different *modes* of behaviour over time: a mode can be defined as a collection of states or times in which the system is carrying out a particular process, a subprocess of the overall system process. For example, in the lubricants manufacturing plant of Figure 7.8, the system passes through four clearly defined phases:

- Reactant **A** is pumped into the vessel via pump 1 and valve 1, then
- reactant **B** is pumped into the vessel via pump 2 and valve 2, then
- reactant **C** is manually added to the vessel, then
- the system starts recirculating the material via pump 3 and valve 3.

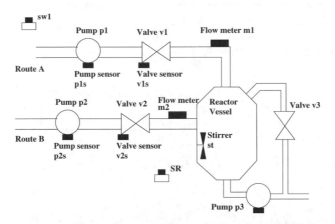

Figure 7.8: Lubricants Factory

Additionally there are modes where the system is discharging the completed product material, and where the system is being cleaned, etc.

In mode decomposition we define a separate software subsystem to control the system in each separate phase. Unlike horizontal decomposition, these subsystems will often control common actuators (for example the stirrer in the reaction vessel must be on during the loading B, loading C and recirculation phases, and off otherwise) and receive input from common sensors (all mode controllers must deactivate if the emergency stop button is pressed, for example). There will not normally be direct dependencies between different mode controllers however, because no more than one mode controller will be active at any time. Mode decomposition is analogous to the application of the state design pattern: each mode controller responds to system sensor events while the mode that it controls is active. When a new mode becomes active, the controller for that mode takes over the event handling instead. In Java the mode controllers can be expressed as subclasses of a class which represents the system controller.

Figure 7.9 shows the structure of a typical phase decomposition.

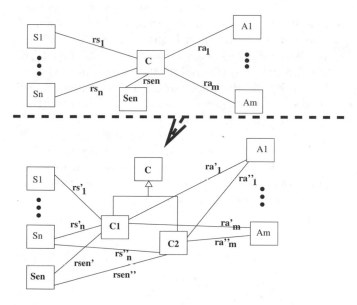

Figure 7.9: Phase Decomposition Structure

In RSDS a mode decomposition can be automatically applied, using the states of a selected sensor as the different modes. In the case of the gas burner, for example, the modes could be based on the states **on** and **off** of the switch. Then the mode controller for **on** would have the invariants:

$$\mathbf{gv} = \mathbf{open}$$
$$\mathbf{av} = \mathbf{open}$$
$$\mathbf{fd} = \mathbf{absent} \;\Rightarrow\; \mathbf{ig} = \mathbf{On}$$
$$\mathbf{fd} = \mathbf{present} \;\Rightarrow\; \mathbf{ig} = \mathbf{Off}$$

For **off** there are the invariants:

$$\mathbf{fd} = \mathbf{absent} \;\Rightarrow\; \mathbf{av} = \mathbf{closed}$$
$$\mathbf{fd} = \mathbf{present} \;\Rightarrow\; \mathbf{av} = \mathbf{open}$$
$$\mathbf{gv} = \mathbf{closed}$$
$$\mathbf{ig} = \mathbf{Off}$$

Although this decomposition has resulted in simpler invariants, in this case there are many common actuators (all three) between the two modes, so it is not necessarily a good design approach for this system.

7.2.3   Hierarchical Decomposition

In cases where several subsystems need to be coordinated at the same time to carry out the processing of the system, we can define a supervisor controller which manages the interactions of these subsystems. The subsystem controllers again do not directly depend on each other, but only via the supervisor. The supervisor may compute a function of the state of one subsystem it manages, and communicate this to another subsystem which needs this information.

For example, in the robot production cell of Figure 7.5, the feed belt and table subsystems need to be coordinated, because the feed belt should only move a blank off its right hand end onto the table if the table is in the correct position (at the top of its range) and does not already hold a blank. So this condition of the table state needs to be communicated to the feed belt controller by a coordinator controller of the two subsystems.

Figure 7.10 shows the typical structure of a hierarchical decomposition. Hierarchical decomposition is related to the chain of responsibility design pattern: a sensor event (request) may be handled partly by a supervisor controller and then passed on to the subordinate controllers, each of which may themselves be supervisors of smaller subsystems organised hierarchically.

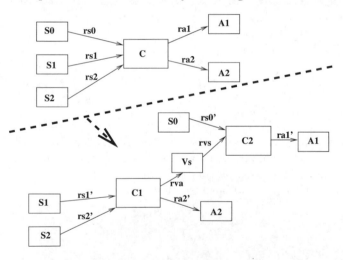

Figure 7.10: Hierarchical Decomposition

7.3   Fault Detection

A reactive system usually makes some assumptions about the set of possible states and behaviours of the EUC, these assumptions are similar to preconditions in the sense that the control algorithm is designed so that it works correctly if they hold true, but makes no guarantees if they fail. For example, the elevating table in the production cell has position sensors **ts** at the top of the range of motion of the table, and **bs** at the bottom of the tables' range of motion. An environmental assumption here would be that not both of these can be detecting the table at their position at the same time:

$$\neg \, (\mathbf{ts} = \mathbf{On} \, \& \, \mathbf{bs} = \mathbf{On})$$

If this fails then it indicates that something is wrong with the EUC, either an obstruction has entered the table to trigger the sensors, or the sensors themselves have failed. The system should therefore take some fault recovery action if this condition is detected: the simplest form of this would be to shut the plant down:

```
if (Mts.ts == On && Mbs.bs == On)
{ controller.shutdown(); }
```

More specific environmental assumptions would be that a sensor event α should not occur unless a condition **G** holds:

$$\alpha \; \Rightarrow \; \mathbf{G}$$

For example, a blank should only become present in the table if the table is at the top position:

$$\mathbf{s3on} \; \Rightarrow \; \mathbf{ts} = \mathbf{On}$$

The corresponding fault detection rule is:

```
public void s3on()
{ if (Mts.ts == On)
  { controller.s3on(); }
  else
  { controller.shutdown(); }
}
```

In both cases we can separate out responsibility for fault detection to a *fault detection controller* (Fdc) which intercepts events before they reach the main controller of a subsystem, and generates the appropriate fault detection action if an event occurs which violates the environmental assumptions. Figure 7.11 shows the structure of this fault detection architecture. This is also related to the chain of responsibility design pattern.

7.4   Scheduling

Often it is the case that some resource (an actuator, group of actuators, or more generally, a subsystem) within a reactive system may be subject to multiple demands at a single point in time. For example in a lift system serving several floors, the lift can only respond to one request to go to a floor at a time, the other requests will have to be queued in some manner, i.e. *scheduled* according to some scheduling policy such as *first come, first served*.

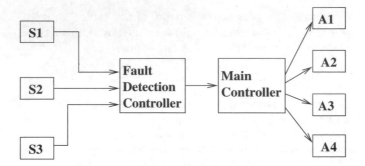

Figure 7.11: Fault Detection Architecture

When developing a reactive system which involves such a resource, we would like to separate the processing involved in scheduling the resource from the processing involved in controlling it (in the lift case the control aspect concerns moving the lift to the next floor specified by the schedule, stopping it, opening and closing its doors, etc.). In other words, there should be separate subsystems for the scheduling and control responsibilities within the system.

This is a useful design approach because it simplifies both the control and scheduling code, and makes it easier to change these parts of the system independently. For example in the lift case we might want to change the scheduling algorithm so that requests from the penthouse suite at the top of the building always get priority over any other requests, i.e. they always go to the front of the queue when they occur. Only the scheduling module would need to change in this case, the algorithm for controlling the lift to a scheduled destination is unaffected.

There are several ways to achieve this separation. We will describe one simple approach, which is supported by the RSDS tool. In this, we assume that particular sensor events indicate a request for the resource. In the lift system these events are **buttonPressed(n)** events on floor button **n** either inside or outside the lift. In addition, we assume that to each of these request events **req** is associated a corresponding command **act** which is the action to be carried out to give the resource to the request once **req**'s turn to have the resource has been reached. This may be an action on an actuator component, such as **sig1Setgreen** (set signal 1 green) or a command to a subsystem, **moveLift(n)**, "move the lift to floor **n**" in the case of the lift system. A scheduling architecture is considered relevant if there are system invariants of the form

$$\textbf{req} \ \Rightarrow \ \textbf{AF}(\text{act})$$

That is, "if **req** occurs, then eventually **act** will occur." **AF** is the temporal logic operator *eventually*, meaning that the property, in this case the occurrence of event **act**, holds in the current or in some future state.

A **Scheduler** controller is then synthesised, which sits between the controller which detects the **req** events, and the resources/controllers for the resources (Figure 7.12). The scheduler will ensure the invariant, provided the

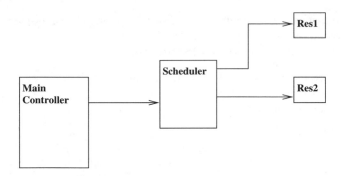

Figure 7.12: Scheduler Controller Architecture

scheduling policy is fair, and that requesters always eventually release the resource. The scheduler controller has two variables: **schedule**, which is a list of outstanding requests, and **status** which is either **IDLE** (no use is being made of the resource), **BUSY** (the resource is being used but there are no waiting requests in the schedule) or **SCHEDULING** (the resource is being used and there are outstanding requests). The controller has an operation for each request event **req**, which either puts **req** on the schedule list (in a position which depends on the scheduling policy in force) if **status** ≠ **IDLE**, or invokes the corresponding **act** for **req** if **status** = **IDLE**. It also has an operation **complete** which is invoked by the main controller in response to any event that indicates that the resource has been released from use. The scheduler controller responds to this command by invoking **act** for the request **req** at the head of the schedule, if the schedule is non-empty.

As a simple example, consider a pair of railway routes which cross a bridge (Figure 7.13). Because of the narrowness of the bridge, only one train can be on it at any time. Thus the bridge is a schedulable resource: when two trains are waiting we must make a decision as to which is to be let onto the bridge first.

The request events and actions are:

- **ents1on** – a train is detected at the entry sensor to route 1. The action to

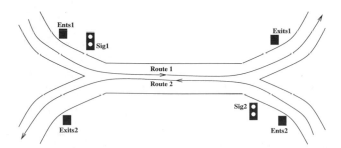

Figure 7.13: Railway Bridge Example

be taken when the resource is allocated to this request is **sig1Setgreen**:
set signal 1 to allow entry to route 1 across the bridge;

- **ents2on** – with corresponding action **sig2Setgreen**.

Completion of use of the resource is indicated by the events **exits1off** or **exits2off** which occur when a train has completely cleared the bridge.

The resulting Java code for the scheduler, generated by RSDS, is:

```java
import java.util.Vector;
import java.util.List;

class Scheduler
{ private List schedule = new Vector();
  private static final int IDLE = 0;
  private static final int BUSY = 1;
  private static final int SCHEDULING = 2;
  private int status = IDLE;

  public void ents1on()
  { if (status == BUSY || status == SCHEDULING)
    { schedule.add(new Integer(0));
      status = SCHEDULING;
    }
    else
    { Actuatorsig1.sig1Setgreen();
      status = BUSY;
    }
  }

  public void ents2on()
  { if (status == BUSY || status == SCHEDULING)
    { schedule.add(new Integer(1));
      status = SCHEDULING;
    }
    else
    { Actuatorsig2.sig2Setgreen();
      status = BUSY;
    }
  }

  public void complete()
  { if (schedule.size() == 0)
    { status = IDLE; }
    else
    { Integer iob = (Integer) schedule.get(0);
      int ii = iob.intValue();
      schedule.remove(0);
      if (ii == 0)
      { Actuatorsig1.sig1Setgreen(); }
      else
      if (ii == 1)
```

```
      { Actuatorsig2.sig2Setgreen(); }
      if (schedule.size() == 0)
      { status = BUSY; }
    }
  }
}
```

This is a standard template which can be applied to any single-resource scheduling problem, provided we know what sensor events constitute requests for the resource, the corresponding resource allocation actions, and the events that indicate release of the resource.

This architecture can also be seen as an example of the chain of responsibility pattern: if a request cannot be immediately dealt with by the resource it is passed on to the scheduler for processing.

For scheduling of multiple (interchangeable) instances of a resource, such as two lifts running between the same set of floors, an additional **Allocator** component is needed to decide which resource instance is to be provided to a given requester. The allocator holds a circular queue of resource instances to implement a "least recently used" policy to promote fair use of these instances.

7.5   Coordination Contracts in Reactive Control Systems

There are some similarities between coordination contracts and controllers in a reactive system: both detect events and generate responses based on these events; both are designed for use in situations where the elements being controlled/coordinated are relatively fixed and stable, but the algorithm for coordination or control may be required to change quite frequently. In the lubricants plant of Figure 7.8, for example, a wide variety of different products can be manufactured by varying the ratio of ingredients A and B and C, changing the recirculation duration, etc. These "recipes" for different products can be expressed as coordination contracts between the plant interface (requests to start and stop the complete manufacture cycle) and the local controllers of each route. In this case the components coordinated by the contracts are the (relatively stable) subsystem controllers. The contracts specify parameters of these controllers, such as the length of time a pump should be on, etc.

Contracts may also be used to ensure that invariants which connect any two subsystems are maintained. This allows us to completely separate two subsystems such as the table and feed belt controllers in the production cell, with any necessary coordination (that the feedbelt should stop if the table becomes occupied, for example) being handled by a contract external to the controllers. An outline of a suitable contract in this case would be:

```
contract TableFeedbeltSupervisor
participants
  table: TableController;
  feedbelt: FeedbeltController;
```

```
coordination
  unsafeToMove1: when *->> table.s3on()
    after { feedbelt.stmoff(); };

  unsafeToMove2: when *->> table.tsoff()
    after { feedbelt.stmoff(); };
end contract
```

7.6   RSDS

The RSDS toolset provided on the CD includes all of the facilities described above for reactive system design: construction of statecharts and invariants, consistency and completeness checking of invariants, derivation of invariants, generation of operational invariants, generation of Java and B controllers, and architectural decomposition using horizontal, mode and hierarchical approaches, and fault-detection and scheduling architectures. DFD or class diagram views of a system structure can be used. Figure 7.14 shows an example of the RSDS tool interface, on the specification of the lubricants plant system. On the CD the RSDS specifications of the gas burner and railway bridge systems are provided, in the files **gb.rsds** and **bridge.rsds**, which can be loaded and processed using the tool.

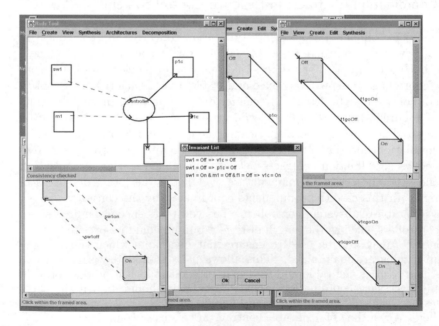

Figure 7.14: Specification Interface of RSDS Tool

Conclusions

This chapter has described design processes for reactive control systems, and we've seen that the same principles of modularity and system decomposition can be applied to such systems as for more general software systems. On the CD and website for the book you will find a version of the RSDS tool for reactive system design, which implements the approach described here.

Exercises

1 The controller invariants for the elevating table discussed in the chapter are:

$$\textbf{ts} = \textbf{Off} \ \& \ \textbf{s3} = \textbf{Off} \ \Rightarrow \ \textbf{tablemotor} = \textbf{Up}$$
$$\textbf{ts} = \textbf{On} \ \& \ \textbf{s3} = \textbf{Off} \ \Rightarrow \ \textbf{tablemotor} = \textbf{Off}$$
$$\textbf{bs} = \textbf{Off} \ \& \ \textbf{s3} = \textbf{On} \ \Rightarrow \ \textbf{tablemotor} = \textbf{Down}$$
$$\textbf{bs} = \textbf{On} \ \& \ \textbf{s3} = \textbf{On} \ \Rightarrow \ \textbf{tablemotor} = \textbf{Off}$$

where **bs**, **ts** and **s3** are binary sensors with states **Off** and **On**, and transitions

$$\textbf{bson} : \textbf{Off} \rightarrow \textbf{On}$$
$$\textbf{bsoff} : \textbf{On} \rightarrow \textbf{Off}$$
$$\textbf{tson} : \textbf{Off} \rightarrow \textbf{On}$$
$$\textbf{tsoff} : \textbf{On} \rightarrow \textbf{Off}$$
$$\textbf{s3on} : \textbf{Off} \rightarrow \textbf{On}$$
$$\textbf{s3off} : \textbf{On} \rightarrow \textbf{Off}$$

(**s3** is the sensor that detects if a blank is on the table or not) and the **tablemotor** is a three state actuator with commands **setUp**, **setDown** and **setOff** to move it into each of these states.

Derive the operational invariants for this system, and write a Java method for the **s3on** event.

2 Formalise invariants for the following system, and propose a suitable controller decomposition of it into subcontrollers.

The system is used to measure out a precise quantity of reactant for use in a chemical process. The equipment consists of a measure tank (Figure 7.15) with sensors **N1**, **N2** and **M2** at the points indicated. These are all binary **Off**/**On** state devices, they read **On** if water is present at their position. There are also three push buttons in a radio-button configuration (i.e. only one of the three can be engaged at any time): **fill**, **discharge** and **shutdown**. If **fill** is engaged, the system must fill the tank to the level **N2** using the feed valve **fv** only, **ev** must be closed. **rv** should be opened and **fv** closed if the level is above **M2**. **rv** should be closed if the level is below **N2**.

If **discharge** is engaged then **fv** and **rv** should be closed, and **ev** should be open if the level is above **N1**, otherwise **ev** should be closed. If **shutdown** is engaged then all valves should be closed. All valves are binary state actuators with states **closed/open** and are initially closed.

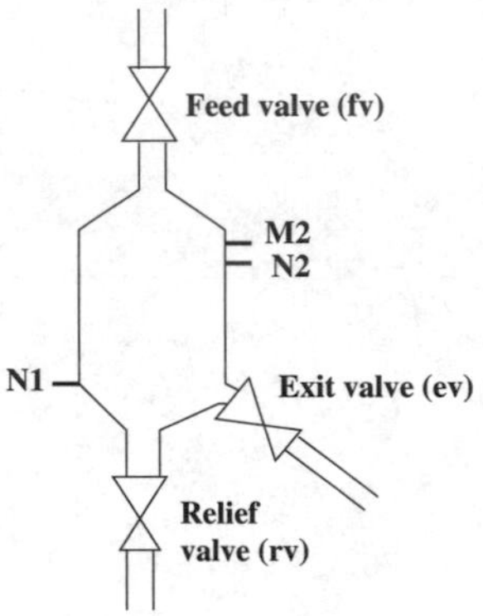

Figure 7.15: Measure Tank System

3   Define a scheduler for the lift system discussed above. Consider the case where there are three floors, with request events **f1pressed**, **f2pressed** and **f3pressed**, and completion of a visit to a floor is indicated by the event **ldcloses** (the lift doors close). A **LiftController** manages the lift motor and doors, and has commands **moveToFloor1**, **moveToFloor2**, **moveToFloor3** to move the lift to the respective floors.

Chapter 8

Distributed and Internet Applications

This chapter describes design techniques for systems that use the internet to support distributed processing: online banking applications, e-commerce, web-based teaching applications, etc. We describe technologies that can be used to implement such systems and give guidelines for modular design. An online booking function for the restaurant system will be used as a running example.

Software engineering of internet applications is an area which has been relatively neglected, as the emphasis has been instead on the rapid introduction of new technologies and languages. However, standard frameworks for internet applications, such as J2EE [25], are now beginning to appear, and provide the basis for more systematic design of such systems.

8.1 Architectures for Internet Applications

In order to provide wide, sometimes global, access to a particular set of information or resources, many applications are designed to operate in a *distributed* manner, that is, they involve processing on two or more physically separate hosts. For an application which is only intended for use within a particular organisation, the local area network (LAN) of this organisation is usually sufficient to link these different hosts, but for applications intended for more general use the internet can be used instead to coordinate distributed processing and support communication between the hosts executing parts of the application.

The key aspect of this approach is the separation between the *client*: the process requesting a service, e.g. a web browser on a customers PC, and the *server*: the process providing a service, e.g. a web server on a remote host where the web pages being browsed are stored. An internet-based application can use a mixture of *client-side* and *server-side* processing to carry out its functionality. Figure 8.1 shows the basic architecture of such applications. In many cases the processing at the server side is further distributed into an *applications* server which does the substantial server-side processing, and a *database* server, which manages a repository for the data. This architecture is called a *distributed three tier* structure, as shown in Figure 8.2.

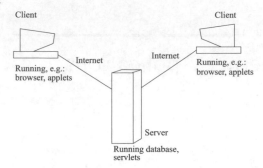

Figure 8.1: Client/Server Internet Architecture

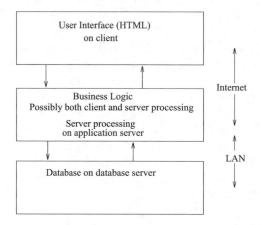

Figure 8.2: Distributed Three Tier Architecture

The most general architecture for internet applications in current use is a five-tier architecture consisting of the levels:

Client tier: This has the responsibility to display information to the user and receive information from the user and transmit this to the presentation tier. It may be either a *thin client* with minimal processing apart from its visual interface functionality, or a *fat client* doing more substantial computation. The overall trend is towards thin clients, typically using web browsers to achieve maximum portability: any machine with a browser and an internet connection can provide an interface to the application. Such clients are called *web clients*.

Presentation tier: This has the responsibility of managing the presentation of information to the client: which pages to send to the client, for example, an error report page versus a confirmation page for an on-line restaurant booking, and what sequence of interaction to follow. It also relays user requests to the business tier.

Business tier: This tier contains the business rules of the application. For example, rules concerning what days bookings will be accepted for, what maximum size of party can be accepted, etc.

Integration tier: This tier mediates between the business tier and the resource tier. It manages the detail of data retrieval, using interfaces such as JDBC. It insulates the business tier and higher tiers from direct knowledge of how the data is stored and retrieved. An example could be a method to insert a new booking into a database table, using a JDBC connection to a database, and SQL statements.

Resource tier: This has responsibility for storage of data and interaction with external resources such as credit card authorisation services or business-to-business services. It usually involves an external commercial piece of software such as a relational database.

In the J2EE architecture [25] the presentation tier is called the *web tier*, and the integration and resource tiers are bundled together as the *EIS tier*.

8.1.1   Internet Application Components

The basic components of a typical internet application are:

- Web pages, consisting of HTML, often combined with some scripting language code which provides dynamic processing of the page data and modification of its visual appearance.
- Program files, for example in Java, which perform the main computations and decision-making activities of the application. The input data for these components may come from HTML forms completed and submitted by the client, and their output data can consist of web pages in text form to be returned to the client for viewing on their browser.
- Configuration files, specifying system parameters, such as the location and name of a database and database driver. These files are often written in a structured text format such as XML [54]. They enable the application to be quickly deployed on a different server by separating out the data which varies between servers from the main application code.

The program components are subdivided further into:

- **Controller** components, which do substantial processing, such as selecting what set of web pages to return to a client based on their login id.
- **Session bean** components, which encapsulate information and operations specific to a particular client session (a connection by one browser process to the server). Their data does not persist beyond this session. Session beans are further divided into:
    - *Stateless session beans*: session beans without data. They typically provide utility functions to other components of the application, such as operations on dates.

   – *Statefull session beans*: session beans with stored data, which persists for the duration of the session. An example could be a shopping cart, as shown below.

- **Entity bean** components, which provide access to persistent data, such as that stored in a database. Typically they provide an object-oriented view of the tables of a relational database: each entity bean class corresponds to a database table, and it has **getAtt** and **setAtt** methods for each of its attributes which correspond to the columns of that table. Each object of the bean corresponds to a row of the table.

The following class is an example of a statefull session bean which could be used on an e-commerce web site to keep track of the items a customer intends to purchase:

```java
import java.util.HashMap;
import java.util.Set;
import java.util.Iterator;

public class BasketBean
{ private HashMap contents = new HashMap();

  public void addItem(Long itemid)
  { updateItem(itemid,1); }

  public void updateItem(Long itemid, int quantity)
  { if (quantity > 0)
    { contents.put(itemid,new Integer(quantity)); }
    else
    { deleteItem(itemid); }
  }

  public Set getItems()
  { return contents.keySet(); }

  public int getquantity(Long itemid)
  { return ((Integer) contents.get(itemid)).intValue(); }

  public void deleteItem(Long itemid)
  { contents.remove(itemid); }

  public void emptybasket()
  { contents.clear(); }

  public int numberofitems()
  { return contents.size(); }

  public static void main(String[] args)
  { BasketBean basket = new BasketBean();
    basket.addItem(new Long(10014));
    basket.updateItem(new Long(20332),4);
```

```
Set contents = basket.getItems();
Iterator iter = contents.iterator();
Long itemid;
int quantity;
while (iter.hasNext())
{ itemid = (Long) iter.next();
  quantity = basket.getquantity(itemid);
  System.out.println("Item number " + itemid.toString() +
                     " is in the basket " + quantity +
                     " times.");
}
}
}
```

8.1.2   Internet Application Programming Languages

A wide range of technologies exist to support distributed and internet applications, many of which are Java-based. Some client-side examples are:

- *Applets* – these consist of Java code which is invoked when a browser views a particular web page held on the server. The code executes on the client and normally is prevented from modifying the state of the client machine (creating, deleting or updating data in particular), but may use its display to present or receive information, and can connect, using Java sockets or remote method invocation (RMI), back to the server host to transmit data to or retrieve data from this host.
- *JavaScript* – this is a Java-like scripting language (a simplified programming language) which executes on the client when the client browser views web pages containing embedded JavaScript. There are a number of similar languages such as Microsoft's *JScript*, and *VBScript*, based on Visual Basic instead of Java.

The advantage of client-side processing is that it reduces the amount of work that the server needs to do, which is particularly important if many different clients may be connected to the server at the same time. However server-side processing increases flexibility (for example, complete customised web pages can be generated by the server and sent to the client) and efficiency (when the application needs to frequently refer to the database). It is also more secure, because it may be possible for a client to view or decompile code used for client-side processing, thus potentially exposing commercially sensitive business rules. Client side processing, such as form validation, also may not occur because the client browser may have disabled scripts/applets or be unable to execute the client-side language used.

Some server-side technologies are:

- *ASP* – server-side scripting for Windows servers, scripts to be executed on the server are embedded in the web pages that trigger them, and can access and update server data directly. The results of processing are presented by generating a web page and returning this to the client browser.

- *Perl* – server-side text processing and scripting language for generating web pages.
- *JSP* – JavaServer Pages. These embed Java statements in HTML, these statements are executed on the server when the page is viewed by a client browser. As with ASP, the results of processing are returned as web pages.
- *Java Servlets* – a pure Java server-side technology: methods of servlet classes generate web pages for display on the client.

In the following sections we describe the JavaScript, JSP and Servlet technologies, and give design guidelines for their use.

8.2   JavaScript

JavaScript was originally developed by Netscape as a means of adding dynamic functionality such as animations, context-sensitive help, etc., to web pages. The notation is very close to that of Java and many of the standard Java statements and control structures may be used in JavaScript. However there are significant differences at the level of data types and program structure.

Here is a simple JavaScript program which checks that two numbers entered by a user represent a valid date:

```
<! DOCTYPE html PUBLIC "-//W3C//DTD HTML 4.0 Transitional//EN">
<HTML>
<HEAD>
<TITLE>Date Check Program</TITLE>

<SCRIPT LANGUAGE = "JavaScript">
  var firstNumber,  // first string entered
      secondNumber, // second string
      number1,      // 1st string as number
      number2;      // 2nd string as number

  // read in numbers as strings:
  firstNumber = window.prompt("Enter month (1--12)", "1");
  secondNumber = window.prompt("Enter day (1--31)", "1");
  // convert from strings to numbers:
  number1 = parseInt(firstNumber);
  number2 = parseInt(secondNumber);
  if (1 <= number2 && number2 <= 31 &&
      (number1 == 1 || number1 == 3 || number1 == 5 ||
       number1 == 7 || number1 == 8 || number1 == 10 ||
       number1 == 12))
  { document.writeln("<H1>Date is correct</H1>"); }
  else if (1 <= number2 && number2 <= 30 &&
```

```
            (number1 == 6 || number1 == 4 ||
            number1 == 9 || number1 == 11))
    { document.writeln("<H1>Date is correct</H1>"); }
    else if (1 <= number2 && number2 <= 29 && number1 == 2)
    { document.writeln("<H1>Date is correct</H1>"); }
    else
    { document.writeln("<H1>Date is not correct!</H1>"); }
</SCRIPT>
</HEAD>

<BODY>
Click Refresh or Reload to run script again
</BODY>
</HTML>
```

This script pops up simple dialog entry boxes for the two numbers (very similar to the **JOptionPane** input dialog of Java Swing), checks if the date entered is valid, and then prints a message to the current web page.

The features of JavaScript illustrated here are:

- Variable declarations, written as:

  ```
  var identifier;
  ```

  Unlike in Java, no explicit type for the variable **identifier** is given in the declaration, instead any value (string, array, object, number or boolean) can be stored in a JavaScript variable.
- The **if** statement, which has identical syntax to **if** in Java.
- Reading values from a dialog, using **prompt**. As in Java, these values are strings and need to be converted to numbers, using **parseInt**, before numeric processing can be used on them.
- **document.writeln(s);** This statement writes the string **s** back to the current web page, and **s** is then interpreted by the browser. Therefore HTML tags can be, and usually are, used in **s** to format the output.

  Other means of communicating information to the user are to write to the browser window's information bar by an assignment **window.status = s;** where **s** is the message string, or to open an *alert* dialog using **window.alert(s);**
- The JavaScript program is written within a <SCRIPT> tag pair in the head of the document, with **JavaScript** identified as the script language being used, so that the browser can correctly execute the program statements.

Evaluation of arithmetic expressions follows the same rules as in Java, and the same comparison operators ==, ! =, <, >, <= and >= are used.

There is an array data structure in JavaScript which is similar to that of Java, but with a slightly different syntax. To declare an array of 10 elements, we write:

```
var arr1 = new Array(10);
```

Numbering of elements starts from 0, as in Java, the size of an array is **arr1.length**, and individual elements are referred to by the notation **arr1[index]**. However, unlike Java, arrays can grow dynamically: if we assign a value to **arr1[10]** then this value will be stored and **arr1** extended to have length 11.

JavaScript also adopts the **while**, **do** and **for** loops of Java, and these are written in the same way as their Java counterparts except that a **for** loop has the form:

```
for (var x = 0; x < val; x++)
{ ... statements ... }
```

with a JavaScript-style declaration of the index variable. These loops are often used to write out an HTML table, with each row being generated by one iteration of the loop.

JavaScript programs are structured by being broken up into *functions*, corresponding to methods of a Java class. This is a return to the more primitive structuring capabilities of languages such as C and Pascal, but is appropriate for a scripting language whose programs will generally be carrying out quite simple processing.

Here is an example illustrating **for** loops, and function definition and invocation:

```
<!DOCTYPE html PUBLIC "-//W3C//DTD HTML 4.0 Transitional//EN">
<HTML> <HEAD>
<TITLE>Squares and Cubes of 1..10</TITLE>

<SCRIPT LANGUAGE = "JavaScript">
  document.writeln("<TABLE BORDER = '1' WIDTH = '60%'>");
  document.writeln("<TR><TD WIDTH = '20%'>Number</TD> " +
    "<TD WIDTH = '20%'>Square</TD> " +
    "<TD WIDTH = '20%'>Cube</TD> </TR>");
  for (var i = 1; i <= 10; i++)
  { document.writeln("<TR> <TD> " + i +
                      " </TD> <TD> " + square(i) +
                      " </TD> <TD> " + cube(i) +
                      " </TD> </TR>");
  }
  document.writeln("</TABLE>");
  // end of main function

  function square(x)  // function definition
  { return x*x; }

  function cube(x)
  { return x*square(x); }
</SCRIPT>
</HEAD>  <BODY>  </BODY>
</HTML>
```

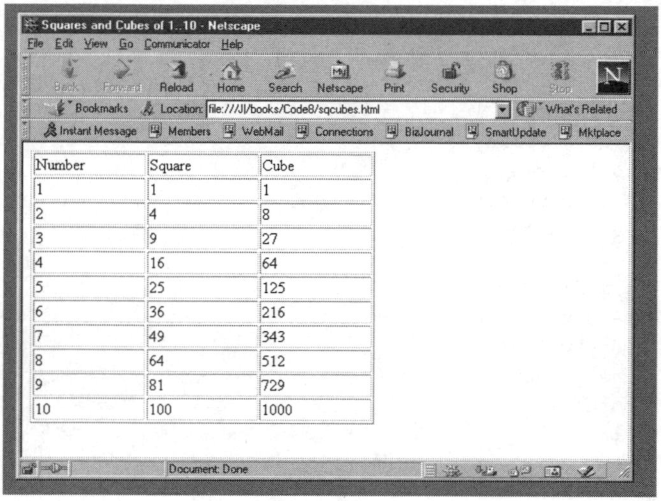

Figure 8.3: Output of Squares/Cubes script

Figure 8.3 shows the web page produced by this program.

Much of the power of JavaScript as a client-side processing and interface language comes from the ability to detect user events such as mouse clicks or other actions on the browser interface, and to invoke functions in response to these events.

A list of common events to which JavaScript event handlers can be attached is given in Table 8.1.

Event	*HTML Syntax*
Page is loaded	< **BODYONLOAD** = "function()" >
Button is pressed	< **INPUTTYPE** = "button"
	VALUE = "Command"
	ONCLICK = "function()" >
Mouse is moved	< **BODYONMOUSEMOVE** = "function()" >
Mouse over element	< ...**ONMOUSEOVER** = "function()" >
Mouse leaves element	< ...**ONMOUSEOUT** = "function()" >
Form entry active	< **INPUT** ... **ONFOCUS** = "function()" >
Form entry inactive	< **INPUT** ... **ONBLUR** = "function()" >

Table 8.1: Browser Events

Here is an example of event handling, where we have packaged up the date-checking code in a function:

```
<HTML>
<HEAD>
<TITLE>Date Check Program</TITLE>

<SCRIPT LANGUAGE = "JavaScript">
// An array which holds number of days in each month:
```

```
var maxDaysInMonth =
  [31, 29, 31, 30, 31, 30, 31, 31, 30, 31, 30, 31];

function checkDate()
{ var smonth,  // month as a string
      sday,    // day as a string
      nmonth,  // month as a number
      nday;    // day as a number

  // Get values from form fields:
  smonth = document.date.month.value;
  sday = document.date.day.value;
  // convert from strings to numbers:
  nmonth = parseInt(smonth);
  nday = parseInt(sday);
  if (1 <= nmonth && nmonth <= 12 && 1 <= nday &&
      nday <= maxDaysInMonth[nmonth-1])
  { window.status = "Date is correct"; }
  else
  { window.status = "Date is not correct!"; }
}
</SCRIPT>
</HEAD>

<BODY>
<FORM NAME="date">
<STRONG>What month (1--12)?</STRONG><br>
<INPUT NAME = "month" TYPE = "text" SIZE = "2"
 MAXLENGTH = "2"></P>

<STRONG>What day (1--31)?</STRONG><br>
<INPUT NAME = "day" TYPE = "text" SIZE = "2"
 MAXLENGTH = "2"></P>

<INPUT TYPE="button"
 VALUE="Check Date" ONCLICK="checkDate()">
</FORM>
</BODY>
</HTML>
```

Figure 8.4 shows the resulting interface. Within JavaScript we can also control which page is loaded into the browser. For example we could show alternative pages based on the **navigator.appName**: the name of the browser program being used, such as "Microsoft Internet Explorer". In an application front end where a number of successive forms need to be filled in, this facility can also be used to take the user from one form to the next. If the first form was the date entry page given above, we could write:

```
if (... date is correct ...)
{ document.location = "booktable.html?day=" + nday +
                      "&month=" + nmonth; }
```

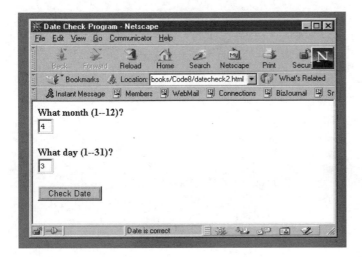

Figure 8.4: Interface of Date Check Program

```
else
{ ... don't go on to next form ... }
```

This loads the next form into the browser if the date is valid, and passes on the date as parameters of this page.

The **booktable.html** file can read these parameters by examining the **location.search** string. This has the form ?**day** = **v**&**month** = **w** in this case. The values **v** and **w** are extracted and placed in hidden form elements, so they can be passed on to the server program **test.jsp**:

```
<! DOCTYPE html PUBLIC "-//W3C//DTD HTML 4.0 Transitional//EN">
<HTML>
<HEAD>
<TITLE>Booking Details</TITLE>

<SCRIPT LANGUAGE = "JavaScript">
var searchString = location.search;
var sub = searchString.slice(1,searchString.length); // remove '?'
var arr = sub.split("=");  // divide into substrings
var parts = new Array(4);
var p = 0;

for (var i = 0; i < arr.length; i++)
{ var arr2 = arr[i].split("&");  // divide again
  for (var k = 0; k < arr2.length; k++)
  { parts[p] = arr2[k];  // the attributes and their
    p++;                 // values, in order.
  }
}

// Day is parts[1], Month is parts[3]:
```

```
function copyparams()
{ document.tableform.day.value = parts[1];
  document.tableform.month.value = parts[3];
  document.tableform.day2.value = parts[1];
  document.tableform.month2.value = parts[3];
}
</SCRIPT>
</HEAD>

<BODY ONLOAD="copyparams()">
<FORM NAME = "tableform"
 METHOD="GET" ACTION = "http://localhost:8080/test.jsp">

<STRONG>Day</STRONG>
<INPUT NAME="day2" TYPE = "text" SIZE = "2"></P>

<STRONG>Month</STRONG>
<INPUT NAME="month2" TYPE = "text" SIZE = "2"></P>

<INPUT NAME="day" TYPE = "hidden" SIZE = "2"></P>

<INPUT NAME="month" TYPE = "hidden" SIZE = "2"></P>


<STRONG>What is your name?</STRONG><br>
<INPUT NAME = "name" TYPE = "text" SIZE = "30"></P>

<STRONG>How many people is your booking for?</STRONG><br>
1 or 2
<INPUT NAME="number" TYPE="radio" VALUE="1 or 2">
3 to 6
<INPUT NAME="number" TYPE="radio" VALUE="3 to 6" CHECKED>
More than 6
<INPUT NAME="number" TYPE="radio" VALUE="more than 6">
<P>

<STRONG>Smoking or non-smoking?</STRONG><BR>
Non-smoking
<INPUT NAME="smoke" TYPE="radio" VALUE="non smoking" CHECKED>
Smoking
<INPUT NAME="smoke" TYPE="radio" VALUE="smoking">
<P>

<INPUT TYPE="submit" VALUE="Submit data">
</FORM>
</BODY>
</HTML>
```

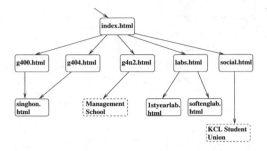

Figure 8.5: Site Map of BSc Website

8.2.1 Software Engineering Guidelines for JavaScript

Writing a JavaScript program is similar to defining a single Java class, so many of the guidelines for simple Java programs apply to JavaScript:

- Structure the program by dividing it into functions with clear specifications, and a single unambiguous purpose.
- Limit the length of functions by using helper functions.
- Factor sections of code that occur in several different places in the program into helper functions.
- Name functions, variables and constants using Java conventions, and with meaningful names.
- Divide the GUI into a set of HTML files, each file should have a clear simple purpose and a name that reflects that purpose (although the initial file normally has the name `index.html`).

For any website we can draw a graph, similar to a state machine, which shows the web pages as states and the jumps from one page to another, via links or explicit page loading, as transitions between these states. For example, Figure 8.5 shows the structure of a web site giving information to prospective students at a college. States with dashed outlines denote pages on remote sites. In a conventional website such a graph shows how easy or difficult it will be for a viewer to navigate from one page to another, i.e. how many steps they will need to take. In a web site programmed using JavaScript it shows also the sequence of processing states or modes that the web-based GUI can go through[1].

8.3 HTTP GET and POST Requests

There are two main ways in which the client side of an internet application sends information to the server side using the *Hypertext transfer protocol (HTTP)*:

---

[1]Such graphs are essentially the notorious "flow charts" of the 1960's, in the days before structured programming. Care is needed using these to design a system, since they permit control flows which are not expressible in terms of **while** or **if** and hence are very difficult to understand or debug.

- GET requests send information to the server as part of the request URL. These data values appear after a ? sign in the URL, for example: http://www.serv.org?param1=val1&param2=val2.
- POST requests send information to the server in a separate message body (not the URL). They are therefore more secure because the data being sent is not visible in the browser URL display. POST requests are used for updating server data, e.g. entering details from a form into a database.

Another disadvantage of GET is that some browsers may place a limit on the length of a URL, thus restricting the amount of data that can be appended as part of the GET request. This limit may be as low as 255 bytes (characters).

The choice of which method to use is specified in the FORM tag in HTML. For example, the **booktable.html** file given above used GET to submit restaurant booking information:

```
<HTML>
<BODY>
<FORM NAME = "tableform"
 METHOD="GET" ACTION = "http://localhost:8080/test.jsp">
....
</FORM>
</BODY>
</HTML>
```

In this case the data is sent using GET to the server-side program, a JSP file, specified in the ACTION clause.

8.4   JavaServer Pages (JSP)

JSP plays the same role for the server side of a web application that JavaScript does for the client side: adding processing capabilities to HTML pages. However JSP code will generally be much more complex than JavaScript, because it may implement the business rules, the "middle tier" in a distributed three tier application. JavaScript code is usually restricted to input validation, as in the examples above, or help facilities, page animation and visual effects, etc. Because of this, JSP programming needs particular care, and a structured and systematic approach, using *beans*, pluggable Java components, is recommended.

A simple example of a JSP page, **test.jsp**, which simply echoes back parameters it receives from an HTTP request (GET or POST), is as follows:

```
<HTML>
<HEAD><TITLE>Echo Parameters</TITLE></HEAD>
<BODY>
Thank you, <%= request.getParameter("name") %> for
your booking. You requested a table for
<%= request.getParameter("number") %> people, in a
<%= request.getParameter("smoke") %> area,
```

```
on day <%= request.getParameter("day") %>
of month <%= request.getParameter("month") %>.
</BODY>
</HTML>
```

The code within the <% and %> brackets is executed on the server, in contrast to JavaScript code written between <SCRIPT> and </SCRIPT> tags, which execute on the client. The directive <%= **exp**%> evaluates the Java expression **exp**, placing the result, as a string, into the web page which is returned to the client as the response to the HTTP query. **request** is a Java object representing the HTTP request, and **getParameter(att)** returns the value of the **att** parameter of this request, as a string. Java code fragments written in a JSP page are often called *scriptlets*.

The JSP here seems simple enough, however for more complex processing, mixing Java code fragments with HTML can lead to an incomprehensible mess, extremely difficult to maintain or debug. In fact this is just the problem of mixing GUI and back-end code which we discussed in Chapter 3, and which multi-tier applications are supposed to avoid.

Also, simply echoing back request parameters is not very useful, in most cases the server side of an application would take these parameters and use them as the basis for a query or update to a database on the server: the third tier of a distributed three-tier application. Typically such databases are wrapped in entity beans, which are simply Java objects with **get** and **set** methods for all the attributes to be queried/stored by the JSP code. These methods may use JDBC to access a database, or may use files or other techniques to make data persistent.

A version, **test2.jsp**, of the above JSP file using beans is as follows:

```
<jsp:useBean id="booker" class="BookingBean"/>
<jsp:setProperty
 name="booker" property="month" param="month"/>
<jsp:setProperty
 name="booker" property="day" param="day"/>
<jsp:setProperty
 name="booker" property="name" param="name"/>
<jsp:setProperty
 name="booker" property="number" param="number"/>
<jsp:setProperty
 name="booker" property="smoking" param="smoke"/>

<HTML>
<HEAD><TITLE>Echo Parameters</TITLE></HEAD>
<BODY>
Thank you, <jsp:getProperty name="booker" property="name" /> for
your booking. You requested a table for
<jsp:getProperty name="booker" property="number" />
people, in a
<jsp:getProperty name="booker" property="smoking" /> area,
on day <jsp:getProperty name="booker" property="day" />
```

```
of month <jsp:getProperty name="booker" property="month" />.
</BODY>
</HTML>
```

This page writes and reads data to an instance, **booker**, of the bean class
BookingBean, defined as:

```
public class BookingBean
{ private int month;
  private int day;
  private String name;
  private String number;
  private boolean smoking;

  // All bean classes must provide a
  // no-argument constructor:
  public BookingBean() { }

  public void setMonth(String mon)
  { month = Integer.parseInt(mon); }

  public String getMonth()
  { return "" + month; }

  public void setDay(String d)
  { day = Integer.parseInt(d); }

  public String getDay()
  { return "" + day; }

  public void setName(String nme)
  { name = nme; }

  public String getName()
  { return name; }

  public void setNumber(String num)
  { number = num; }

  public String getNumber()
  { return number; }

  public void setSmoking(String smoke)
  { if (smoke.equals("smoking"))
    { smoking = true; }
    else
    { smoking = false; }
  }
```

```
  public boolean isSmoking()
  { return smoking; }
}
```

A complete version of **BookingBean** would contain a database connection and a **confirm** operation to write its data to the database.

The JSP statements in **test2.jsp** create, update and read a particular object, **booker**, of the **BookingBean** class:

1. < **jsp** : **useBean id** = "booker" **class** = "BookingBean"/ >
   This corresponds to the Java statement:

   ```
   BookingBean booker = new BookingBean();
   ```

   if **booker** does not already exist.

2. < **jsp** : **setProperty name** = "booker" **property** = "month" **param** = "month"/ >
   This corresponds to the Java statement:

   ```
   booker.setMonth(request.getParameter("month"));
   ```

   where **request** is a Java object representing the HTTP request, and **getParameter** extracts the value of the **month** parameter of this request. A similar translation applies for the other **jsp:setProperty** tags.

3. < **jsp** : **getProperty name** = "booker" **property** = "name"/ >
   This corresponds to the Java statement:

   ```
   booker.getName();
   ```

   In the case of boolean properties such as **smoking**, **booker.isSmoking()** is called instead.

These conversions are performed automatically (in fact the JSP files are translated to pure Java Servlets, as described in Section 8.5), all the programmer has to provide are the appropriate methods of the bean class. Note that the bean object is named by the **id** clause in the **useBean** tag, but by the **name** clause elsewhere[2].

Beans can have four different levels of scope or persistence, as shown in Table 8.2. If we omit a scope specifier for a bean, then **page** scope is assumed.

We can use the normal Java conditional and loop statements within a JSP page, for example, in a login script which returns alternative sets of available commands to a user depending on their user id, or a script, **testdate.jsp**, which checks the date entered in one form before allowing the user to proceed to another:

---

[2]There are many such quirks and inconsistencies in JSP. No spaces are allowed either side of the "=" sign in the above tags, for example, and if a submitted request parameter has empty value then the corresponding bean attribute is not modified by the **setProperty** ... **param** tag at all, instead of being set to the empty string, or to **null**!

Scope	Persistence of bean object	Purpose
page	Only exists while page is loaded	local page data/ processing
request	Exists while particular request is being processed. Valid in declaring page and any page it forwards request to	data related to a given request
session	Exists for duration of a browsing session, i.e. connection by a particular execution of browser to the server	holds session data such as a customer number
application	Exists for duration of server application	application level data, such as a database connection pool.

Table 8.2: Bean Scopes and Persistence

```
<jsp:useBean id="booker"
 scope="session" class="BookingBean"/>
<jsp:setProperty
 name="booker" property="month" param="month"/>
<jsp:setProperty
 name="booker" property="day" param="day"/>
<HTML>
<% if (booker.dateError())
    { out.println("<H2>Error in data: Press Back to re-enter</H2>"); }
    else
    {
%>
<BODY>
<FORM NAME = "tableform"
 METHOD="GET" ACTION = "http://localhost:8080/test3.jsp">

<STRONG>What is your name?</STRONG><br>
<INPUT NAME = "name" TYPE = "text" SIZE = "30"></P>

<STRONG>How many people is your booking for?</STRONG><br>
1 or 2
<INPUT NAME="number" TYPE="radio" VALUE="1 or 2">
3 to 6
<INPUT NAME="number" TYPE="radio" VALUE="3 to 6" CHECKED>
More than 6
<INPUT NAME="number" TYPE="radio" VALUE="more than 6">
<P>

<STRONG>Smoking or non-smoking?</STRONG><BR>
Non-smoking
<INPUT NAME="smoke" TYPE="radio" VALUE="non smoking" CHECKED>
Smoking
<INPUT NAME="smoke" TYPE="radio" VALUE="smoking">
```

```
<P>

<INPUT TYPE="submit" VALUE="Submit data">
</FORM>
</BODY>
<% } %>
</HTML>
```

In this JSP file we switch back and forth between Java (inside the <% and %> brackets) and HTML with JSP tags. Great care is needed in getting this bracketing correct. A helpful editor which shows up the different parts of JSP files in different colours, is Edit Plus (http://www.editplus.com).

In the above script the **day** and **month** values are copied from the HTTP request into the session bean, which provides a method **dateError(): boolean** to determine if the date is valid or not. If it is invalid, the message "Error in data: Press Back to re-enter" is returned to the client browser, otherwise a further HTML form, **bookingform.html**, is returned. This calls the following JSP page, **test3.jsp**, when it is submitted:

```
<jsp:useBean id="booker"
 scope="session" class="BookingBean"/>
<jsp:setProperty
 name="booker" property="name" param="name"/>
<jsp:setProperty
 name="booker" property="number" param="number"/>
<jsp:setProperty
 name="booker" property="smoking" param="smoke"/>

<HTML>
<HEAD><TITLE>Echo Parameters</TITLE></HEAD>
<BODY>
Thank you, <jsp:getProperty name="booker" property="name" /> for
your booking. You requested a table for
<jsp:getProperty name="booker" property="number" />
people, in a
<jsp:getProperty name="booker" property="smoking"/> area,
on day <jsp:getProperty name="booker" property="day"/> of
month <jsp:getProperty name="booker" property="month"/>.
</BODY>
</HTML>
```

The bean object will not be created by this script, since it was previously created by **testdate.jsp** within the same session. Instead the additional parameter values are copied into it.

The control flow diagram of this application is shown in Figure 8.6. This control flow is acceptable because it corresponds to a **do-while** loop. It also represents a form of the chain of responsibility pattern: if **testdate.jsp** cannot handle the request itself (because the date is correct), it forwards the processing on to **bookingform.html**.

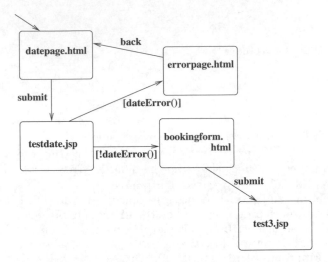

Figure 8.6: Control Flow of Booking Program in JSP

8.4.1   Server-side Includes

Often two web pages in an application will be very similar in content. For example, one page could consist of a data-entry form and another could consist of the same form but with an additional error message, telling the user that they entered data incorrectly and must re-enter the data. It is possible to textually include one page in another, e.g. to define the form plus error message by importing the form page into the extended page, by using *server-side includes*.

A server-side includes directive is written as:

```
<%@ include file="message.inc" %>
```

where **message.inc** is the file to be included. The text of this file is then inserted into the document by the server whenever the page is translated into a servlet for execution, and so this insertion is done before any script on the page is executed.

8.4.2   Guidelines for JSP Design

As with JavaScript, the main unit of modularity in JSP is the file or web page, with dependencies between pages due to control flow transfers or shared data. To improve the clarity of JSP code and the ability to debug JSP programs, as much of the Java code as possible should be placed in separate bean classes. Server-side includes can also be used to factor out common parts of pages into separate files.

8.4.3   Installing JSP on a Web Server

Many web servers provide the capability to execute JSP files, for example Apache Tomcat (http://www.apache.org), Jigsaw (http://www.w3.org/Jigsaw) and Resin (http://www.caucho.com/products/resin). We will illustrate the process of setting up a web server using Resin, under Linux.

Resin is a commercial web server, which is free for educational uses such as student projects. Downloads for Windows and Unix systems are available at `http://www.caucho.com/products/resin`. Having downloaded Resin for Unix, uncompress and untar (from the Unix command line) the download:

```
uncompress resin-2.0.4.tar.Z
tar -xvf resin-2.0.4.tar
```

The result is a directory **resin-2.0.4** which contains all the source code, libraries, binaries and documentation for this version of Resin. To run, Resin needs the **tools.jar** Java archive to be in the class path. To check if it is already in the path, type:

```
echo $CLASSPATH
```

If **tools.jar** occurs in this path, no further work should be needed. Otherwise, find the location of this archive on the system (e.g. in **/usr/local/lib**) and put the following lines in your startup shell script **shellrc** (for the **sh** shell):

```
CLASSPATH="$CLASSPATH:/usr/local/lib/tools.jar"
export CLASSPATH
```

Type **source shellrc** to update the classpath. Resin can then be started by typing **./httpd.sh** in the **resin-ver/bin/** directory:

```
kcl@pc779 ~/resin-2.0.4/bin $ ./httpd.sh
Resin 2.0.4 (built Thu Nov 15 17:56:24 PST 2001)
Copyright(c) 1998-2001 Caucho Technology.  All rights reserved.

Starting Resin on Thu, 07 Feb 2002 08:09:09 +0000 (GMT+00:00)
http listening to *:8080
srun listening to 127.0.0.1:6802
[2002-02-07 08:09:14.319] initializing application /examples/login
[2002-02-07 08:09:14.321] initializing application /examples/tags
[2002-02-07 08:09:14.322] initializing application /examples/xsl
[2002-02-07 08:09:14.339] initializing application /examples/templates
[2002-02-07 08:09:14.340] initializing application /java_tut
[2002-02-07 08:09:14.340] initializing application /examples/navigation
[2002-02-07 08:09:14.341] initializing application /examples/basic
[2002-02-07 08:09:14.341] initializing application /
[2002-02-07 08:09:14.342] initializing application /examples/tictactoe
```

To use JSP, place JSP files in the **resin-ver/doc/** directory. The **class** files of beans should be placed in the **resin-ver/doc/WEB-INF/classes** directory. The **URL** to use to connect to a JSP file **test.jsp** on the current machine is `http://localhost:8080/test.jsp`, or `http://machine:8080/test.jsp` on a remote host **machine** given as an IP address or fully qualified host name.

8.5   Java Servlets

Servlets are a pure Java technique for defining server-side processing in internet applications, in contrast to the hybrid HTML/Java notation of JSP. Therefore they are usually easier to debug and understand.

8.5.1   Servlet Example

The following Servlet corresponds to the **test.jsp** program shown in the previous section. It represents a controller component, and servlets are usually more appropriate for this kind of component than JSPs. Notice that we import both the general **servlet** package **javax.servlet** and its subpackage **javax.servlet.http** which is specifically for the HTTP protocol.

```
import java.io.*;
import java.util.*;
import javax.servlet.http.*;
import javax.servlet.*;

public class BookingServlet extends HttpServlet
{
  public BookingServlet() {}

  public void doGet(HttpServletRequest  req,
                    HttpServletResponse res)
  throws ServletException, IOException
  { res.setContentType("text/html");
    PrintWriter pw = res.getWriter();
    String name = req.getParameter("name");
    String number = req.getParameter("number");
    String smoke = req.getParameter("likes");
    String day = req.getParameter("day");

    pw.println("<!DOCTYPE HTML PUBLIC \"-//W3C//DTD " +
               "HTML 4.0 Transitional//EN\">");
    pw.println();
    pw.println("<head>");
    pw.println("<meta http-equiv=\"Content-Type\" " +
               "content=\"text/html; charset=ISO-8859-1\">");
    pw.println();
    pw.println();
    pw.println("<title>Booking Details</title>");
    pw.println("</head>");
    pw.println();
    pw.println("<body bgcolor=#FF69CC>");
    pw.println();
    pw.println("<h1>Thank you, " + name + " for booking. </h1>");
    pw.println("<h1>You booked for: " + number + " people </h1>");
    pw.println("<h1>In a " + smoke + " area </h1>");
```

```
    pw.println("<h1>On " + day + ".</h1>");
    pw.println();
    pw.println("</body>");
    pw.close();
  }

  public void doPost(HttpServletRequest req,
                     HttpServletResponse res)
  throws ServletException, IOException
  { doGet(req,res); }
}
```

doGet handles HTTP **GET** requests from the client. **req** holds the data which has been sent, and it has parameters for each named input item in the source form. **res** has an output print writer, **pw** in the above example, to which HTML text can be sent, which is the servlet's response to the request. We have defined **doPost** to simply call **doGet** as there is no need for specific processing of **POST** requests in this case.

This servlet responds to **GET** requests from the following form:

```
<HTML>
<BODY>
<FORM METHOD="GET"
 ACTION="http://localhost:8080/servlet/BookingServlet">

<STRONG>What is your name?</STRONG><br>
<INPUT NAME = "name" TYPE = "text" SIZE = "30"></P>

<STRONG>How many people is your booking for?</STRONG><br>
1 or 2
<INPUT NAME="number" TYPE="radio" VALUE="1 or 2">
3 to 6
<INPUT NAME="number" TYPE="radio" VALUE="3 to 6" CHECKED>
More than 6
<INPUT NAME="number" TYPE="radio" VALUE="more than 6"> <P>

<STRONG>Smoking or non-smoking?</STRONG><BR>
Non-smoking
<INPUT NAME="likes" TYPE="radio" VALUE="non smoking" CHECKED>
Smoking
<INPUT NAME="likes" TYPE="radio" VALUE="smoking"> <P>

<STRONG>Day:</STRONG>
<SELECT NAME="day">
<OPTION SELECTED>Monday
<OPTION>Tuesday
<OPTION>Wednesday
<OPTION>Thursday
<OPTION>Friday
<OPTION>Saturday
<OPTION>Sunday
```

```
</SELECT> <P>

<INPUT TYPE="submit" VALUE="Submit data">
</FORM>
</BODY>
</HTML>
```

Directly writing HTML text within a servlet is a very primitive way of dealing with requests. For more complex processing we can use Java classes such as **HtmlPage** and **HtmlForm** which represent the corresponding HTML constructs[3]. These allow a web site to be represented internally within a Java program and make it easy to copy or adapt pages by simply creating suitable objects.

For example, here is a class (a statefull session bean) which represents an HTML page that is shown if there is some error in the booking data.

```
public class ErrorPage extends HtmlPage
{ private String month;
  private String day;
  private String name;
  private String number;
  private String smoke;

  public ErrorPage(String mon, String d, String nme,
                   String numb, String sm)
  { super();
    month = mon;
    day = d;
    name = nme;
    number = numb;
    smoke = sm;
  }

  public boolean isError()
  { // checks that all fields are non-null and valid.
    if (month == null || day == null || name == null ||
        name.equals(""))
    { return true; }
    int monthint;
    int dayint;
    try
    { monthint = Integer.parseInt(month);
      dayint = Integer.parseInt(day);
    }
    catch (Exception e) { return true; }
    return dateError(monthint,dayint);
  }

  private boolean dateError(int mon, int d)
```

---

[3]Complete versions of these classes are available on the CD.

```
{ /* returns true if mon, d is invalid date, false otherwise */ }

public void buildPage()  // if an error
{ HtmlHead head = new HtmlHead("Errors in Booking");
  HtmlBody body = new HtmlBody();
  HtmlText title = new HtmlText("Errors in Booking", "H2");
  HtmlText mess =
    new HtmlText("Press Back and re-enter data in form","P");
  body.add(title);
  if (month == null)
  { HtmlText monthrep =
      new HtmlText("Month not specified!", "P");
    body.add(monthrep);
  }
  if (day == null)
  { HtmlText dayrep =
      new HtmlText("Day not specified!", "P");
    body.add(dayrep);
  }
  if (name == null || name.equals(""))
  { HtmlText namerep =
      new HtmlText("Name not specified!", "P");
    body.add(namerep);
  }
  body.add(mess);
  setHead(head);
  setBody(body);
  }
}
```

This is used in the following version of the booking servlet:

```
import java.io.*;
import java.util.*;
import javax.servlet.http.*;
import javax.servlet.*;

public class BookingServlet2 extends HttpServlet
{ public BookingServlet2() {}

  public void doGet(HttpServletRequest  req,
                    HttpServletResponse res)
  throws ServletException, IOException
  { res.setContentType("text/html");
    PrintWriter pw = res.getWriter();
    String month = req.getParameter("month");
    String day = req.getParameter("day");
    String name = req.getParameter("name");
    String number = req.getParameter("number");
    String smoke = req.getParameter("likes");
```

```
    pw.println("<!DOCTYPE HTML PUBLIC \"-//W3C//DTD " +
              "HTML 4.0 Transitional//EN\">");
    pw.println();
    ErrorPage ep =
      new ErrorPage(month,day,name,number,smoke);
    if (ep.isError())
    { ep.buildPage();
      pw.println(ep.getHtml());
    }
    else
    { pw.println("<head>");
      pw.println("<meta http-equiv=\"Content-Type\" " +
                "content=\"text/html; charset=ISO-8859-1\">");
      pw.println();
      pw.println();
      pw.println("<title>Booking Details</title>");
      pw.println("</head>");
      pw.println();
      pw.println("<body bgcolor=#FF69CC>");
      pw.println();
      pw.println("<h1>Thank you, " + name +
                " for your booking. </h1>");
      pw.println("<h1>You booked for: " + number + " people </h1>");
      pw.println("<h1>In a " + smoke + " area </h1>");
      pw.println("<h1>On day " + day + ".</h1>");
      pw.println();
      pw.println("</body>");
    }
    pw.close();
  }
}
```

This servlet displays an error report if there is some mistake in the data, or displays a confirmation page. This is a much clearer and simpler program than the JSP version described in the previous section.

The **HtmlPage** class used above is defined in outline as:

```
public class HtmlPage implements HtmlComponent
{ private HtmlHead head = new HtmlHead(" ");
  private HtmlBody body = new HtmlBody();

  public HtmlPage() { }

  public void setHead(HtmlHead h)
  { head = h; }

  public void setBody(HtmlBody b)
  { body = b; }

  public String getHtml()
  { return "<HTML> \n" + head.getHtml() + "\n" +
```

```
            body.getHtml() + "\n </HTML>";
  }
}
```

where:

```
public interface HtmlComponent
{ public String getHtml(); }
```

is the interface declaring the **getHtml** method common to all HTML components. **HtmlHead** represents the header of an HTML document. JavaScript code would be inserted into a returned page by using an **HtmlHead** object.

```
public class HtmlHead implements HtmlComponent
{ private String title = "";

  public HtmlHead(String t)
  { title = t; }

  public String getHtml()
  { return "<HEAD> <TITLE> " + title +
          " </TITLE> </HEAD>";
  }
}
```

HtmlBody represents the body of an HTML page as a sequence of HTML components.

```
import java.util.Vector;

public class HtmlBody implements HtmlComponent
{ private Vector contents = new Vector();
  /* Of HtmlComponent */

  public void add(HtmlComponent c)
  { contents.add(c); }

  public String getHtml()
  { String res = "";
    for (int i = 0; i < contents.size(); i++)
    { HtmlComponent c = (HtmlComponent) contents.get(i);
      res = res + "\n " + c.getHtml();
    }
    return res;
  }
}
```

Individual HTML elements such as anchors or text can be defined in the same way:

```
public class HtmlText implements HtmlComponent
{ private String text = "";
  private String format = "P";
```

```
public HtmlText(String s, String f)
{ text = s;
  format = f;
}

public String getHtml()
{ return "<" + format + "> " + text + " </" +
        format + "> ";
}
}
```

Care is needed over the use of instance variables in a servlet: such variables are shared between all instances of the **doGet** method which may be executing at a particular time, i.e. in response to requests from multiple clients. Therefore any data which is local to a specific request must be defined as local variables of **doGet** or **doPost**.

8.5.2   Managing Sessions

A servlet can record and read information concerned with a particular client session, i.e. interaction between the servlet and a particular client, by creating an **HttpSession** object. For example, to record someone's login id from the opening login prompt of a website, we could write:

```
String userid = request.getParameter("userid");
HttpSession session = request.getSession(true);
session.putValue("login",userid);
```

in the **doPost** method that receives the request from this prompt. The parameter **true** in **getSession** indicates that a session object should be created for the client (for whom **doPost** is being executed) if one does not already exist for this client. If a session already exists, it is returned, otherwise the new session is returned.

The session can be referred to in another method, and its values extracted:

```
HttpSession session = request.getSession(false);
if (session != null)
{ String userid = (String) session.getValue("login");
  ...
}
```

If this code is called within the same browsing session, for example, by the client submitting data from another form, then the session object will exist and the login value stored by the initial request will be returned. This can be used to check authorisation for taking an action or giving information. The **false** parameter in **getSession** indicates that a new session should not be created if one does not already exist, instead **null** is returned.

Traditionally, session information was recorded on the client, using *cookies*, or hidden HTML fields in web pages returned to the client. While servlets enable programmers to use such techniques, it is generally recommended that server-side storage of session data is used, to improve security and efficiency.

8.6 Three Tier Applications

Database connections can be validly shared between several requests, so they can be placed in servlet instance variables. The connection could be created in the **init** method of the servlet, which is executed when the servlet is initialised by the server, before any client requests are handled. Each client request can then use the shared database connection to read or write data, although only one request should use the connection at a time, i.e. the database update and enquiry methods should be declared as **synchronized**. The code for establishing and operating on the database connection should be encapsulated in a separate class to the servlet, in order to achieve a separation of the database tier of the system from the business logic tier.

We will illustrate the construction of a three tier application using the booking example, and a database table **Booking** which stores the relevant attributes (Table 8.3). We will use the **PostgreSQL** database management system [40] to construct a database to hold this table, and use JDBC to link the middle tier servlet classes to this database, as in Chapter 3.

PostgreSQL is an open source, free DBMS which provides similar capabilities to commercial databases such as Oracle or Access. It runs on Linux. The following steps are needed to set up a PostgreSQL database installation for the first time:

1. Create a directory **pgdata** in your home directory to hold the database files, then **cd** to this directory.
2. Run **initdb**.

Once this settup is complete, the database server process can be started to deal with database creation, queries and updates:

```
postmaster -i > server.log &
```

To create a database called **bookingdb**, run:

```
createdb bookingdb
```

bookingid	name	month	day	number	smoke
1	"Felix Ali"	12	18	1	Y
2	"Linda Pel"	11	22	3	N

Table 8.3: Booking Table Example

The tables of this database can then be defined using the interactive **psql** program:

```
kcl@pc779 ~/pgdata $ psql bookingdb
Welcome to psql, the PostgreSQL interactive terminal.

Type:  \copyright for distribution terms
       \h for help with SQL commands
       \? for help on internal slash commands
       \g or terminate with semicolon to execute query
       \q to quit

bookingdb=# CREATE TABLE booking
bookingdb-# (bookingid INT2,
bookingdb(#  name CHAR(30),
bookingdb(#  month CHAR(3),
bookingdb(#  day CHAR(2),
bookingdb(#  number CHAR(10),
bookingdb(#  smoke CHAR(1),
bookingdb(# PRIMARY KEY (bookingid));
```

This SQL statement creates a new table called **booking** in the **bookingdb** database. We can view its structure by the psql **\d** command:

```
bookingdb=# \d booking
         Table "booking"
 Attribute |   Type   | Modifier
-----------+----------+----------
 bookingid | smallint | not null
 name      | char(30) |
 month     | char(3)  |
 day       | char(2)  |
 number    | char(10) |
 smoke     | char(1)  |
Index: booking_pkey
```

Rows can be added to **booking** using the SQL INSERT command:

```
bookingdb=#  INSERT INTO booking
bookingdb=# VALUES(001,'Felix Ali','12','18','1','Y');
INSERT 18801 1
```

The table can be viewed by using **SELECT * FROM booking;** as usual. All commands are standard SQL commands, as we used with Access in Chapter 3. To quit from **psql** type **\q**. To shut down the database server, identify its Unix process ID by using **ps**, then type **kill id** where **id** is the ID of the **postmaster** process.

To connect to a PostgreSQL database from Java programs, the archive **postgresql.jar** needs to be in the CLASSPATH. This provides a database driver for PostgreSQL. An interface class (an entity bean) which uses this driver to connect to the above database can be defined as:

```
import java.io.*;
import java.sql.*;

public class BookingDBI
{ private Connection conn;
  private Statement stat;

  /** Construct a database connection and
      statement for "bookingdb" with username "kcl" */
  public BookingDBI()
  { try
    { Class.forName("org.postgresql.Driver");
      conn =
        DriverManager.getConnection(
              "jdbc:postgresql:bookingdb", "kcl", "");
      stat = conn.createStatement();
    }
    catch (Exception e)
    { e.printStackTrace(); }
  }

  /** Add a new booking to the database. */
  public synchronized void addBooking(String name,
                          String month, String day,
                          String number, String smoke)
  { int maxId = getMaxId();
    String numb;
    String sm;
    maxId++;

    if (number.equals("1 or 2"))
    { numb = "1"; }
    else if (number.equals("3 to 6"))
    { numb = "3"; }
    else
    { numb = "6"; }

    if (smoke.equals("non smoking"))
    { sm = "N"; }
    else
    { sm = "Y"; }

    try
    { stat.executeUpdate("INSERT INTO booking " +
                       "VALUES (" + maxId + ",'" + name + "','" +
                              month + "','" + day + "','" +
                              numb + "','" + sm + "')");
      conn.commit();
    }
    catch (Exception e)
```

```
      { e.printStackTrace(); }
  }

  private int getMaxId()   // Returns max primary key
  { int maxId = 0;         // value used in database.
    try
    {
      String sQuery = "SELECT MAX(bookingid) " +
                      "AS MaxId FROM booking";
      ResultSet res = stat.executeQuery(sQuery);
      while (res.next())
      { maxId = res.getInt("MaxId"); }
    }
    catch(SQLException e)
    { System.err.println("Error in getting max id");
      e.printStackTrace();
    }
    return maxId;
  }

  /** Close connection to database. */
  public synchronized void logoff()
  { try
    { stat.close();
      conn.close();
    }
    catch (Exception e)
    { e.printStackTrace(); }
  }
}
```

In a professional application, the name of the database, the table and database driver should not be hard-coded into the database interface class, but instead defined in a separate *configuration file*.

The above interface can then be used by the booking servlet to record bookings:

```
import java.io.*;
import java.util.*;
import javax.servlet.http.*;
import javax.servlet.*;

public class BookingServlet extends HttpServlet
{ private BookingDBI dbi; // Interface to database

  public BookingServlet() {}

  public void init(ServletConfig cfg)
  throws ServletException
  { super.init(cfg);
    dbi = new BookingDBI();
```

```
}

public void doGet(HttpServletRequest req, HttpServletResponse res)
  throws ServletException, IOException
{
  res.setContentType("text/html");
  PrintWriter pw = res.getWriter();
  String name = req.getParameter("name");
  String month = req.getParameter("month");
  String number = req.getParameter("number");
  String smoke = req.getParameter("smoke");
  String day = req.getParameter("day");

  pw.println("<!DOCTYPE HTML PUBLIC \"-//W3C//DTD HTML 4.0" +
             " Transitional//EN\">");
  pw.println();
  pw.println("<head>");
  pw.println("<meta http-equiv=\"Content-Type\" " +
             "content=\"text/html; charset=ISO-8859-1\">");
  ErrorPage ep = new ErrorPage(month,day,name,number,smoke);
  if (ep.isError())
  { ep.buildPage();
    pw.println(ep.getHtml());
    pw.close();
    return;
  }
  pw.println();
  pw.println("<title>Booking Details</title>");
  pw.println("</head>");
  pw.println();
  pw.println("<body bgcolor=#FF69CC>");
  pw.println();
  pw.println("<h1>Thank you, " + name +
             " for your booking. </h1>");
  pw.println("<h1>You booked for: " + number + " people </h1>");
  pw.println("<h1>In a " + smoke + " area </h1>");
  pw.println("<h1>On day " + day + " of month " +
             month + ".</h1>");
  pw.println();
  pw.println("<HR>");
  if (dbi != null)
  { dbi.addBooking(name,month,day,number,smoke);
    pw.println("<H2>Booking added to database</H2>");
  }
  else
  { pw.println("<H2>Booking NOT added to database</H2>"); }
  pw.println("</body>");
  pw.close();
}
```

```
public void doPost(HttpServletRequest req, HttpServletResponse res)
throws ServletException, IOException
{ doGet(req,res); }

public void destroy()
{ dbi.logoff(); }
}
```

The **init** method establishes the database connection, whilst **destroy** closes it down. In more intensively-used applications where there may be hundreds of client sessions running concurrently, database connections would need to be acquired from a connection pool when needed by a client and released once a database operation was complete.

This servlet can be invoked by HTTP requests from a web page such as the **booktable.html** file of Section 8.3, where we use **servlet/BookingServlet** instead of **test.jsp** as the recipient program.

To make all this work, we need three external pieces of software running at the same time:

1. The database server needs to be running, i.e. the **postmaster** process needs to be invoked as shown above.
2. A web server such as Resin needs to be running, with the **BookingServlet.java** and **BookingDBI.java** files placed in the appropriate **WEB-INF/classes** directory.
3. A web browser is needed to view the web pages.

Figure 8.7 shows the connections and messages between these components.

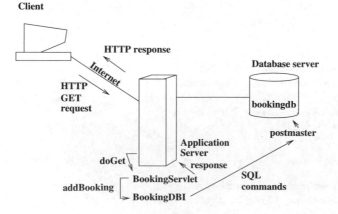

Figure 8.7: Structure of Example 3-Tier Application

8.6.1 Installing Servlets

To install a servlet in Resin, we simply place the **java** files of the servlet in the **resin-ver/doc/WEB-INF/classes** directory.

8.6.2 Comparing JSP and Servlets

Table 8.4 gives a comparison of JSP and Servlets as server-side technologies. JSP could be regarded as "web programming for people who can't program", enabling JSP pages to be written by HTML developers instead of (more expensive) Java programmers. For people confident in Java however, servlets are probably the better choice. The guidelines for Servlet development are simi-

Property	*JSP*	*Servlets*
Efficiency	Delay when first compiled	No compilation delay
Separation of HTML and code	By using beans	By using **HtmlPage**, **HtmlForm**, etc.
Debugging	Very difficult	Using Java tools
Structuring	Using files and server-side includes.	Using classes.

Table 8.4: Comparison of JSP and Servlets

lar to those for normal Java applications, i.e. appropriate use should be made of classes to break a system up into relatively independent modules dealing with separate responsibilities. Classes to represent HTML pages as objects should be used in preference to directly writing large chunks of HTML in a servlet. Session objects should be used to organise session-specific processing, such as shopping carts. Care is needed because of the inherent concurrency of a servlet: any updates/accesses to instance-level data should be protected by encapsulating these updates/accesses within **synchronized** methods.

8.7 Design Patterns for Internet Applications

The chain of responsibility pattern is clearly relevant for organising internet applications, since different components, such as JSP pages or servlets, may either handle a request directly themselves or delegate the request to a further component (often via an HTML page which submits further details of the request to this component, as in Figure 8.6 above). With servlets, the pattern can be made explicit in the application code.

Internet applications also have their own specific patterns, such as connection pooling for database connections, related to the proxy and singleton patterns; guest books; session tracking; and shopping carts. Patterns for J2EE applications are described in [16] and include:

Front Controller (presentation tier): Centralises the handling of client requests in a single component (usually a servlet) instead of providing multiple entry points to a system, e.g. by multiple JSP pages directly referenced in web page ACTION attributes. This avoids duplication of code for authentication of the client, etc. The front controller component may delegate the choice of view to be presented to the client in response to a request to a dispatcher.

Composite View (presentation tier): View construction using composition of subviews, such as separate parts of a web page which provide independent information groups (news headlines, a sidebar with navigation links, share price alerts, etc., in a share management system). The composition can be carried out using JSP server-side includes, or by automated generation of HTML page fragments using the **HtmlBody** and related classes given in Section 8.5 above. Figure 8.8 shows the general structure of a composite view, based on the GoF composite design pattern [21].

Value Object (business tier): A value object is a group of data returned from the integration tier, which will be used by the business tier. Providing a group of data, such as a complete booking record, avoids the need for expensive multiple query operations to obtain individual attributes.

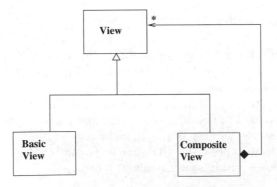

Figure 8.8: Composite View Pattern

Underlying many of the internet application design patterns is the intention to structure the application to separate out components which have clear and specific roles, such as views versus persistent data, and to coordinate these via controller objects. More flexible organisation of the connections between components could be achieved by using concepts such as coordination contracts to completely externalise control of components from the components themselves. Particular contracts would have responsibility for maintaining suitable properties relating components of the application. For example a contract managing a connection pool would be trying to maintain the constraint:

$$client\ connection\ exists\ \Rightarrow\ a\ live\ database\ connection\ exists$$

A contract in a share-trading site could be given the responsibility of maintaining the constraint:

$$client\ connection\ exists\ \Rightarrow$$
$$a\ live\ connection\ to\ a\ share\ price$$
$$site\ with\ prices\ \leq\ 15\ mins\ old\ exists$$

and so forth.

Summary

We have shown some basic techniques for using JavaScript, JSP and Servlets, and we have described architectures and design aproaches for internet applications.

Exercises

1   Write a JavaScript program which takes as input two integers **i** and **j** from a form, and when the user presses a **Display Table** button, displays the table of squares and cubes of integers from **i** to **j** inclusive.

2   Write a JSP program which displays a table of the first 10 squares and cubes, as in the JavaScript example of Figure 8.3.

3   Write a servlet for a student course registration system which processes the following login form, records the user name and password, and if these check against a stored data record (in a file **passwd.txt**), then displays a further form to the user with buttons **View Registrations**, **Update Registrations**.

```
<HTML>
<BODY>
<FORM NAME = "loginform"
 METHOD="POST" ACTION = "http://localhost:8080/servlet/Login">

<STRONG>User Id</STRONG>
<INPUT NAME="userid" TYPE = "text" SIZE = "10"></P>

<STRONG>Password</STRONG>
<INPUT NAME="password" TYPE = "password" SIZE = "10"></P>

<INPUT TYPE="submit" VALUE="Submit data">
</FORM>
</BODY>
</HTML>
```

4 Extend the three-tier application to check if a table is available on the requested date before confirming the booking. A table is available if there are fewer than **MAX_TABLES** bookings in the database for a given date. If a table is not available, do not enter the booking in the database, but ask the user to specify a different date.

Appendix A

Java in Five Easy Pieces

This appendix will give a rapid introduction to Java, up to the level needed in the rest of the book, for those new to Java programming. Java is becoming one of the most widely used general purpose programming languages in industry[1], and is also frequently used as the main teaching language in universities. It is a high quality language, with object-oriented structuring, good support tools and extensive libraries, enabling programmers to quickly build sophisticated graphical interfaces, "applets" (programs which run in a web browser) and the server side processing of web applications. In Section 1 we introduce basic Java programs and the elementary data types out of which all Java classes are ultimately built. In Section 2 we describe how to define classes to represent real-world entities. In Section 3 we cover conditional and loop statements. Section 4 deals with subclass definitions and Section 5 with data structures.

A.1 Basic Java Programs and Data Types

A.1.1 Java Program Structure

Just as a book consists of a number of chapters, and each chapter in turn consists of a number of sections, and sections consist of paragraphs, etc., so a Java program is built up out of simpler parts and subparts. A Java program consists of a set of files (with extension **.java**), each file can contain one or more *class* definitions. In turn each class definition consists of a list of local data declarations and *method* definitions:

```
class Name
{ <definitions of local data of the class>

  <method definition 1>
  ...
  <method definition n>
}
```

---

[1]The number of Java programmers grew from 0 in 1994 to 2.5 million in 2002.

Each method definition consists of a method *header* and a method *body*. A method body consists of a list of *statements*:

```
public Type methodName(parameters)   // method header
{ <definitions of local data>        // method body
                                     // between {  }
  <statement 1>                      // brackets.
  ...
  <statement m>
}
```

(Compare with a section in a chapter consisting of a section header and section contents.) At the most basic (sentence) level in Java, each statement may be of one of several kinds: assignments, method calls, constructor calls, if, while, do and for statements, and others. Each Java statement ends with a ;.

At least one class in each file must be declared as a `public class`. The name of the file must be the same as this class. For example, the following class definition:

```
public class Hello
{  /* Writes a simple message on the screen. */
   public static void main(String[] args)
   {  System.out.println("Hello, World!"); }
}
```

should be written in a file **Hello.java**. This class definition contains no local data and only one method, called **main**. A comment (between /* and */ brackets, or written after //) precedes this method definition. In turn, this method has no local data, and a single statement in its body:

```
  System.out.println("Hello, World!");
```

When this statement is executed, the message `Hello, World!` will appear on the screen (e.g. in the DOS or Unix window that we executed it in). The program terminates at the end of the **main** method.

To run this program, type:

```
  javac Hello.java
```

in a DOS or Unix/Linux window to compile it, then, if no compilation errors occur, type:

```
  java Hello
```

to execute the compiled code.

The method **println** "print line" always adds a new line after the text it displays. In this case, on the standard terminal display denoted by **System.out**.

Here is another very simple Java program, this time with two statements in its **main** method instead of one:

```
public class Hello2
{  /* Writes a simple message on the screen. */
   public static void main(String[] args)
```

```
{ System.out.println("Hello, World!");
    System.out.println("See you later.");
}
}
```

We can put as many statements as we need in the **main** method. Each statement must end with a ";". In any Java program the **main** method is the starting point for execution, it is always executed first when we type **java Prog**, and normally the program terminates when **main** does.

A.1.2   Objects and Methods

Java provides many built-in *objects*. **System.out** is an object, representing the output display for the program. Strings such as "Hello, World!" are also objects (of class **String**). Java programs deal with objects and also "primitive values" such as integers and real numbers: 165, 45.565, etc. We can also define our own new classes (like **Hello** above) and create objects of these classes.

The execution of a Java program consists of a series of *method calls*. For example:

```
System.out.println("Hello, World!");
```

This statement is an application of the method **println** to the object **System.out**.

A class lists all the methods that its objects can respond to. **Hello** responds to only one method **main**: this method is automatically invoked when a Java program is started (by **java Hello** on the command line). We will see in Section 2 that we can define as many methods as we need in a class, in order to carry out the functions our program is supposed to provide.

A.1.3   Numbers and Operations on Numbers

Suppose I visit the USA, and I have 8 pennies, no nickels, 5 dimes and 6 quarters. How much have I got altogether? To work out the answer, we need to know that a penny is a 1 cent coin, a nickel is worth 5 cents, a dime is worth 10 cents, and a quarter is worth a quarter of a dollar or 25 cents.

EXAMPLE 1.1

```
public class Change1
{ /* Calculate how much money you have (in cents) if you
      have 6 quarters, 5 dimes, no nickels, and 8 pennies. */

  public static void main(String[] args)
  { System.out.print("You have ");
    System.out.print(6*25 + 5*10 + 0*5 + 8);
    System.out.println(" cents.");
```

```
    }
}
```

---

main contains three statements. When it is run, these produce three parts of a single line of output:

- Statement 1: writes "You have " (no new-line).
- Statement 2: writes "208" (no new-line).
- Statement 3: writes " cents." (plus new-line).

So we get:

You have 208 cents.

on the screen.

This program used the * and + operators on numbers. In Java programs the following operators can be used in arithmetic expressions (Table A.1).

Operator	Name	Example
+	addition	3.4 + 7
-	subtraction (also used for -number)	5887 - 356
*	multiplication	12*12
/	division	24/6
%	remainder	23%6

Table A.1: Arithmetic Operators

In Java, numbers are either integers or floating-point numbers. If a numeric value is written without a decimal point, e.g. 4, it is treated as an integer. If it is written with a decimal point, e.g. 4.0, it is treated as a floating-point number.

Because of this difference, the division operator, /, has two different meanings. If used with two integers then it denotes *integer division*. For example: 11 / 4 = 2, (-11) / 4 = -2.

If used with two floating-point values, or one integer and one floating-point value, it denotes ordinary arithmetic division. For example: 10.5 / 2 = 5.25.

The remainder operator is only used with two integers. For example: 11%4 = 3 and (-11)%4 = -3. It is an error to attempt to evaluate **m/n** or **m%n** where **n** is zero, and the result will be an exception in the case of integer division, or **NaN** "not a number" or a constant representing positive or negative infinity, for arithmetic division.

The Java operators *, / and % bind more tightly than + and -. So, for example, 3+4*5 means 3+(4*5), not (3+4)*5.

In an expression with several + and - operators in a row, or several *, / and % operators in a row, the operators are applied from left to right. So, for example, 3-4-5 has the same meaning as (3-4)-5, not 3-(4-5). Similarly 3/4/5 means (3/4)/5, not 3/(4/5) (which will produce an error).

Recommendation: always bracket explicitly in such cases to show the intended meaning!

A.1.4 Variables

Variables are the way we, as programmers, can store values in the memory of the computer, so that they can be used in several places in a program. A *variable* has a name, and holds a value. Using that name in an expression results in the value of the variable with that name being retrieved from memory and being used at that point in the expression. For example in the following program, the variable **total** represents the total amount of money that we have.

EXAMPLE 1.2

```
public class Change2
{  /* Calculate how much money you have in dollars
      and cents if you have 6 quarters, 5 dimes,
      no nickels, and 8 pennies. */

   public static void main(String[] args)
   {  int total = 6*25 + 5*10 + 0*5 + 8; // Store 208 in total
      System.out.print("You have ");
      System.out.print(total/100); // Get value, 208, of total,
                                   // print 208/100
      System.out.print(" dollars and ");
      System.out.print(total%100); // Get value, 208 of total,
                                   // print 208%100
      System.out.println(" cents.");
   }
}
```

---

total is a *local* variable of the **main** method: it can be used within this method after it has been declared, but not in any other method of the class or in other classes. This is called the *scope* of the variable: the area of the program text where it is defined. For a variable declared at the beginning of a method, such as **total**, its scope is the remainder of the method following its declaration.

By convention, variable names always begin with a lowercase letter, and we use capitals to separate words within the name, for example `taxRate`.

The statement

```
int total = 6*25 + 5*10 + 0*5 + 8;
```

says: create a variable called **total** and set its value to the result of the expression $6 * 25 + 5 * 10 + 0 * 5 + 8$. (i.e. to 208). The word **int** means that the value stored in **total** is always an integer value.

This statement is called a *variable declaration* (or variable definition). Once defined, an integer variable can be used in arithmetic expressions in its scope in any way that a literal integer value can, as in the statements **System.out.println(total/100);** and **System.out.println(total%100)** above, which display 2 and 8 respectively. In the following example we define further local variables of **main** to hold the number of each kind of coin:

EXAMPLE 1.3

```
public class Change3
{ /* Calculate how much money in dollars and cents is
      6 quarters, 5 dimes, no nickels, and 8 pennies. */

  public static void main(String[] args)
  { int quarters = 6;
    int dimes = 5;
    int nickels = 0;
    int cents = 8;

    int total =
          quarters*25 + dimes*10 + nickels*5 + cents;

    System.out.print("You have ");
    System.out.print(total/100);
    System.out.print(" dollars and ");
    System.out.print(total%100);
    System.out.println(" cents.");
  }
}
```

This program produces the same output as the previous one. The variables **quarters**, **dimes**, etc. are simply intended to make the program easier for someone to understand. In larger programs, it becomes very important to keep the program code as simple and easy to understand as possible, otherwise huge amounts of time will be wasted trying to comprehend and modify it.

Each variable has a name and a piece of memory. We call the value held in the piece of memory the value *assigned* to the variable. This value can be changed as the program runs, for example the following program starts by creating two variables called **stones** and **pounds** set to someone's weight in stones and pounds (1 stone is 14 pounds). Then it executes the statement

```
pounds = 14*stones + pounds;
```

This calculates the value of the expression **14*stones + pounds**, and stores the result in the variable **pounds**.

EXAMPLE 1.4

```
public class Weight1
{ /* Calculate someone's weight in kilos
      given their weight in stones and pounds. */

  public static void main(String[] args)
```

```
{  int stones = 10;
   int pounds = 8;    /* Initialisation of pounds */

   pounds = 14*stones + pounds; /* Update pounds to 148 */
   double kilos = pounds * 0.4536;
   System.out.print("You weigh ");
   System.out.print(kilos);
   System.out.println(" kilos.");
  }
}
```

The declaration of **kilos**:

```
double kilos = pounds * 0.4536;
```

is an example of the use of a floating-point value. It says: create a variable called **kilos** of type **double**, and assign it the value **pounds*0.4536**. A variable of type **double** holds a double length floating point number.

The product of an integer and a floating-point number is calculated in floating-point. In this case the result will be 67.1328. The last three statements output the answer:

```
You weigh 67.1328 kilos.
```

A.1.5 Assignments

The statement

```
pounds = 14*stones + pounds;
```

is called an *assignment statement*. The general form of an assignment statement is:

```
variable = expression;
```

When this executes, the **expression** is evaluated, producing a value **val**, and this value is then stored in **variable**. Note that it is wrong to repeat the type of the variable before its name in an assignment statement:

```
int pounds = 14*stones + pounds;    // ERROR!
```

This would be a (re)declaration of **pounds**, which is invalid. We can assign values to a variable as many times as necessary, each time the variable retains the value until it is replaced by the next assignment to it.

A shorthand for the above assignment is:

```
pounds += 14*stones;
```

"Add **14*stones** to **pounds**". One of the commonest examples of this kind of statement is when we want to add 1 to the value of a variable:

```
x += 1;
```

However, there is an even shorter abbreviation for this:

```
x++;
```

Similarly, to subtract 1 from x, we can write x--.

A.1.6   Constants

Constants are used to hold values which are read but not changed by a program, for example

```
final int DAYS_PER_YEAR = 365;
```

```
System.out.println("Number of days in " + n + " years is: " +
                DAYS_PER_YEAR*n);
```

The **final** keyword means that any assignments to **DAYS_PER_YEAR** after its declaration/initialisation are invalid.

Constants are usually written all in upper case, with "_" as the word separator.

A.1.7   Casts

A *cast* expression has the form **(Type) expression**. This says: evaluate the **expression** and convert, if possible, its value to a value of type **Type**. For example:

```
int n = 4;
int m = 3;
double x = ((double) m) / n;
```

By putting the **(double)** cast in front of **m**, we are asking Java to convert the value of **m** to a double value, i.e. a 64-bit floating-point value. Once it has done this, it will apply the / operator with one **double** value and one **int** value. So we get floating-point division, and the value 0.75 is produced and stored in **x**. Without the cast the value 0 would be produced. In this case the type being cast to is "wider", more general, than the type of the value. But we can also use a cast to restrict a **double** value to an integer, for example:

```
int wholeKilos = (int) kilos;
```

assigns the integer part of **kilos** to **wholeKilos**, in Example 1.4 this is 67. Casts are also often used with class types to "downcast" a variable declared to be of a very general type to a value of a specific class, if we know that the variable actually holds an object of such a class at runtime.

A.1.8 Strings

String values in Java are written between double quotes:

```
"the dog"
```

Strings are a sequence of characters. We can have strings which are a sequence of no characters. These are called the *empty string* and are written as: "".

Control characters such as tabs and newlines can be written in strings by preceding them with the \ character, the same applies to literal quotes. For example, **\n** denotes a newline, **\t** a tab, **\"** denotes ", etc.

We can define variables of type String:

```
String animal = "dog";
```

Because strings are treated like objects in Java, **animal** will actually store a memory address: the address where the string object for **"dog"** is stored.

A very frequently used operator on strings is *concatenation*, denoted by "+". If **st1** and **st2** are strings, then **st1 + st2** denotes the string consisting of all the characters of **st1** followed by all the characters of **st2**.

For example, if variable **animal** has been assigned the value **"dog"**, then the expression

```
"The " + animal + " ran away."
```

evaluates to the string value

```
"The dog ran away."
```

So the statement

```
System.out.println("The " + animal + " ran away.");
```

displays the message **"The dog ran away."** on the screen.

Java allows numbers and strings to be combined using the + operator. For example, if **howMany** is an integer variable with value 10, then the expression

```
"The " + animal + " ran away " + howMany + " times".
```

evaluates to the string value

```
"The dog ran away 10 times."
```

To evaluate $x + y$ where x and y are either numbers or strings, Java will:

1. If x and y are both strings, concatenate them.
2. If one of x and y is a string and the other is a number, it will convert the number to a string and concatenate it with the other.
3. If x and y are both numbers, it will add them.
4. $x + y + z$ is evaluated as $(x + y) + z$.

Some other important methods that can be applied to string objects are:

- **substring**: If **st** denotes a string, and **m** and **n** denote integer values, then the expression

```
st.substring(m,n)
```

returns the string made up of the characters of **st**, starting at position **m** and ending at position **n** − 1. So for example, if the variable **animal** has been assigned the value "elephant", then the expression

```
animal.substring(5,8)
```

returns the string "ant":

```
e l e p h a n t
          | | |
0 1 2 3 4 5 6 7 8
```

Notice that the characters within a string are numbered starting at 0, this is common to all data structures in Java, and is a legacy of the C language, from which Java borrows much of its syntax.
- **st.length()**: Returns the number of characters in **st**. For example "Alice Brown".length() returns value 11.
- **st.toLowerCase()**: Returns lowercase version of **st**. For example "Alice Brown".toLowerCase() returns "alice brown".
- **st.toUpperCase()**: Returns uppercase version of *st*. For example "Alice Brown".toUpperCase() returns "ALICE BROWN".

A.1.9   Reading Input Values

Java provides a large number of built-in *dialogs* to read values entered by a user. The simplest is a **JOptionPane** input dialog which pops up a dialog containing a single text field:

```
String reply =
  JOptionPane.showInputDialog("Enter value:");
```

This produces the dialog of Figure A.1. When the user presses the **OK** or

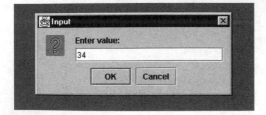

Figure A.1: Basic Input Dialog

Cancel buttons the dialog closes, and in the case of **OK** the string typed in the text field is transferred to the **reply** variable.

Here is a new version of the weight conversion program using dialogs. Notice we must *import* the swing and awt libraries to use **JOptionPane**:

EXAMPLE 1.5

```
import java.awt.*;     // make the awt and swing
import javax.swing.*; // packages available
                      // to the program.

public class Weight2
{  /* Read user's weight in stones and pounds,
      and output their weight in kilos. */

   public static void main(String[] args)
   { System.out.println("Tell me your weight.");
     String s =
       JOptionPane.showInputDialog("How many stones:");
     int stones = Integer.parseInt(s);
     String p =
       JOptionPane.showInputDialog("How many pounds:");
     int pounds = Integer.parseInt(p);

     pounds = 14*stones + pounds;
     double kilos = pounds * 0.4536;
     System.out.print("You weigh ");
     System.out.print(kilos);
     System.out.println(" kilos.");
   }
}
```

Integer.parseInt(s) converts a string **s** into the integer it represents, i.e. a string "547" will be converted to the integer value 547.

A.1.10 Summary

We have seen the general template structure for a simple Java program:

```
public class Test
{ // start of class
  public static void main(String[] args}
  { // start of main method
    // declarations and statements
  } // end of main method
} // end of class
```

Any name can be used in place of "Test", although by convention class names begin with a capital letter, and any valid sequence of declarations and statements can be placed inside the **main** method. We have seen the general form of a declaration:

```
Type variable = initialValue;
```

and the assignment statement:

```
variable = value;
```

plus statements **System.out.println(s);** for outputting information to the user, and **JOptionPane.showInputDialog(s);** for reading information from the user.

Key Points

- **What is a class?** A class is a group of attributes (data) and methods. If the class **C** represents a program, then it must be declared as **public class C** in a file **C.java**, and must have a *main* method, which is where execution starts when we type **java C** on the command line.
- **What is a method?** A method is a named piece of executable code. When the method is executed, the statements inside it are executed in order (from top to bottom of the method text).
- **What is a variable?** A variable is a named piece of computer memory. So far, we have only seen *local* variables, defined within a method. Once declared, these variables can be written to and read from in the rest of the method. We can store integers in an **int** variable, rational numbers in a **double** variable, and strings – sequences of characters – in a **String** variable.

A.2   Defining Classes

Classes provide a way to represent almost any entity from the real world inside a program, e.g. students, bank accounts, railway networks, etc. As a simple example, we will consider the task of building a program which will store information about students in a computer science department, keeping track of what course they are on, what their year of study is, etc.

A.2.1   Student Database Application

To develop: a database program in Java that will record information about all students studying in a computer science department.

This program will use many different kinds of objects:

- objects that represent individual students;
- an object that holds the list of all students in the database;
- objects that represent courses, lecturers, etc.

Here we will consider the **Student** class. This class forms a template for student objects, it defines the attributes (variables) and operations (methods) which all student objects will have, although different student objects will normally have different values stored in their attributes. Figure A.2 gives a graphical representation of such a class, in UML notation.

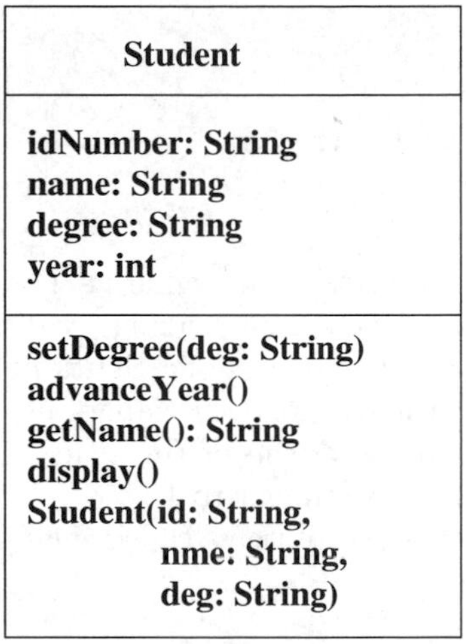

Student
idNumber: String **name: String** **degree: String** **year: int**
setDegree(deg: String) **advanceYear()** **getName(): String** **display()** **Student(id: String,** 　　　　**nme: String,** 　　　　**deg: String)**

Figure A.2: UML Class Diagram of Student Entity

The **Student** entity can be coded up in Java as a piece of program called a *class definition*. We start by identifying what are the required operations for this class:

1. It should be possible to change a student's degree programme. So we need a method **setDegree** that replaces a student's current degree programme with a new one.
2. It should be possible to change a student's year of study on from 1 to 2, 2 to 3 or 3 to 4. So we need to define a method **advanceYear** to do this.
3. We need a method **getName** to get a student's name.
4. It should be possible to display all details of a student on the screen. We need a method **display** to do this.
5. It will be necessary to create new **Student** objects. We need a method that takes the student's ID number, name and degree programme and creates a year 1 student object with this data.

The final operation here is carried out by a *constructor*. A constructor is like a method in that it has a body, a name and parameters. However, the name must always be the same as the class it belongs to. So the name of this constructor will be **Student**. As indicated in Figure A.2, it will take three parameters **id**, **nme** and **deg** representing the ID number, name and degree of the student to be represented. No return type is needed with a constructor. For **Student** the constructor is written in Java as:

```
/* Create a new student with the given ID number,
   name and degree.  Year will be set to 1. */
public Student(String id, String nme, String deg)
{ idNumber = id;
  name = nme;
  degree = deg;
  year = 1;
}
```

A constructor is invoked by a **new** statement. This has the form

```
new Student(val1,val2,val3);
```

in the case of **Student**. When this statement is executed, the value **val1** is stored in the **id** parameter of the constructor (so **val1** must be a string), **val2** is stored in **nme** and **val3** is stored in **deg**, then the code of the **Student** constructor is executed, which copies the values in the parameter variables into the corresponding attributes **idNumber**, **name** and **degree** of the student instance that is being created, and sets the year of this student to 1.

The structure of a class consists of a number of separate items called *members* or *features*. There are three kinds of members:

1. *Variables/attributes.* These record the data of the object. For example, a **Student** object will have a variable that contains the student's name. These variables are sometimes called *fields* (or *instance variables*). Unlike local variables, they can be used by any of the methods of the class in which they are declared: their scope is the entire class text following their declaration.

2. *Methods.* These carry out operations that can be performed on an object. They typically update and read the attributes of the class, and may define their own local variables to carry out local computations within the method.

3. *Constructors.* These create objects belonging to the class. They typically initialise some or all of the attributes.

Each feature is declared to be either *public* or *private*. Public features can be used by any class in the application. Private features can only be used within the class that declares them.

Each **Student** object contains the following four items of information:

1. Student ID number.
2. Name.
3. Degree programme.
4. Year of study.

Each will be held in an attribute of the appropriate type:

```
public class Student
{ private String idNumber;
  // The student's ID number.
  private String name;
  // The student's name.
  private String degree;
  // The student's degree programme.
  private int year;
  // The student's year
  // of study (1, 2, 3 or 4).

  /* Create a new student with the given ID number,
     name and degree.  Year will be set to 1. */
  public Student(String id, String nme, String deg)
  { idNumber = id;
    name = nme;
    degree = deg;
    year = 1;
  }
}
```

This is a valid class definition, but not a very useful one as yet, since no methods have been defined to read or modify a student.

Every instance of **Student** will have its own copy of the four variables. For example if we created two student objects using the **Student** constructor:

```
Student s1 = new Student("038923","J. Patel","CS");
Student s2 = new Student("037722","N. Malik","CS/Man");
```

then there are eight variables which have been created and initialised as a result of these constructor calls, four in each object. **s1** has the variables

1. **s1.idNumber** with value "038923"
2. **s1.name** with value "J. Patel"
3. **s1.degree** with value "CS"
4. **s1.year** with value 1.

and **s2** has variables:

1. **s2.idNumber** with value "037722"
2. **s2.name** with value "N. Malik"
3. **s2.degree** with value "CS/Man"
4. **s2.year** with value 1.

The class **Student** acts as a *template* for its instances: it describes their common structure. But each separate instance is completely independent of the others, we can modify **s1** without changing **s2**, for example. Figure A.3 shows that objects correspond to real-world entities, in this case students, usually in

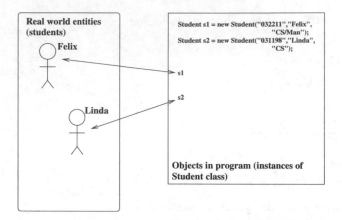

Figure A.3: Objects Represent Real-world Entities

a 1-1 manner, i.e. each different student in the CS department has a unique object that represents themselves and some of their characteristics.

We could define initial values for the fields, e.g.

```
private int year = 1;
```

although often these are left for the constructor to define instead.

It is usual for instance variables to be **private**. This prevents one class from referring directly to the internal structure of another class, and so reduces inter-class dependencies. Thus direct reference to the values **s1.name**, etc., are not allowed. In contrast methods are normally **public**, so that other classes can call these methods, e.g. as: **s1.advanceYear();** to modify or read student objects. For the same reason the constructor is normally **public**.

The first method of **Student** is **setDegree**. This changes a student's degree programme. When it is called (i.e. executed), it takes the name of the new degree programme as a *parameter* variable. In general, methods and constructors can have any number of parameters. **setDegree** has just this one, called **deg** here. Parameter variables are very similar to local variables, their scope is the method of which they are a parameter. But they are initialised by the call, and in this way transfer data from the calling program to the called method.

The body of a method consists of a sequence of statements that will carry out whatever actions are needed.

In this case, only one action is needed: the new degree programme (i.e. the parameter **deg**) should be stored in the **degree** attribute:

```
degree = deg;
```

Here is the complete definition of **setDegree**:

```
/* Change the student's degree programme to deg. */
public void setDegree(String deg)
{ degree = deg; }
```

The first line is a comment, the next line is the method heading:

1. `public` says the method can be used anywhere in the program.
2. `void` says the method does not return any value.
3. `setDegree` is the name of the method.
4. `(String deg)` is the list of all the method's parameters.

Finally comes the body of the method, enclosed in {}.

To use this method we need to create a **Student** object, stored in a variable, e.g. called **fred**. Then if the programmer wants to set this student's degree programme to "CS/Man", they can invoke the method **setDegree("CS/Man")** on this object:

```
Student fred = new Student("021199","Janice Smith","CS");
fred.setDegree("CS/Man");
```

The second statement says: execute method **setDegree** from the **Student** class on the object **fred**, using the parameter value "CS/Man".

When this statement is executed, the value "CS/Man" is copied to the **deg** parameter of the method, then the method body is executed, which is the assignment **degree = deg;** So the value of **deg** is evaluated – this value is still the string "CS/Man" of course – and copied to the **degree** attribute of the object **fred**. In other words the effect of the method call **fred.setDegree("CS/Man");** is equivalent to the assignment `fred.degree = "CS/Man";` being performed.

advanceYear is simpler than **setDegree** because it has no parameters. All the body of this method does is add 1 to the **year** attribute:

```
/* Increase the student's year of study by 1. */
public void advanceYear()
{ year++; }
```

The next method is **getName**. Unlike the two previous methods, it does "return a value". For example, the method is called when Java executes the statement:

```
String st = fred.getName();
```

Java will create the string variable **st**, then it will execute the method call

```
fred.getName();
```

The method will return the name of this student (e.g. "Janice Smith" in the above example), and Java will store it in the variable **st**.

fred.getName() is used as an expression, in the same way that **Math.sqrt(1.5)** is used as an expression in:

```
double x = 1 - Math.sqrt(1.5);
```

Methods that return values are always used like this.

The body of **getName** is a single statement. It says: return the value of the **name** attribute to the caller of the method.

```
return name;
```

This is called a *return statement*. The outcome is effectively that the assignment
`String st = fred.name;` is carried out.

EXAMPLE 2.1:   *Complete Student class*

```java
/* A Student object is a record of a BSc/MSci student. */
public class Student
{ private String idNumber;
  // The student's ID number.
  private String name;
  // The student's name.
  private String degree;
  // The student's degree programme.
  private int year;
  // The student's year
  // of study (1, 2, 3, 4).

  /* Create a new student with the given ID number,
     name and degree.  Year will be set to 1. */
  public Student(String id, String nme, String deg)
  { idNumber = id;
    name = nme;
    degree = deg;
    year = 1;
  }

  /* Change this student's degree programme to deg. */
  public void setDegree(String deg)
  { degree = deg; }

  /* Increase this student's year by 1. */
  public void advanceYear()
  { year++; }

  /* Return this student's name. */
  public String getName()
  { return name; }

  /* Display details of this student on the screen. */
  public void display()
  { System.out.println("Student number: " + idNumber);
    System.out.println("Name: " + name);
    System.out.println("Degree programme: " + degree);
    System.out.println("Year: " + year);
  }
}
```

The **display** method simply prints out the values of all the attributes of
the object.

Finally here is a very simple program that makes use of a **Student** object. It consists of a single **main** method, placed in the class **TestStudent**:

EXAMPLE 2.2

```java
import java.awt.*;
import javax.swing.*;

public class TestStudent
{ /* Read details of a student.
     Then create the corresponding Student object,
     and display that object's details.
   */
  public static void main(String[] args)
  { /* Read information about a student
       and create an object for them. */
    String i =
      JOptionPane.showInputDialog("Enter student's ID number:");
    String n =
      JOptionPane.showInputDialog("Enter their name:");
    String d =
      JOptionPane.showInputDialog("Enter their degree:");

    Student st = new Student(i,n,d);
    /* Change the student's year and degree,
       and display the student's details. */
    st.advanceYear();
    st.setDegree("CS with Man");
    System.out.println();
    st.display();
  }
}
```

A.2.2 Reference Values

When a Java program is running, each variable either contains a primitive value such as an integer or boolean value, or it contains a reference to an object. Similarly, if an expression is evaluated, the result will either be a primitive value or a reference to an object. References behave differently to primitive values because they identify locations in memory. For example, in the code:

```java
Student st1 = new Student("0912345", "Brown, Alice",
                          "Maths and CS");
Student st2 = st1;
st1.setDegree("CS");
st2.display();
```

the degree programme displayed for **st2** is "CS" because **st1** and **st2** are *aliased* by the assignment **st2 = st1**: after this assignment they hold the same object reference, so a method call **s.m(x)** on either affects *both* variables identically.

A **null** reference can be assigned to any variable that normally holds a reference value. For example:

```
Student st = null;
```

In the student database program this could be useful if we had a method which searches the database for a student with a particular ID number. If such a student object is found, the method returns a reference of this object. If no student with the given ID number is found, the method could return **null**.

If an object **st** is **null** we cannot invoke any method on it:

```
st.setDegree("CS");
```

will produce a run-time error, **NullPointerException**. Thus it is usual to test if an unknown object is non-null before attempting to execute a method on it:

```
if (st != null)  // if statement, see following section
{ st.setDegree("CS"); }
```

A.2.3   Example 2: Cats

As another example of a class defined to represent an entity type, consider a class of **Cat**s, as for example used by a pedigree cat breeder to record details of their animals:

```
public class Cat
{ private String name = "";
  private int age = 0;
  private String breed = "";
  private Cat sire = null; // Breeding partner
  private int numberKittens = 0;

  public Cat(String nme, int ag, String brd)
  { name = nme;
    age = ag;
    breed = brd;
  }

  public String getName()
  { return name; }

  public String getBreed()
  { return breed; }

  public String toString()
  { return "Cat: " + name + " is " + age + " years old, of breed " +
```

```
        breed;
  }

  public void birthday()
  { age++; }  // Only for live cats.

  public void breedWith(Cat s)
  { sire = s; }
}
```

This class has an attribute for each of the important properties of a cat that we want to record: its name, age, breed and any mating partner. The **toString()** method returns a string representation of each cat object, so these objects can be directly used within a **println** statement:

```
public class TestCat
{ public static void main(String[] args)
  { Cat c1 = new Cat("Fifi-Trixibelle",2,"Burmese");
    Cat c2 = new Cat("Alexander",3,"Burmese");
    System.out.println(c1);  // Implicitly calls c1.toString()
    System.out.println(c2);
  }
}
```

This produces the output:

```
Cat: Fifi-Trixibelle is 2 years old, of breed Burmese
Cat: Alexander is 3 years old, of breed Burmese
```

A.2.4 Summary

In this section we have seen how to define classes which have several methods, and variables of a class, called **attributes**, which can be used in all the methods of the class. We have seen several additional statements:

- **new C(values);** – a **new** statement, which invokes the constructor of class **C** to create a new object of **C**.
- **return expression;** – a **return** statement, used to return the value of **expression** to the caller of the method that the statement occurs in. The statement also terminates the execution of the method.
- method calls **obj.m(values);** – which execute by copying the values (if any) into the parameter variables of **m**, then executing the body of **m** on object **obj**, reading and modifying its attributes and optionally returning a value using **return**.

The following general template can be used to define a class representing an entity **Ent** with attributes **att1: Type1**, ..., **attn: Typen**:

```
public class Ent
{ private Type1 att1;
```

```
...
private Typen attn;

public Ent(Type1 p1, ..., Typen pn)
{ att1 = p1;
  ...
  attn = pn;
}

public Type1 getAtt1()
{ return att1; }

...

public Typen getAttn()
{ return attn; }

... entity specific updater methods ...
}
```

As we saw in the **Student** and **Cat** examples above, not every attribute of a class may be supplied with a value via a parameter of the constructor: the value may always be the same for every new object, like 1 for the **year** attribute of a student, so it needs no parameter. Also not every attribute will need a corresponding **get** method to read its value.

Key Points

- **What is an object?** An object **x**, say, is an instance of some class, **C**: it has particular values **x.att** for each attribute **att** of **C**, and methods **m** of **C** can be applied to **x**: **x.m(params);** to modify/read these values. Two different objects **x** and **y** are completely independent collections of data.
- **What are parameters?** Parameter variables pass information into a method, allowing its code to be used with many different values. For example, a cube calculator method: **public int cube(int n) { return n*n*n; }** could be supplied with value 6: **cube**(6), and returns value 216, or with value 9: **cube**(9), returning 729.

A.3   Conditional and Loop Statements

A.3.1   Conditional Statements: `if`

`if` statements are used to make decisions and to select from two alternative actions which will be carried out next. For example:

```
if (ans == 6048)
{ System.out.println("Well done!"); }
else
{ System.out.println("Wrong."); }
```

This is what this statement says:

> If the value of **ans** is equal to 6048, display the message "Well done!", otherwise display the message "Wrong."

Note that the expression

```
ans == 6048
```

stands for the condition (test) "**ans** equals 6048". The symbol == is used for the equality relation, rather than =, to avoid confusion with assignments.

Here is a program using this `if` statement. It starts by asking the user to do a simple calculation: what is 72 times 84? It reads the user's answer, stores it in variable **ans**, then an `if` statement checks if the user gave the right answer.

EXAMPLE 3.1

```
import java.awt.*;
import javax.swing.*;

public class Multiply1
{   /* Ask the user to input the value of
       72 times 84, and check their answer. */

    public static void main(String[] args)
    { String a =
         JOptionPane.showInputDialog("What is 72 times 84?");
      int ans = Integer.parseInt(a);
      if (ans == 6048)
      { System.out.println("Well done!"); }
      else
      { System.out.println("Wrong."); }
    }
}
```

The general form of an `if` statement is given below. A *Boolean expression* is any expression that may be true or false.

```
if (BOOLEAN-EXPRESSION)
{ STATEMENT(s)-1 }
else
{ STATEMENT(s)-2 }
```

When Java executes this statement, it checks whether the BOOLEAN-EXPRESSION is true or false. If it is true, STATEMENT(s)-1 are executed. If it is false, STATEMENT(s)-2 are executed.

There is a shorter form of the `if` statement which misses out the `else` and second branch:

```
if (a < b)
{ System.out.println("The smaller value is " + a); }
```

This says: if **a** is less than **b** then display the message, otherwise do nothing.

It has the same effect as:

```
if (a < b)
{ System.out.println("The smaller value is " + a); }
else
{}  // empty statement, has no effect
```

We can have several if statements following each other, just as with any other kind of statement. For example, suppose the variables **a**, **b**, **c** and **d** contain four numbers. The following code stores the smallest of these values in the variable **s**:

```
s = a;
if (b < s)
{ s = b; }  // s is min(a,b) after this if.
if (c < s)
{ s = c; }  // s is min(c,min(a,b)) after this if.
if (d < s)
{ s = d; }  // s is min(d,min(c,min(a,b))) after this if.
```

Here is another example of a one-branch `if` statement. The program uses **Math.sqrt** to calculate square roots. If the user enters a negative number, it prints out an error message, and then executes a **return** statement.

This just consists of **return;** (with no return value). It means: finish obeying the method and return to its caller. In this case this means return to the DOS or Unix terminal that executed the program. Such a return statement can only occur in a method with **void** return type, whereas the **return e** statement must occur in a method with non-**void** type **T** compatible with **e**'s type.

EXAMPLE 3.2

```
import java.awt.*;
import javax.swing.*;

public class Sqrt
```

```
{  /* Ask user to input a number
      then output its square root. */

   public static void main(String[] args)
   { String s =
        JOptionPane.showInputDialog("Enter a number:");
     double x = Double.parseDouble(s);
     if (x < 0)
     { System.out.println("Number should be >= 0.");
       return;    // Exit the main method.
     }
     System.out.println("The square root is " + Math.sqrt(x));
   }
}
```

if statements can be cascaded, to provide a multi-way choice. For example, to get a student grade from a mark we could have the cases:

- mark in range 70 – 100: grade = A
- mark in range 60 – 69: grade = B
- mark in range 50 – 59: grade = C
- mark in range 40 – 49: grade = D
- mark in range 0 – 39: grade = F

If the variable **mark** contains the numeric mark, we can write:

```
if (mark >= 70) { grade = "A"; }
else if (mark >= 60) { grade = "B"; }
else if (mark >= 50) { grade = "C"; }
else if (mark >= 40) { grade = "D"; }
else { grade = "F"; }
```

The same technique can be used to test a series of conditions one after another and carry out appropriate actions.

The general form of a conditional statement has **n** Boolean expressions and **n + 1** statements:

```
if (B1)
{ S1 }
else if (B2)
{ S2 }
else if (B3)
{ S3 }
  ...
  ...
else if (Bn)
{ Sn }
else
{ T }
```

Just as with the two-branch **if** statement, only one of the branches **S1**, ..., **Sn**, **T** will ever be executed. If **B1** holds, **S1** is executed, if **B1** is false but **B2** holds, then **S2** is executed, and so on, until **T**, which only executes if none of the **Bi** are true.

A.3.2   The Data Type boolean

A Boolean expression such as **ans** $==$ 6048 can be evaluated to get one of the values `true` and `false`. These are called *Boolean values*. Together they form the primitive data type called *boolean*. We can define variables of boolean type, e.g.

```
boolean ok = (x > 0);
```

Boolean expressions include relations between numbers. Table A.2 gives examples of the common cases. These can be used between any expressions

Operator	Name	Example
$==$	equals	$26 == 2 * 13$
$!=$	not equals	$5 \mathrel{!=} 3$
$<$	less than	$9 < 23$
$<=$	less than or equal to	$10 <= 10$
$>$	greater than	$51 > 3 * 3$
$>=$	greater than or equal to	$2 * 5 >= 9$

Table A.2: Boolean-valued Arithmetic Operators

that denote integer or floating-point values.

Other Boolean expressions are:

1. The literal values `true` and `false`.
2. **obj instanceof C**: this expression is true iff **obj** is an instance of class **C**, e.g. if **obj** $=$ **new C(params)** has been executed.
3. Method calls, where the method returns a Boolean value.

Complex Boolean expressions can be built from simpler ones using logical operators. (B1 and B2 are any Boolean expressions):

operator	meaning
B1 && B2	B1 and B2
B1 || B2	B1 or B2
! B1	not B1

When Java evaluates B1 && B2, it will evaluate B1 first. If B1 is false it does not go on and evaluate B2, because B1 && B2 is bound to be false. This "lazy" way of evaluating B1 && B2 is sometimes very helpful, if B2 only has a well-defined value when B1 is true:

```
grade != null && grade.equals("A")
```

Java also evaluates B1 || B2 in a "lazy" way. If B1 is true then B2 is not evaluated, because the value of B1 || B2 is bound to be true. The expression !B1 is true if B1 is false, and false if B1 is true.

&& and || are less binding than the other operators we have met. || is less binding than &&. So for example, Java interprets the expression

```
n >= 0 && n < 10 || n >= 20 && n < 30
```

as

```
((n >= 0) && (n < 10)) || ((n >= 20) && (n < 30))
```

The "not" operator, !, is more binding than other operators. The assignment operator = is less binding than all the other operators we have seen. So it is not necessary to use brackets in the statement

```
boolean ok = (x > 0);
```

We can simplify complicated boolean expressions by using the equivalencies:

> !(**P1** && **P2**) is equivalent to !**P1** || !**P2**
> !(**P1** || **P2**) is equivalent to !**P1** && !**P2**
> !(!**P1**) is equivalent to **P1**
> !(**x** < **y**) is equivalent to **x** >= **y**
> !(**x** == **y**) is equivalent to **x** ! = **y**
> !(**x** <= **y**) is equivalent to **x** > **y**

The first two are the *De Morgan* rules, essentially they allow us to move a negation inside a conjunction or disjunction. The other rules allow us to eliminate negations from certain basic formulae.

A.3.3 Comparing Strings

If **s1** and **s2** are strings, **s1.equals(s2)** returns **true** if **s1** has exactly the same sequence of characters as **s2**, and **false** otherwise.

The == operator is never normally used to test if two strings are the same. The reason is that the condition

```
E1 == E2
```

where **E1** and **E2** are expressions that denote strings, evaluates **E1** and **E2**. This gives two reference values: the memory locations of the strings. So **E1** == **E2** tests if these reference values are equal. That is, it tests if **E1** and **E2** are at the same physical location in memory. But this isn't the test we want, because two strings can easily have identical values (sequences of characters) without being at the same place in memory.

A useful alternative to **equals** is:

- **st1.equalsIgnoreCase(st2)** – returns **true** if **st1** and **st2** are two strings that consist of the same characters, if upper and lower case versions of the same letter are counted as equal. Otherwise return **false**.

For example, if **st1** is "the dog" and **st2** is "The Dog", then the method will return true.

An example of a method using string comparison is the following additional method of the **Cat** class of Section 2:

```
public Cat giveBirth()  // Only for female cats with a sire
{ String kittenBreed = breed;    // default breed for kitten
                                 // is my breed.
  if (sire != null)
  { String matedWith = sire.getBreed();
    if (breed.equals(matedWith)) // pure bred kittens -- do nothing
    { }
    else
    { kittenBreed = kittenBreed + "Cross" + matedWith; }
    Cat kitten = new Cat(name + "_" + sire.getName() + "_" +
                         numberKittens, 0, kittenBreed);
    numberKittens++;
    return kitten;
  }
  return null;  // No sire, so I can't breed
}
```

If the cat and her partner are of the same breed, then their kittens are also of this breed, otherwise the kittens are of breed **breed1Crossbreed2**.

A.3.4   Loop Statements

Java provides three statements for repeating actions a set number of times, or until a condition is satisfied: *while, do-while* and *for* statements.

The simplest Java loop statement is the **while** statement. This has the syntax:

```
while (BOOLEAN-EXPRESSION)
{ STATEMENT(s) }
```

This means:

> Keep repeating the STATEMENT(s). Each time, before the STATE-
> MENT(s) are executed, check that the BOOLEAN-EXPRESSION
> is true. If it is false, finish immediately.

An example of while loops is given by *Euclid's algorithm*: Suppose we want to work out the highest common factor of two integers, e.g. 338 and 546. Euclid's algorithm for solving this problem is to write down the two numbers, and subtract the smaller number from the bigger one. The smaller one is left unchanged. Keep repeating the subtraction step until the two numbers are equal. This value is the hcf of the original two numbers.

The process can be expressed by the following while loop. Assume that **a** and **b** initially hold the two integers we are trying to find the hcf of:

```
while (a != b)
{ if (a > b)
  { a = a-b; }
  else
  { b = b-a; }
}
```

The body of this loop repeatedly subtracts the smaller of the two values from the larger. This process is repeated until the numbers are equal.

Note that if **a** > 0 and **b** > 0 initially then they will be so at the end of every iteration, so the loop must eventually terminate.

A while statement starts by carrying out the loop test. A do-while statement starts by executing the body of the loop, then does the test:

```
do
{ STATEMENT(s) }
while (BOOLEAN-EXPRESSION);
```

This means:

> Keep repeating the STATEMENT(s). Each time, after the STATEMENT(s) have been executed, check that the BOOLEAN-EXPRESSION is true. If it is false, finish immediately.

These loops are used if there is always going to be at least one execution of the body, otherwise they are used exactly as for while loops.

*Beware: this is one of the few cases where it is correct to write a ; immediately after a test. Don't try this with **while** or **if** statements!*

The final type of loop are *for loops*. These are used whenever a predetermined number of iterations is needed (instead of iterating until a general condition becomes true).

For example, if we want to display a table of values of **cos**(**x**) for **x** being: 0, 5, 10, 15, ..., 85, 90, we could do this using a while loop:

```
int x = 0;
while (x <= 90)
{  Display the value of x and cos(x).
   x = x+5;
}
```

However any loop of this form (with a known number of iterations and fixed step/increment) should be expressed using a for loop which has the general syntax:

```
for (First; Continue; Next)
{ STATEMENTS }
```

First is a statement that sets the index variable of the loop to its first value. **Continue** is a boolean expression, which tests if the index variable has not passed its final value. **Next** is a statement defining how the index variable is updated. The equivalent while loop is:

```
First;
while (Continue)
{ STATEMENTS;
  Next
}
```

So using a `for` loop to produce the cosine table, we get:

```
for (int x = 0; x <= 90; x = x + 5)
{ System.out.println("\t" + x + "\t" + Math.cos(x)); }
```

for loops with integer indices are very frequently used to process arrays and lists, as described in Section 5.

Loops can be nested inside other loops (because any statements can be written inside a loop), for example:

```
for (int i = 1; i <= 12; i++)
{ System.out.println("Times table for " + i);
  for (int j = 1; j <= 12; j++)
  { System.out.println(i + " times " + j + "\t = " + i*j); }
  System.out.println();
}
```

prints out the times tables from 1 to 12.

A.3.5   Recursion

Another way of repeating some processing is to use *recursion*, that is, to define a method which calls itself. The following gives a simple example of a recursive method, **power(x,n)**, which calculates the **n**th power of **x**:

EXAMPLE 3.3

```
public class PowerProg
{ /* Read two integers, x and y, where y >= 0.
     Output the value of x to the power y. */

  public static void main(String[] args)
  { String arg = JOptionPane.showInputDialog("Enter argument");
    int x = Integer.parseInt(arg);
    String pow = JOptionPane.showInputDialog("Enter power");
    int y = Integer.parseInt(pow);
    System.out.println(x + " to the power " + y +
                       " = " + power(x,y));
  }

  /* If n >= 0, return x to the power n. */
  private static int power(int x, int n)
  { if (n == 0)
    { return 1; }
```

```
      else
      { return power(x,n-1)*x; }  // call to itself
   }
}
```

If this program is executed, and the user inputs values 2 and 4, Java will call **power(2,4)**, which leads to a call of **power(2,3)** in the expression **power**$(x, n - 1) * x$.

This call leads to a call to **power(2,2)**, **power(2,1)** and finally **power(2,0)**, which returns with result 1. The execution of **power(2,1)** returns the value 1*2, i.e. 2. This is used in the execution of **power(2,2)**, which returns 4. And so on.

In this case a simple non-recursive solution is possible:

```
private static int power(int x, int n)
{ int answer = 1;
  for (int i = 0; i < n; i++)
  { answer = answer * x; }
  return answer;
}
```

Generally non-recursive solutions are more efficient than recursive programs, because they have no overhead of creating/deleting local and parameter variables for nested method calls. However, a recursive version may be considerably simpler than any possible iterative version, for example in binary search. Recursive solutions are natural if the problem itself is recusive, e.g. manipulating a tree structure, or the "towers of Hanoi" problem. In these cases recursive solutions are reasonable provided the loss of efficiency is not significant.

A.3.6   Static Methods

In the above program, the **power** method had the keyword **static** before its definition, as have all the **main** methods we have seen so far. This keyword indicates that the method uses none of the instance variables of the class (in **PowerProg** there are no instance variables anyway), in other words that it is independent of any particular object of the class. This is normally the case for methods that compute a mathematical function of their input values, such as **sqrt(x)** and **sin(x)**. For such methods we invoke them from outside their class by prefixing them with their class name, instead of any object name. So the **sqrt** and **sin** methods of the built-in **Math** class are invoked by **Math.sqrt(x);** and **Math.sin(x);**. Similarly, if **power** above was **public**, we could invoke it by **PowerProg.power(x,n)**.

Key Points

- **What is an if statement?**   This is a statement
  if (**E**) { **C1** } else { **C2** } which enables a program to make
  a choice in its execution: if **E** is true, **C1** is executed, otherwise **C2** is executed. **C1** and **C2** can be any statements or
  sequences of statements.
- **What is a loop statement?** This is a statement which repeats another statement/sequence of statements until a condition becomes false. There are three kinds of loop in Java:
  while, **for** and **do**.
- **What is recursion?** This is a programming technique which
  repeats some process by using a method which calls itself.

A.4   Inheritance and Subclasses

A.4.1   Defining Subclasses in Java

Java, along with all other object-oriented languages, supports the idea of one
class being a *subclass* of another. This enables Java programs to accurately
represent those situations in the real world where all instances of one sort of
entity are also instances of another (more general) sort.

For example: all monkeys are mammals; all medical students are students;
all Ford Pintos are vehicles, etc.

Going back to the **Student** class from Section 2, there are extra, specialised
kinds of student, such as **PlacementStudent**, which contain additional information (such as the organisation they are doing their placement at) and
methods to modify/read this information.

In general, suppose we have a class **A**, and we want to define a new class,
B, whose objects have all the features of objects of **A**, plus additional features.
We can define B like this:

```
public class B extends A
{  Additional variables, methods and constructors of B.
   (Do NOT repeat definitions of A's features here.)
}
```

B is said to *extend* **A**. Also, **B** is called a *subclass* of **A**, and **A** is called
a *superclass* of **B**. This situation corresponds to a UML class diagram such
as Figure A.4. **B** objects will have all the features (variables, methods and
constructors) given in the definition of **A**. B is said to *inherit* the features of
A.

We can also define new methods of **B** objects, and give new definitions for
some old methods of **A**. In the second case the new method is said to *override*
the old one. For **B** objects the definition of the method given in **B** takes effect,

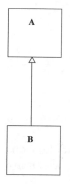

Figure A.4: Inheritance of **A** by **B**

replacing the definition given in **A**, which only applies for **A** objects. **B** also usually has its own constructors.

In effect, a **B** object has a dual personality. It can be used strictly as a **B** object, e.g. one of the new methods from the definition of **B** can be used with it. Or it can be used as a special case of an **A** object. Java will allow any code written for **A** objects to be applied to **B** objects. This feature of Java is known as *polymorphism*.

Since Java is willing to treat **B** objects as if they are **A** objects, we can think of **B** objects as if they actually belong to class **A**. It is for this reason that **B** is called a subclass of class **A** (every instance of **B** can be treated as an instance of **A**, i.e. the set of instances of **B** is a subset of the set of instances of **A**).

Here is how we could define the **PlacementStudent** subclass of **Student**:

```
class PlacementStudent extends Student
{ private String placedAt = "";

  public PlacementStudent(String id, String nme, String deg)
  { super(id,nme,deg); } // invoke Student constructor

  public void setPlacement(String org)
  { placedAt = org; }

  public void display()
  { System.out.println("Student " + getName());
    System.out.println("Placement at: " + placedAt);
  }
}
```

A test program using this class could be:

```
public class TestPlacementStudent
{ public static void main(String[] args)
  { PlacementStudent pstud =
      new PlacementStudent("021134", "Xavier", "CS");
```

```
    pstud.setPlacement("Accenture");
    pstud.advanceYear();
    pstud.display();
  }
}
```

We can use **Student** methods on **PlacementStudent** objects: **pstud.advanceYear()**, etc., but also the new methods of the subclass, to set its placement: **pstud.setPlacement("Accenture")**.

Every class inherits a class called **Object** which contains default definitions of general methods such as **equals(Object obj)**, **toString()**, etc., which are applicable to any class (Figure A.5).

We can override these methods in our own classes to provide more specific versions. For example we can define a method, in **PlacementStudent**, which decides if two placement students are equal:

```
public boolean equals(Object obj)
{ if (obj instanceof PlacementStudent)
  { PlacementStudent other = (PlacementStudent) obj;
    if (other.getName().equals(getName()))
    { return true; }
  }
  return false;
}
```

This means that **st.equals(st1)** will return **true** for two placement student objects **st** and **st1** provided their names are the same, regardless of the values of other attributes[2].

Probably a better definition of equality in this case would be to use the **idNumber** attributes, as these are intended to be unique to individual students. However **idNumber** is a private attribute of **Student**, so we cannot refer to it in this subclass. The solution to this is given in the following section. **toString()** returns a string representation of any object. It is implicitly called whenever we use the object within a string expression, e.g. `System.out.println(stud);` where **stud** is an object, will try to convert the object into a string by invoking **stud.toString()**. For students we can define:

```
public String toString()
{ return "Student number: " + idNumber + "\n" +
        "Name: " + name + "\n" +
        "Degree programme: " + degree + "\n" +
        "Year: " + year + "\n";
}
```

This means that **display()** in **Student** can be simplified to:

```
public void display()
{ System.out.print(toString()); }
```

---

[2]This method gives an example of downcasting: once we know that **obj** is a **PlacementStudent** instance, we can apply a **(PlacementStudent)** cast to convert this **Object** value to a **PlacementStudent** value.

Figure A.5: Inheritance Hierarchy

A.4.2   Protected Access

idNumber is private in **Student**, so it cannot be accessed in **PlacementStudent** or in any other class. This gives the designer of the **Student** class the freedom to make changes to such private features of **Student**, e.g. to improve the performance of the code, without affecting any other class, provided the public features perform according to their specifications.

However, Java allows the designer of a class to give its members a level of access in between private and public. Methods and attributes can be declared to be `protected`. This means they can be accessed from any class that extends the original class, but not by other classes.

If we change the **idNumber** declaration in **Student** to:

```
protected String idNumber;
```

we can define

```
public boolean equals(Object obj)
{ if (obj instanceof PlacementStudent)
  { PlacementStudent other = (PlacementStudent) obj;
    if (other.idNumber.equals(idNumber))
    { return true; }
  }
  return false;
}
```

in **PlacementStudent**.

Alternatively, and preferably, we can provide accessor methods to return values of private fields: **getIdNumber()** in this case.

A.4.3   Defining Common Superclasses

We've covered the situation where we have a class **A**, and we extend it to produce a subclass **B** whose objects consist of **A** objects with additional features. Another common situation is when two different classes of objects, **B1** and **B2**, have common properties, and need to be processed in similar ways. For example, we might want to create a list of objects made up of a mixture of **B1** objects and **B2** objects, and apply the same methods to each of the list objects.

To do this, we define a common superclass **A** of both **B1** and **B2** (Figure A.6). Often **A** is *abstract*, that is it will never have any real instances of its own, all its instances will either be instances of **B1** or of **B2**. In Java terms this means that calls **new A(...)** of **A**'s constructor are disallowed.

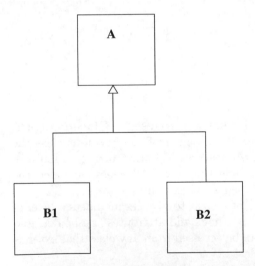

Figure A.6: Superclass **A** of **B1** and **B2**

The common operations applicable to both **B1** and **B2** objects can be programmed as methods of **A**. Since **B1** objects and **B2** objects are going to be treated alike at times, is quite likely they will have some attributes and methods in common. All these common features can be defined in **A**.

For example, consider classes that might be used in a simple database system that records users of a department's computer systems. There are two kinds of user: student users and staff users. So there will be classes called **CSStudent** and **Staff**. A superclass that contains both student and staff objects could be called **User** (Figure A.7).

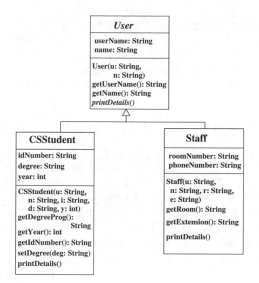

Figure A.7: Class Diagram of CSStudents and Staff

A **CSStudent** object has the following attributes:

1. String userName
2. String name
3. String idNumber
4. String degree
5. int year

The attributes for **Staff** objects are:

1. String userName
2. String name
3. String roomNumber
4. String phoneNumber

The last field is a four-digit telephone extension.

CSStudent and **Staff** both have **userName** and **name** fields, so these can be moved to the **User** class. Each class will have its own constructor to create a new object and initialise its fields.

The **User(u,n)** constructor creates a **User** object and sets its username to **u** and name to **n** (because **User** is abstract we cannot however use this constructor directly in a **new User(u,n)** statement). The constructors of **CSStudent** and **Staff** are **CSStudent(u,n,i,d,y)** and **Staff(u,n,r,p)** respectively.

Most of the methods in this example are *accessor* methods, i.e. they return the values of attributes. The methods **getUserName** and **getName** of **User** will be inherited by both **CSStudent** and **Staff**. A method **printDetails** will display values of all the attributes of an object: so there will be one version of **printDetails** for the **CSStudent** class, and a different version in the **Staff** class.

A variable of type **User** can be declared. Because **User** is a superclass of both **Staff** and **CSStudent**, such a variable can hold either a **CSStudent** object, or a **Staff** object:

```
User u = new Staff("gatesb", "Gates, Bill", "3D", "2144");
u.printDetails();
u = new CSStudent("rayf", "Felix Ray", "012233", "CS", 1);
u.printDetails();
```

In the first line we assign a **Staff** object to a variable of type **User**. This is always valid, since **Staff** is a subclass of **User**, but assignment of a **User** object to a **Staff** or **CSStudent** object is forbidden, since **User** is a strictly larger type than its subclasses: there are staff who are not students, and conversely.

Because of this capability, it is necessary to define common methods of the subclasses, such as **printDetails**, in the **User** class. For the call **u.printDetails()** to be valid, **User** must have a **printDetails** method. We can declare it as an *abstract* method (i.e. without a body):

```
abstract public void printDetails();
```

At run-time, when the statement

```
u.printDetails();
```

is executed, **u** will actually be a member of either **Staff** or **CSStudent**. The Java system will determine which subclass **u** belongs to, and will call the **print-Details** method defined for *that* subclass. This is known as *dynamic binding*.

EXAMPLE 4.1 (User, CSStudent and Staff classes)

```
/** A User object represents a user
    of the CS Department facilities. */

public abstract class User
{ private String userName;
  private String name;

  /** Create a User with username u and name n. */
  public User(String u, String n)
  { userName = u;
    name = n;
  }

  /** Print details of the user. */
  abstract public void printDetails();

  /** Return username of the user. */
```

```java
  public String getUserName()
  { return userName;  }

  /** Return name of the user. */
  public String getName()
  { return name; }

  /** Program for testing User, Student and Staff classes. */
  public static void main(String[] args)
  { User u = new Staff("gatesb", "Gates, Bill",
                        "3D", "2715");
    u.printDetails();
    System.out.println();
    u = new CSStudent("wonga", "Wong, Alice", "9912345",
                        "Maths and CS", 2);
    u.printDetails();
  }
}
```

The comments /** ...   */ are used by the *javadoc* program to produce HTML documentation of Java programs.

```java
/** A CSStudent object represents a student user. */
class CSStudent extends User
{ private String idNumber;
  private String degree;
  private int year;

  /** Create new CSStudent object with given username,
      name, ID number, degree programme and year. */
  public CSStudent(String u, String n, String i,
                   String d, int y)
  { super(u,n);
    idNumber = i;
    degree = d;
    year = y;
  }

  /** Print details of the student. */
  public void printDetails()
  { System.out.println("STUDENT");
    System.out.println("Username: " + getUserName());
    System.out.println("Name: " + getName());
    System.out.println("ID number: " + idNumber);
    System.out.println("Degree: " + degree);
    System.out.println("Year: " + year);
  }
```

```
/** Return student's ID number. */
public String getIdNumber()
{ return idNumber; }

/** Return student's degree programme. */
public String getDegreeProg()
{ return degree; }

/** Return student's year. */
public int getYear()
{ return year; }
}


/** A Staff object represents a member of staff
    who is a user. */
class Staff extends User
{ private String roomNumber;
  private String phoneNumber;

  /** Create new Staff object with given username,
      name, room number and extension. */
  public Staff(String u, String n, String r, String e)
  { super(u,n);
    roomNumber = r;
    phoneNumber = e;
  }

  /** Print details of the member of staff. */
  public void printDetails()
  { System.out.println("STAFF");
    System.out.println("Username: " + getUserName());
    System.out.println("Name: " + getName());
    System.out.println("Room: " + roomNumber);
    System.out.println("Ext: " + phoneNumber);
  }

  /** Return the staff member's room number. */
  public String getRoom()
  { return roomNumber; }

  /** Return staff member's extension. */
  public String getExtension()
  { return phoneNumber; }
}
```

These three class definitions are all in a single text file `User.java`. Generally each class should be in a separate text file, but if several classes are put in a single file they should be closely related, and (1) only one class in the file can be `public`, and (2) the name of the file must be the same as that of the public class.

Any public class can have a main method with the usual heading:

```
public static void main(String[] parameters)
```

This is often used to test the class by creating some objects of the class and applying methods of the class to them, as for **User** above.

A.4.4   Subclass Constructors

Think of each **CSStudent** and **Staff** object as being built around a **User** object. A constructor for a subclass, say **CSStudent**, must start by constructing the superclass object at the core of the subclass object. This is done by the statement:

```
super(parameters);
```

where `parameters` must be a list of parameter values that matches the declared parameters of one of the superclass's constructors.

So the constructors in **CSStudent** and **Staff** both start with this statement:

```
super(u,n);
```

where **u** and **n** are the initial values for the username and name attributes.

Other superclass methods can also be used in a similar way. For example, we can save work in subclass methods like **printDetails** by putting any common code of these methods in the superclass:

```
public abstract class User
{  private String userName;
   // User's username.
   private String name;
   // User's name.

  public void printDetails()
  { System.out.println("Username: " + userName);
    System.out.println("Name: " + name);
  }


  ...
}
```

This can then be called in subclass **printDetails()** methods as **super.printDetails()**:

```
  public void printDetails()
  { System.out.println("STAFF");
    super.printDetails();
    System.out.println("Room: " + roomNumber);
    System.out.println("Ext: " + phoneNumber);
  }
```

and similarly for **CSStudent**. Unlike the superclass constructor, **super.m(e)** can be called anywhere in a subclass method.

A.4.5   Interfaces

An *interface* definition specifies a type which classes can implement. It consists of a list of methods:

```
interface InterfaceName
{ returntype1 m1(args1);
  returntype2 m2(args2);
  ...
}
```

or:

```
interface Interface2
{ returntype3 m3(args3); }
```

The methods are (by default) public and abstract. No code can be given for them: the interface is simply asserting that any implementing class must provide such methods (e.g. any class implementing the **List** interface must define the **add**, **remove**, **size**, etc., methods of this interface). An implementing class is written as:

```
public class C implements InterfaceName, Interface2
{ ...
  public returntype1 m1(args1)
  { ... definition of m1 ... }

  public returntype2 m2(args2)
  { ... definition of m2 ... }

  public returntype3 m3(args3)
  { ... definition of m3 ... }
  ...
}
```

Classes can implement *several* different interfaces. In contrast they can only extend one class.

Key Points

- **What is a subclass?** A subclass **B** of a class **A** is a specialised extension of **A**, with all the features of **A** plus some of its own, and possibly redefining some of **A**'s methods. An instance of **B** can be stored in a variable of type **A**: **A x = new B();** is valid. But **B y = new A();** is invalid: there may be **A** instances that are not **B** instances.

> **Key Points**
>
> - **What is an abstract class?** This is a class declared as **public abstract class C**. The statement **new C(args);** is invalid for such classes, as they have no elements of their own, only elements of their non-abstract (*concrete*) subclasses. If a class contains an abstract method definition then it must be abstract. Abstract classes are used to group together common features that belong to all their subclasses, to avoid repetition of these features in subclasses.

A.5   Data Structures

Programs often deal with thousands or even millions of items of information. To store such data within a program, programming languages provide structures such as *arrays*, *lists* and *maps*.

A.5.1   Arrays

An array in Java is a special kind of object. It consists of a sequence of variables, called the *elements* of the array.

The elements of an array do not have individual names, instead they are numbered: 0, 1, 2, ... The number of an element is called its *index* (or subscript). An array element can be any type of variable, but all elements in an array must be of the same type. So, for example, we can have an array whose elements are all of type **int**. The type of such an array is denoted by **int**[]. Similarly we can have an array of type **String**[] whose elements hold references to strings, or an array of type **Student**[] which holds references to **Student** objects, and so on.

The number of elements in an array is called the *length* of the array. Once an array has been created, its length is fixed. Although we can change the individual values stored in array elements, we cannot add new elements, or remove existing elements. If **a** denotes an array, **a.length** denotes its length[3].

Suppose that a variable **row** contains a reference to an array of type **int**[] of length 5. There are then 5 individual integer variables **row[0]**, **row[1]**, **row[2]**, **row[3]** and **row[4]** contained in **row**. The element with index **i** is denoted by **row[i]**. We can treat it just like any other **int** variable. For example, we can assign value 0 to **row[2]**:

```
row[2] = 0;
```

or output the value of **row[4]**:

---

[3] As the syntax indicates, this is a public attribute of the array object, not a method, such as **s.length()** for strings **s**.

```
System.out.println(row[4]);
```

Or output the values of all elements of **row**:

```
for (int i = 0; i < row.length; i++)
{ System.out.println(row[i]); }
```

Whenever an expression such as **row[4]** is used to denote an array element, Java will check that the array really does have an element with the given index (4 in this case). If not, a run-time error **IndexOutOfBoundsException** occurs.

To declare an integer array of length 5, we write:

```
int[] row = new int[5];
```

This can be read as "integer array **row** becomes equal to a new integer array of size 5".

The five elements **row[0]**, **row[1]**, **row[2]**, **row[3]** and **row[4]** of this array will each be given a default value. The default value for numbers is 0, the default value for objects, including strings, is **null**, and so on.

Alternatively we can set initial values for elements in the declaration:

```
int[] row = {4, 9, 11, 0, 26};
```

This creates an array of length 5, with the initial values for its elements as shown, i.e. **row[0]** has initial value 4 and so on.

Similarly, for the initialisation of string arrays:

```
String[] animals = { "cat", "dog", "fox" };
```

This creates three string variables **animals[0]** with initial value "**cat**", **animals[1]** with initial value "**dog**", and **animals[2]** with initial value "**fox**".

Two-dimensional arrays are declared as arrays of arrays, for example:

```
int[][] places = new int[3][3];
```

declares a 3-by-3 array of integer elements, as an array of three integer arrays each of size 3. We can read this declaration as "integer array array **places** becomes equal to a new integer array (each of size 3) array of size 3." Elements of two-dimensional arrays are referred to by the corresponding expression notation, for example, **places[i][j]**.

A.5.2   The List Interface

Linked lists are an alternative way of storing a long sequence of values such as might be stored in an array. We could define a class called **DataList**, say, which has a field containing a data value, and another field containing a reference to another **DataList** object:

```
class DataList
{ private Object data;      // data of this cell
  private DataList next;    // link to next cell

  public DataList(Object val, DataList tail)
  { data = val;
    next = tail;
  }

  public Object get() { return data; }

  public DataList next() { return next; }

  public String toString()
  { return data + " -> " + next; } // recursive call of toString()
}
```

This second field can be used to link together a number of these objects in a long chain terminated by a null pointer **next == null** (Figure A.8).

For some situations linked lists are more suitable than arrays. This is the case when elements are frequently added to, or removed from the interior of a structure: this is easy to achieve with a couple of assignments in a linked list. But if we want to access a value quickly using index numbers, then arrays will be much more efficient.

Java provides an interface called **List** which describes a set of methods for handling sequences of values, independent of the implementation (array or linked list) of the sequences.

We can declare variables that refer to sequences of values as being of type **List**, and then use any of the wide range of methods in the **List** interface. The only time we have to specify the implementation that is used for a particular list is when calling a constructor to create the list object.

Some of the **List** interface methods are:

- **l.add(v)** – Add value **v** to the end of list **l**. **v** can be any object (but not a primitive value such as an **int**).
- **l.get(i)** – Return value stored in element **i** of list **l**. Elements of lists are numbered 0, 1, ... as usual. The value returned will be of type **Object**, as far as the compiler is concerned.
- **l.size()** – Return number of values stored in list **l**.
- **l.contains(x)** – Return **true** iff **x.equals(l.get(i))** for some index **i** : **0** .. **l.size()** − **1**.

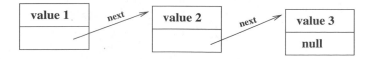

Figure A.8: Linked List Storage

For an array-based implementation of **List** we use the constructor **ArrayList()**. For a linked-list based implementation we use the constructor **LinkedList()**. Another **List** implementation, similar to **ArrayList** in most respects, is **Vector**.

- To store numbers or booleans in lists we use "wrapper" classes: **Integer** for **int**s, **Double** for doubles. To turn a double value **d** into a **Double** object that just contains **d**, we use:

  ```
  Double x = new Double(d);
  ```

  x can then be stored in a list **l** by using **l.add(x)**. To extract its double value use the expression:

  ```
  x.doubleValue()
  ```

- The **get** method has return type **Object**. So the compiler only knows that values extracted from a list are **Object**s. If we know that the value actually is a **Point2D** object (for example), and we are going to apply methods to it that can only be applied to **Point2D** objects (e.g. **getX()**), then we must tell the compiler this, by applying a **(Point2D)** cast to it. For example

  ```
  Point2D pp = (Point2D) points.get(i);
  ```

To use the **List** interface in a program we need to import it from the **java.util** package:

```
import java.util.List;
```

Similarly for **ArrayList**, **Vector**, etc.

A.5.3 Arrays versus Lists

A comparison of the properties of arrays and lists is given in Table A.3. In

Property	*array*	*List*
Extensible	Manually	Automatically
Element type	Any type	Not primitive types
Getting elements	**arr[ind]**	**(Type)** l.get(ind)
Insertion	Complicated	Library method **add**
Deletion	Complicated	Library method **remove**

Table A.3: Lists versus Arrays

general we should use arrays to store a collection if the data size is fixed, otherwise use lists.

A.5.4 The Map Interface

The **List** interface is one of a number of Java interfaces that represent collections of data. They are known as **Collections**. For databases the **Map** interface is often more suitable than List.

Objects which implement the **Map** interface behave like mappings from one set of values, called *keys*, to another set called *values*. Unlike mappings in mathematics, a map can only be applied to a finite number of keys.

We can think of a map as a lookup table. Given a key, a map object tells you the value (instance of the **Object** class) the key maps to/identifies.

A typical example of a map would be **User** objects identified by their **userName**:

$$\{\text{"gatesb"} \mapsto \textbf{staff1}, \text{"wonga"} \mapsto \textbf{stud1}\}$$

where **staff1** is the staff object created by `new Staff("gatesb", "Gates, Bill", "3D", "2715");` and **stud1** the student object created by `new CSStudent("wonga", "Wong, Alice", "9912345", "Maths and CS", 2);`

Some **Map** interface methods are:

- **m.put(k,v)** – Extend map **m** by adding mapping of key **k** to value **v**. This replaces any existing mapping in **m** of **k** to another value.
- **m.get(k)** – Return the value that **m** maps key **k** to. If there is no entry for **k** in **m**, return **null**.
- **m.remove(k)** – Remove mapping for **k**. Returns value that **m** mapped **k** onto. If **m** did not map **k** onto anything, returns **null**.

There are two standard implementations of the **Map** interface, **HashMap** and **TreeMap**. **HashMap** is a good choice if we are not interested in a particular ordering on keys.

So to create the example map given above, we could write:

```
Map m = new HashMap();
User staff1 = new Staff("gatesb", "Gates, Bill",
                        "3D", "2715");
m.put("gatesb",staff1);
User stud1 = new CSStudent("wonga", "Wong, Alice",
                           "9912345", "Maths and CS", 2);
m.put("wonga",stud1);
```

A map is like a simple database, which enables us to look up complex objects such as **CSStudent**s, in the range of the map, using simple values such as strings, in the domain. An array or list **x** can be thought of as a special kind of map, where the domain values are just integers **i**, and the corresponding range values are **x[i]** or **x.get(i)**.

Key Points

- **What is an array?** An array is an indexed sequence of individual values, of fixed length and type. An array of elements of type **T** is declared by **T[] arr = new T[n];** where **n** is the size of the array, or by giving an explicit list {**val1**, ..., **valn**} of **n** values of type **T**. The elements of **arr** are denoted by **arr[0]**, ..., **arr[n − 1]** and can be read and assigned to just like any other variables of type **T**.
- **What is a List?** A list is an extensible sequence of values, with method **ll.add(xx)** being used to add **xx** to the end of list **ll**. A list is declared as: **List ll = new Vector();** or **List ll = new ArrayList();** etc. Only objects can be stored in lists, not integers, doubles, etc. To get the **i**th element of a list, use **ll.get(i)**.
- **What is a Map?** A map is an association of one set of objects to another. Maps are declared by, e.g. **Map mm = new HashMap();** and a pair **x ↦ y** is placed in **mm** by **mm.put(x,y)**. The value that **mm** maps **x** to is **mm.get(x)**.

Further Resources

The key source of information for Java developers is the *applications programmer interface (API)*, which is described at http://java.sun.com/j2se/1.4/docs/api/ for version 1.4 of the Java standard edition.

Appendix B

Design Case Study

In this chapter we will give a case study illustrating the design principles and techniques discussed in Chapters 1 to 4, using the noughts and crosses game project introduced in Section 2.7. The application of design guidelines will be highlighted.

B.1   Architectural and Subsystem Design

A possible division of the system into three subsystems:

- GUI
- Strategy subsystem
- Data storage and retrieval

was discussed in Section 2.7. Figure B.1 shows this in more detail.

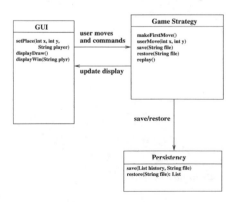

Figure B.1: Architecture of Game Application

Review of this design would consider whether the set of dependencies between subsystems is minimal. In particular the strategy subsystem calls methods on the GUI, which could be avoided by passing back sufficient information as return values of the methods **makeFirstMove** and **userMove** which the GUI calls on the strategy subsystem. However this would increase data dependencies, because both subsystems would share knowledge of this return type.

> **Design Guideline:** Reduce dependencies between subsystems and modules as much as possible, by removing references between modules, and eliminating shared data types except for built-in types and types from the Java libraries.

Each subsystem is already a module and so, having accepted the dependency structure given in Figure B.1, we can proceed to the module design of each of these.

B.2   GUI Design

The GUI must allow the user to make a move, for example by clicking on a button representing a free square with the mouse, and to see the current state of the board, including the program's responses to their moves. The GUI must also provide options for the commands to start a new game, ask the system to move first, to set a strategy, and to save and restore a game. Figure B.2 shows a possible layout of this interface, where the game board is represented as a 3 by 3 grid of buttons, initially blank. To enable a button to know what

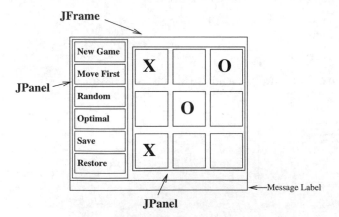

Figure B.2: Interface Design

coordinate it represents, we define a class (internal to the GUI subsystem) of **CoordinateButton**s:

```
class CoordinateButton extends JButton
{ private int x;
  private int y;

  public CoordinateButton(String label, int xx, int yy)
```

```
{ super(label);
  x = xx;
  y = yy;
}

public int getX() { return x; }

public int getY() { return y; }
}
```

There are other ways of finding out the position of a button, for example, we could store an array of the nine buttons in the order of their position on the board (top left being 0 and bottom right being 8), and compare an unknown button with each element of the list in turn until a match is found. The position of the button can then be deduced from the index **i** of the match (the **x** coordinate is i%3, the **y** coordinate is i/3). However this is less efficient. Another approach would be to attach an (anonymous) action listener specific to each button, or to make use of the **setName** and **getName** methods of **JButton** to attach an invisible label to each button. Both of these however are less conceptually clear, and the latter is an abuse of the purpose of the library methods, or in other words, a hack.

The construction of the GUI is therefore:

```
import javax.swing.*;
import javax.swing.event.*;
import java.awt.*;
import java.awt.event.*;

public class NCGui extends JFrame
implements ActionListener
{ private StrategyModule strategy ...;
    // link to Strategy subsystem
  private Container pane;
  private JPanel board = new JPanel();
  private JPanel sidebar = new JPanel();
  private JLabel message =
    new JLabel("Select option or click on board to move");
  private CoordinateButton[][] squares =
                      new CoordinateButton[3][3];
  private JButton clearb =
                  new JButton("New Game");
  private JButton move1stb =
                  new JButton("Move First");
  private JButton strat1b =
                  new JButton("Random Strategy");
  private JButton strat2b =
                  new JButton("Optimal Strategy");
  private JButton saveb =
                  new JButton("Save Game");
  private JButton restoreb =
```

```
                           new JButton("Restore Game");
    private JButton replayb =
                           new JButton("Replay");


    public NCGui()
    { addWindowListener(
        new WindowAdapter()
        { public void windowClosing(WindowEvent e)
          { System.exit(0); }
        });  /* Kills application if main frame is closed */

      // Add components to the window
      pane = getContentPane();
      setTitle("Noughts and Crosses");
      board.setLayout(new GridLayout(3,3,5,5));
      board.setBackground(Color.black);

      Font f = new Font("Sans Serif",Font.BOLD,40);
      for (int i = 0; i < 3; i++)
      { for (int j = 0; j < 3; j++)
        { CoordinateButton cb = new CoordinateButton(".",j,i);
          squares[j][i] = cb;
          addButton(board,squares[j][i]);
          cb.setBackground(Color.white);
          cb.setOpaque(true);
          cb.setFont(f);
        }
      }
      repaint();

      sidebar.setLayout(new GridLayout(7,1));
      addButton(sidebar, clearb);
      addButton(sidebar, move1stb);
      addButton(sidebar, strat1b);
      addButton(sidebar, strat2b);
      addButton(sidebar, saveb);
      addButton(sidebar, restoreb);
      addButton(sidebar, replayb);

      pane.add(board, BorderLayout.CENTER);
      pane.add(sidebar, BorderLayout.WEST);
      pane.add(message, BorderLayout.SOUTH);
    }

    /** Convenience method to add a button */
    private void addButton(Container c, JButton b)
    { b.addActionListener(this);
      c.add(b);
    }
```

In responding to button presses, there are three cases for the buttons on the board:

1. The button pressed has label "." (an empty place): extract the coordinates from the button and attempt a user move at this place. The move may be invalid if it is not the users turn, for example. If it is valid, set the text of the button to "X". The strategy subsystem is responsible for deciding what response move to make and for setting the relevant square to "O".
2. The label is "X": give an error message to tell the user they are already on the square.
3. The label is "O": give an error message to tell the user the place is already occupied.

In the last two cases the board is not changed. The GUI must also respond to the command buttons being pressed. Thus the pseudocode for the **action-Performed** method of **NCGui** is:

```
public void actionPerformed(ActionEvent ev)
{ JButton button = (JButton) ev.getSource();
  String label = button.getText();

  if (".".equals(label)) // user move
  { CoordinateButton b = (CoordinateButton) button;
    if (b.getX(), b.getY() is a valid move)
    { b.setText("X");
      call strategy to generate response move
    }
  }
  else if ("X".equals(label)) // error
  { System.out.println("ERROR: already on that square!"); }
  else if ("O".equals(label)) // error
  { System.out.println("ERROR: already occupied!"); }
  else if ("New Game".equals(label) ||
           "Optimal Strategy".equals(label))
  { create new optimal game;
    clear board;
  }
  else if ("Move First".equals(label))
  { strategy.makeFirstMove(); }
  else if ("Random Strategy".equals(label))
  { create new random game;
    clear the board;
  }
  else if ("Save Game".equals(label))
  { save game; }
  else if ("Restore Game".equals(label))
  { restore game; }
  else if ("Replay".equals(label))
  { clear board;
```

```
      replay game;
    }
  }
}
```

The other methods of the GUI are very simple and can be directly coded:

```
/** Convenience method to clear board */
private void clearBoard()
{ for (int i = 0; i < 3; i++)
  { for (int j = 0; j < 3; j++)
    { squares[i][j].setText(".");
      repaint(1);
    }
  }
}

public void setPlace(int x, int y, String player)
{ squares[x][y].setText(player); }

public void displayDraw()
{ message.setText("Game has been drawn."); }

public void displayWin(String s)
{ message.setText("Player " + s + " has won"); }

public static void main(String[] args)
{ NCGui nc = new NCGui();
  nc.setSize(300,200);
  nc.setVisible(true);
}
}
```

We should review the dependencies between the GUI and strategy subsystems at this point. The data passed from the GUI to the strategy subsystem is: (i) the place selected by the user to move to; (ii) possibly the state of the complete board. The data passed in the other direction is: (i) the location of the system's move; (ii) the player who has won. The two systems also share type information: that the possible values for **x** and **y** coordinates are $0..2$ and that players are represented by the strings "X" for the user and "O" for the system. Can this information sharing and transmission be reduced? The coordinates of a move could be passed as basic integer values, rather than grouped into a class such as **Point2D** which represents pairs of numbers. The state of the board should not be shared, instead the two subsystems will maintain their own separate record of player positions. This requires that all changes made by one subsystem are synchronised with changes made by the other, i.e. there is an invariant or constraint between the subsystems. This could be a candidate for the use of a coordination contract in a larger system. Shared information such as the symbols to be used for players and the size of the board could be placed in an **interface** which is implemented by the main classes of both subsystems. This technique is used within the strategy subsystem.

Also as part of a design review, we could consider alternative representations of the board, for example as a single array

```
IndexedButton[] squares = new IndexedButton[9];
```

instead of a double array, where **IndexedButton** extends **JButton** with a single integer attribute giving the position of the button in the list. While this approach produces a syntactically simpler program, it is more complicated to understand because we need to mentally translate from the 3 by 3 grid of the board into a linear list.

B.3   The Strategy Subsystem

There are two main methods in this subsystem, regardless of what strategy is being used:

```
public void makeFirstMove()
// REQUIRES: the board is clear of pieces
// EFFECTS: updates board by placing a "O" in a place,
//    as determined by the strategy in use. For the
//    random strategy this is a randomly chosen place,
//    for the optimal strategy, it is the center of
//    the board, coordinates (1,1).

public boolean userMove(int x, int y)
// REQUIRES: x: 0..2 and y: 0..2
// EFFECTS: if there is already a piece at (x,y), or
//    if it is not the users turn, returns false and
//    leaves board unchanged.
//     Otherwise, updates internal rep. of board with
//    user move, and selects the responding system move.
//    For the random strategy this is a random free
//    place (if there are any). For the optimal strategy
//    it is a place where some evaluation function is
//    maximal for the system player. This move is then
//    carried out. The operation also checks if a win or
//    draw position has been reached, and informs the gui of this.
```

Refined to pseudocode, these are:

```
public void makeFirstMove()
{ if number of free places is < 9, return;
  Otherwise, set the current player to be "O" and select
  an appropriate place, according to the strategy in use;
  move "O" into this place, updating the gui, removing
  this place from the list of free places, and making
  "X" the next player. Update local representation of
  board;
}
```

```
public boolean userMove(int x, int y)
{ if next player is not "X", return, with value false;
  Likewise if the place identified by (x,y) is not free;
  Otherwise, update internal representation of board
  with user move, display move on GUI, and add to
  history, and switch player;
  Check if win or draw has occurred and notify this to GUI;
  If game is still open, select the responding system move;
  Carry out this move -- update GUI, local data and
  history, and swap players;
  Check if win or draw has occurred and notify this to GUI;
  return true;
}
```

One design pattern would seem immediately relevant to this system: the state pattern, with **RandomGame** and **OptimalGame** subclasses of an abstract class **Game**, and the corresponding alternative code of the above methods placed in the separate subclasses. However, the main parts of the algorithms for **makeFirstMove** and **userMove** do not depend on the strategy, which only affects *which* location is chosen to move to, not any other processing. Therefore, Template Method is a more suitable choice of pattern, with **makeFirstMove** and **userMove** being template methods defined in **Game** and making use of hook methods **selectFirstMove** and **selectMove** which are abstract in **Game** and defined in the separate game subclasses.

There is also a need to factor out the actions which carry out a move:

```
update the position: the internal record of the board;
inform the GUI of the move;
add the move to the history;
swap the players;
```

These actions are repeated three times in the above pseudocode, so they should be used to define a private operation **makeMove** of the module, which is called by **makeFirstMove** and **userMove** as needed. Similarly the code to check for a win or draw is repeated twice in **userMove**, so should be factored into a separate method **detectWinDraw**.

> **Design Guideline:** if a segment **S** of code is used in several operations of a module, then factor this code out into a separate private method of the module, and replace the segments **S** with calls to this new method.

Since several methods of the subsystem refer to the list of free places, it is appropriate to define this as a new explicit association from **Game** to sets of **Place**s (Figure B.3) instead of calculating this list from the **position** each time it is needed.

> **Design Guideline:** if certain data **d**, which is derived as a function
> **d** − **f**(**c**) from other data **c** in the analysis class diagram, is used
> repeatedly or in several operations of a module, then define an
> explicit variable **vd** to hold **d**, and update the value of this variable
> as necessary so that **vd** = **f**(**c**) is maintained. We could call this
> the "Derived Attribute" design pattern.

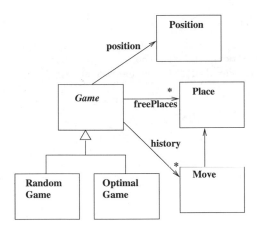

Figure B.3: Design Data Model of Game

We can then write the **Game** class:

```java
import java.util.Vector;
import java.util.Random;
import java.util.List;

/** Interface defining shared data of the
    strategy subsystem classes. */
interface SystemConstants
{ public static final int NONE = 0;
  public static final int NOUGHT = 1;
  public static final int CROSS = 2;

  public static final String[] symbol = { " ", "O", "X" };
}

/** Represents all information about the state of a game. */
abstract public class Game
implements SystemConstants
{ protected Position position = new Position();
  protected Vector freePlaces = new Vector();  // of Place
  protected int nextPlayer = CROSS;  // The users player
  private NCGui gui;
  private Persistency persistency = new Persistency();
  private List history = new Vector(); // of Moves
```

```
public Game(NCGui g)
{ gui = g;
  for (int i = 0; i < 3; i++)
  { for (int j = 0; j < 3; j++)
    { Place pl = new Place(i,j);
      freePlaces.add(pl);
    }
  }
}

/** Internal method to carry out a move, update the
    GUI and history, and change players. Called by userMove
    and makeFirstMove. */
private void makeMove(Place pl)
{ position.move(nextPlayer,pl);
  freePlaces.remove(pl);
  gui.setPlace(pl.getX(), pl.getY(),
             symbol[nextPlayer]);
  history.add(new Move(nextPlayer,pl));
  changePlayer();
}

/** Template method to make first move by system. */
public void makeFirstMove()
{ if (freePlaces.size() < 9)
  { System.err.println("Can't re-make 1st move!");
    return;
  }
  nextPlayer = NOUGHT;
  Place pl = selectFirstMove();
  makeMove(pl);
}

/** Hook method which selects first move for system. */
protected abstract Place selectFirstMove();

/** Alternates the player's turns. */
private void changePlayer()
{ if (nextPlayer == NOUGHT)
  { nextPlayer = CROSS; }
  else
  { nextPlayer = NOUGHT; }
}

/** Template method which carries out user move, if
    valid, and the system's response move. */
public boolean userMove(int x, int y)
{ Place pl = new Place(x,y);
  if (nextPlayer != CROSS)
```

```
  { System.err.println("Cannot move -- not your turn!");
    return false;
  }
  if (! freePlaces.contains(pl))
  { System.err.println("Place already occupied!");
    return false;
  }
  makeMove(pl); // Carry out users move
  boolean over = detectWinDraw();
  if (over)  // Win or draw
  { return true; }
  Place p2 = selectMove();
  if (p2 != null)
  { makeMove(p2);    // System's response move
    detectWinDraw();
  }
  return true;
}


/** Hook method to select place for system's move. */
abstract protected Place selectMove();

private boolean detectWinDraw()
{ String s = position.detectWin();
  if (s == null)  // No-one has won yet
  { boolean draw = position.detectDraw();
    if (draw)
    { gui.displayDraw();
      return true;
    }
    return false; // Neither win or draw
  }
  gui.displayWin(s);
  return true;
}

public void save(String file)
{ call persistence subsystem to save
  history to file;
}

public void restore(String file)
{ set history to data retrieved from file; }

public void replay()
{ replay moves in history, 1 per second; }
}
```

Using the template method pattern, the two types of game are defined as concrete subclasses of **Game** with their own definitions of the hook methods.

An **OptimalGame** moves to the centre square as its first move, and on subsequent moves, evaluates the position produced by trying each element of the free place list as the place to move to, in turn. A place which produces a position with a maximal value is then chosen:

```
class OptimalGame extends Game
{ public OptimalGame(NCGui g)
  { super(g); }

  protected Place selectFirstMove()
  { return new Place(1,1); }

  protected Place selectMove()
  { int bestval = 0;
    Place bestPlace = null;
    for (int i = 0; i < freePlaces.size(); i++)
    { Place pl = (Place) freePlaces.get(i);
      Position newpos = (Position) position.clone();
      newpos.move(nextPlayer,pl);  // Current position + move to pl
      int val = newpos.evaluate(nextPlayer);
      if (val > bestval)
      { bestPlace = pl;    // The best move so far
        bestval = val;
      }
    }
    return bestPlace;
  }
}
```

A **RandomGame** simply selects a random element of the free place list as the place to move to:

```
class RandomGame extends Game
{ private Random generator = new Random();

  public RandomGame(NCGui g)
  { super(g); }

  protected Place selectFirstMove()
  { int index = generator.nextInt(9);  // random int in 0..8
    return (Place) freePlaces.get(index);
  } // or just return selectMove();

  protected Place selectMove()
  { int free = freePlaces.size();
    Place bestPlace = null;
    if (free > 0)
    { int index = generator.nextInt(free);
      bestPlace = (Place) freePlaces.get(index);
    }
    return bestPlace;
```

```
    }
}
```

A **Place** is simply a pair of coordinates:

```
class Place
{ private int x;   /* 0..2 */
  private int y;   /* 0..2 */

  public Place(int xc, int yc)
  { x = xc;
    y = yc;
  }

  public int getX()
  { return x; }

  public int getY()
  { return y; }

  public String toString()
  { return "(" + x + "," + y + ")"; }

  public String toXml()
  { return "<place> \n" +
           "  <x>" + x + "</x>\n" +
           "  <y>" + y + "</y>\n" +
           "</place>";
  }

  public boolean equals(Object obj)
  { if (obj instanceof Place)
    { Place other = (Place) obj;
      return other.getX() == x && other.getY() == y;
    }
    return false;
  }
}
```

We need to define **equals** for **Place** because we used **contains** on the list of free places in **Game**.

A **Move** consists of a player and the place they are moving to:

```
class Move implements SystemConstants
{ private int player;
  private Place place;

  public Move(int mover, Place destination)
  { player = mover;
    place = destination;
  }
```

```
public int getPlayer()
{ return player; }

public Place getPlace()
{ return place; } // or clone it

public String toString()
{ return symbol[player] + " moves to " + place; }

public String toXml()
{ return "<move> \n" +
        "  <player>" + symbol[player] + "</player>\n" +
        place.toXml() + "\n" +
        "</move>";
}
}
```

It is good practice to define **toString** and **toXml** methods for classes representing entity instances. These allow a program to directly display the data of the instances using **println**, in the first case, or to represent the data in a portable structured form, in the second. Similarly **equals** should usually be defined.

> **Design Guideline:** Define **toString** and **toXml** methods for all classes representing analysis model entities. Also define **equals**, in such a way that **ob1.equals(ob2)** implies that **ob1.toString()** equals **ob2.toString()** and likewise for **toXml()**.

A **Position** records the current state of the board, using integer codes corresponding to players, for efficiency reasons:

```
class Position implements SystemConstants
{ private int[][] places = new int[3][3];

  public Position() {}

  /** Create a new position which is a copy of board */
  public Position(int[][] board)
  { places = (int[][]) board.clone(); }

  /** Update board with move of player to pl. */
  public void move(int player, Place pl)
  { int x = pl.getX();
    int y = pl.getY();
    places[x][y] = player;
  }

  /** Heuristic for value of position for the player,
      i.e. how good it is as a candidate move for them. */
```

```
public int evaluate(int player)
{ if (number3lines(player) > 0)
  { return 100; }
  else
  { return number2lines(player) +
          (-50)*intersectingUnblockedLines() +
          numberBlockingLines(player) +
          2*numberBlocking3lines(player);
  }
}

/** Calculate number of 3 lines of the player. */
private int number3lines(int player)
{ int res = 0;

  if (places[0][0] == player && places[0][1] == player &&
      places[0][2] == player)
  { res++; }
  if (places[1][0] == player && places[1][1] == player &&
      places[1][2] == player)
  { res++; }
  if (places[2][0] == player && places[2][1] == player &&
      places[2][2] == player)
  { res++; }
  if (places[0][0] == player && places[1][0] == player &&
      places[2][0] == player)
  { res++; }
  if (places[0][1] == player && places[1][1] == player &&
      places[2][1] == player)
  { res++; }
  if (places[0][2] == player && places[1][2] == player &&
      places[2][2] == player)
  { res++; }
  if (places[0][0] == player && places[1][1] == player &&
      places[2][2] == player)
  { res++; }
  if (places[0][2] == player && places[1][1] == player &&
      places[2][0] == player)
  { res++; }
  return res;
}

private int number2lines(int player)
{ iterate through lines, counting how
  many are unblocked 2-lines for the player;
}

private int numberBlockingLines(int player)
{ iterate through lines, counting
  number that are blocking lines for the player;
```

```
}

private int numberBlocking3lines(int player)
{ iterate through lines, counting number
  that are blocking3lines for the player;
}

private boolean unblocked2line(int a, int b, int c,
                                int player)
{ if (a == player && b == player && c == NONE)
  { return true; }
  if (a == player && b == NONE && c == player)
  { return true; }
  if (a == NONE && b == player && c == player)
  { return true; }
  return false;
}


private boolean blockingline(int a, int b, int c,
                              int player)
{ if (a == player || b == player || c == player)
  { return true; }
  return false;
}


private boolean blocking3line(int a, int b, int c,
                               int player)
{ int other = 3 - player; // Count lines containing
                          // both player and other:
  if (a == player && b == other && c == other)
  { return true; }
  if (b == player && a == other && c == other)
  { return true; }
  if (c == player && a == other && b == other)
  { return true; }
  return false;
}

private int intersectingUnblockedLines()
{ // Identifies the danger situation where opponent
  // has two unblocked 1 lines which intersect with
  // the free place in my own unblocked 2 line: if
  // opponent moves to that place we have lost.
  ...
}

private boolean is3line(int a, int b, int c)
{ return a != NONE && a == b && b == c; }

public String detectWin()
```

```
{ iterate through lines, testing if
  any is a 3-line for a player. That
  players symbol is returned, or null
  is returned if there is no 3-line;
}

/** Returns true iff game is drawn. */
public boolean detectDraw()
{ int blocksX = numberBlockingLines(CROSS);
  if (blocksX < 8) { return false; }
  int blocksO = numberBlockingLines(NOUGHT);
  if (blocksO < 8) { return false; }
  return true;  // No possibility of 3-line for either
}

public String toString()
{ return symbol[places[0][0]] + " | " +
         symbol[places[1][0]] + " | " +
         symbol[places[2][0]] + "\n" +
         "---------\n" +
         symbol[places[0][1]] + " | " +
         symbol[places[1][1]] + " | " +
         symbol[places[2][1]] + "\n" +
         "---------\n" +
         symbol[places[0][2]] + " | " +
         symbol[places[1][2]] + " | " +
         symbol[places[2][2]] + "\n";
}

/** Create copy of the position */
public Object clone()
{ int[][] copy = new int[3][3];
  for (int i = 0; i < 3; i++)
  { for (int j = 0; j < 3; j++)
    { copy[i][j] = places[i][j]; }
  }
  return new Position(copy);
}
}
```

All the **numberX** methods are similar in structure, they iterate through the eight possible lines of 3 places on the board, counting how many of these lines satisfy property **X**. The iterator pattern could clearly be applied in this subsystem to make this processing more concise.

We have made all methods of **Position** private if they are only called within the class, and not by other classes.

> **Design Guideline:** Reduce the interface of a class where possible by making methods **private** if they are not invoked by objects of other classes, or **protected** if they are used by subclasses but not by external classes.

The use of the template method pattern in the strategy subsystem implies that we can simply start a new game in the GUI by invoking the constructor of **OptimalGame**:

```
Game game = new OptimalGame(this);
```

Likewise, a change of strategy to the random strategy could be achieved by:

```
game = new RandomGame(this);
```

But this allows the GUI module to have too much internal information about the strategy subsystem: if we changed the way different kinds of game were represented, the GUI would have to change. Instead the GUI should not refer to the game subclasses, but set the required strategy via the **setStrategy(int i)** method.

> **Design Guideline:** One module should not refer to any classes of another module except the main class of that module, i.e. the class which defines the interface operations of the module.

The main class of the strategy module therefore becomes:

```
public class StrategyModule
{ private Game game;
  private NCGui gui;

  public StrategyModule(NCGui g)
  { game = new OptimalGame(g);
    gui = g;
  }

  public void setStrategy(int s)
  { if (s == 0)
    { game = new RandomGame(gui); }
    else
    { game = new OptimalGame(gui); }
  }

  public void makeFirstMove()
  { game.makeFirstMove(); }

  public boolean userMove(int x, int y)
  { return game.userMove(x,y); }

  public void save(String file)
  { game.save(file); }
```

```
public void restore(String file)
{ game.restore(file); }

public void replay()
{ game.replay(); }
}
```

As part of a design review of the strategy module, we can also consider if the above approach for the optimal strategy is actually the best possible. The heuristic involved was modified until, by exhaustive testing, it appeared to give the best possible response move. The evaluation corresponds to the following general rule:

> If I have an unblocked 2-line, complete it (to win). Otherwise, if opponent has an unblocked 2-line, block it. Otherwise, choose a place that maximises the sum: number of lines with my pieces in them + number of unblocked 2-lines of my pieces. Avoid creating a 2-line whose empty space is also the intersection of two unblocked 1-lines of the opponent.

However there are programming approaches, such as *min-max* game tree evaluation, which provably give optimal moves [13]. These consider the highest value move for a player as being the one which minimises the value of the resulting position for the other player. The evaluation process is therefore recursive, with the tree of possible alternative game histories being expanded until no further move is possible. In noughts and crosses such an approach is feasible, since the maximum depth of the search tree is 9, but in more complex games such as chess, the search has to be bounded. However even for noughts and crosses this search strategy is very expensive in terms of space, because a duplicate of the entire board is made for each projected move, i.e. each node of the search tree. The heuristic approach of **OptimalGame** is preferable for this reason.

A final approach is to use some "ad hoc" rules, such as:

- On the first move, move to the centre place (1,1).
- On the second move, move to the centre if it is vacant, otherwise move to a corner (0,0), (2,0), (0,2) or (2,2).
- On the third move, move to the centre if it is vacant, otherwise move to a corner nearest to the opponents place.

These rules however become extremely complex for the mid part of a game, and are also extremely specific to 3-by-3 noughts and crosses. All the rules would have to change if we wanted to deal with a 4-by-4 variation, for example. The other two approaches are easier to generalise.

B.4 Design Refactorings

The modules in the above version refer directly to each others classes: the **Game** class refers to **NCGui** and **NCGui** refers to **StrategyModule**. To follow the guideline that clients should only depend on *interfaces* of their suppliers, we need to define specification interfaces **GuiInterface** and **Strategy-Interface** of each of these modules, rewrite their code to replace references to classes by references to the interfaces, and declare **NCGui** as implementing **GuiInterface** and **StrategyModule** as implementing **StrategyInterface**. An additional component, **OXOGame**, acts as a coordinator to connect instances of the GUI and back end (Figure B.4). **NCGui** becomes:

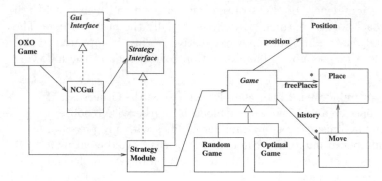

Figure B.4: Implementation Data Model

```
public class NCGui extends JFrame
implements ActionListener, GuiInterface
{ public static final int RANDOM_STRATEGY = 0;
  public static final int OPTIMAL_STRATEGY = 1;
  private StrategyInterface strategy;

  ...

  public void setBackEnd(StrategyInterface s)
  { strategy = s; }

  ...
}
```

To set the random strategy, we call **setStrategy(RANDOM_STRATEGY)** and similarly for the optimal strategy and other operations on the back end. This eliminates all references to **StrategyModule** or any of the strategy module classes within **NCGui**. **StrategyInterface** declares abstractly all the operations of the back end used by the GUI:

```
public interface StrategyInterface
{ public void setStrategy(int s);

  public void makeFirstMove();

  ...
}
```

and **StrategyModule** is defined as implementing this interface. The same approach works to remove all reference to **NCGui** from the back end classes, replacing them by references to **GuiInterface**. **OXOGame** is the only place where explicit reference to classes of both subsystems occurs:

```
public class OXOGame
{ public static void main(String[] args)
  { NCGui gui = new NCGui();
    StrategyModule sm = new StrategyModule(gui);
    gui.setBackEnd(sm);
    gui.setSize(400,300);
    gui.show();
  }
}
```

Other useful refactorings or code transformations in Java are the introduction of explicit **final** parameters of a method:

```
public T m(Type obj)
{ ... Code ... }
```

can be replaced by:

```
public T m(final Type obj)
{ ... Code ... }
```

provided there are no assignments to **obj** in the code of **m**.

We can also replace reference to a class type by reference to the type of some of its properties (this is useful if these types are basic Java types):

```
public T m(final C obj)
{ ... obj.getAtt1() ...
  ... obj.getAtt2() ...
}
```

can be replaced by:

```
public T m(final T1 att1val, final T2 att2val)
{ ... att1val ...
  ... att2val ...
}
```

provided these are the only methods invoked on **obj** in **m**.

B.5   Persistency Subsystem

There are several ways that the game data could be made persistent:

- We could turn the history sequence into three integer arrays, one containing the **x**-coordinates, another the **y**-coordinates, and the third the player number for the successive moves. These could then be saved to a file using an **ObjectOutputStream**:

```
ObjectOutputStream os =
            new ObjectOutputStream(
                new FileOutputStream("out.dat"));
os.writeObject(arrx);
os.writeObject(arry);
os.writeObject(arrplayer);
```

The arrays can be read in using corresponding calls to input streams:

```
ObjectInputStream ois =
            new ObjectInputStream(
                new FileInputStream("out.dat"));
int[] arrx = (int[]) ois.readObject();
int[] arry = (int[]) ois.readObject();
int[] arrplayer = (int[]) ois.readObject();
```

and converted back into a history sequence. **ois** is an **ObjectInput-Stream** for "out.dat". This process is known as *serialisation*. However the resulting file format is binary.

- We could simply write out lines of text to a text file, each line representing one move, e.g.

```
X 1 1
O 0 2
X 0 1
```

representing the users initial move to the centre place, followed by the system's move to the bottom left place, etc.

The first approach is space-efficient but does not produce human-readable files, and it can only be used for data transfer between Java programs. The second uses an ad-hoc text format, which will require special handling in any other program which wishes to import game history data. To overcome such problems, we can use *XML* [54], which is specifically designed as a standardised data exchange format, human-readable and independent of any particular programming language or environment. In XML format the above example history would be:

```
<move>
  <player>X</player>
  <place><x>1</x> <y>1</y></place>
</move>
<move>
  <player>O</player>
  <place><x>0</x> <y>2</y></place>
</move>
<move>
  <player>X</player>
  <place><x>0</x> <y>1</y></place>
</move>
```

To save the history of a game to a file, we write out, in XML format, each of the moves in this history:

```java
import java.io.*;
import java.util.List;
import java.util.Vector;
import javax.xml.parsers.*;
import org.w3c.dom.*;
import org.xml.sax.SAXException;

public class Persistency
{ public void save(List hist, String file)
  { try
    { FileOutputStream fos =
        new FileOutputStream(file);
      PrintWriter pw = new PrintWriter(fos);
      pw.println("<history>");
      for (int i = 0; i < hist.size(); i++)
      { Move mv = (Move) hist.get(i);
        pw.println(mv.toXml());
      }
      pw.println("</history>");
      pw.flush();
      pw.close();
    }
    catch(IOException e)
    { System.err.println("Error saving history"); }
  }
  ...
}
```

The reference to **Move** can be avoided by pre-converting the elements of the list to strings in the strategy subsystem, and simply passing the list of these strings to the above method. Alternatively we could define an interface **XmlPrintable** declaring **toXml** which **Move** and **Place** would implement. The above **save** method could refer to **XmlPrintable** in place of the specific strategy subsystem classes.

> **Design Guideline:** To remove direct reference to the internal classes of one subsystem in another, define interfaces which declare the sets of methods which the client subsystem calls on the supplier classes. The supplier classes then implement the interfaces and the client subsystem uses the interfaces in place of these classes.

Similarly if **Object** supported a **toXml()** method we would not need to cast to **Move**.

In order to parse XML documents efficiently, we need a *Document Type Definition (DTD)* file which describes the allowed syntax of these documents. In the case of histories, the DTD is:

```
<!ELEMENT history (move*)>
<!ELEMENT move (player, place)>
<!ELEMENT player (#PCDATA)>
<!ELEMENT place (x,y)>
<!ELEMENT x (#PCDATA)>
<!ELEMENT y (#PCDATA)>
```

This definition states that documents consist of a **history**, which is a sequence of zero or more **move** elements, these in turn consist of a **player** element followed by a **place** element, **player** consists of "parsed character" data, i.e. string data, and **place**s consist of **x** and **y** elements, etc. Such a DTD can be generated mechanically from the classes being stored as XML.

The class which parses XML files containing history data is:

```java
import java.io.*;
import java.util.List;
import java.util.Vector;
import javax.xml.parsers.*;
import org.w3c.dom.*;
import org.xml.sax.SAXException;

public class HistoryParser implements SystemConstants
{ private DocumentBuilder builder;

  public HistoryParser()
  throws ParserConfigurationException
  { DocumentBuilderFactory factory =
      DocumentBuilderFactory.newInstance();
    builder = factory.newDocumentBuilder();
  }

  public List parse(String file)
  throws SAXException, IOException
  { File ff = new File(file);
    Document doc = builder.parse(ff);
    Element root = doc.getDocumentElement();
    return getHistory(root);
  }

  private static List getHistory(Element e)
  { Vector moves = new Vector();
    NodeList children = e.getChildNodes();
    for (int i = 0; i < children.getLength(); i++)
    { Node cn = children.item(i);
      if (cn instanceof Element) // skip white space
      { Element ce = (Element) cn;
        if (ce.getTagName().equals("move"))
        { Move mv = getMove(ce);
          moves.add(mv);
        }
      }
```

```
    }
    return moves;
}

private static Move getMove(Element e)
{ NodeList children = e.getChildNodes();
  Place pl = null;
  String player = null;
  for (int i = 0; i < children.getLength(); i++)
  { Node cn = children.item(i);
    if (cn instanceof Element)
    { Element ce = (Element) cn;
      String tag = ce.getTagName();
      if (tag.equals("place"))
      { pl = getPlace(ce); }
      else if (tag.equals("player"))
      { Text tn = (Text) ce.getFirstChild();
        player = tn.getData();
      }
    }
  }
  return new Move(intOf(player),pl);
}

private static Place getPlace(Element e)
{ NodeList children = e.getChildNodes();
  int x = 0;
  int y = 0;
  for (int i = 0; i < children.getLength(); i++)
  { Node cn = children.item(i);
    if (cn instanceof Element)
    { Element ce = (Element) cn;
      String tag = ce.getTagName();
      Text tn = (Text) ce.getFirstChild();
      String data = tn.getData();
      if (tag.equals("x"))
      { x = Integer.parseInt(data); }
      else if (tag.equals("y"))
      { y = Integer.parseInt(data); }
    }
  }
  return new Place(x,y);
}

private static int intOf(String p)
{ for (int i = 0; i < symbol.length; i++)
  { if (p.equals(symbol[i]))
    { return i; }
  }
  return -1;
```

```
    }
}
```

This class uses the packages **javax.xml.parsers.***, **org.w3c.dom.*** and **org.xml.sax.SAXException** which are usually part of the Java 2, version 1.4 distribution. Alternatively they can be obtained from **ftp://ftp.gnu.org/pub/ gnu/classpathx**: install the **gnujaxp.jar** archive in a convenient directory and extend the **CLASSPATH** environment variable to include this archive.

Notice that we have made **getHistory**, **getMove**, etc., static, which is valid because they do not use any of the instance variables of the class. They could also be moved into the appropriate strategy system classes, i.e. **getPlace** into **Place**, etc.

> **Design Guideline:** Make methods of a class **static** if they do not use any of the instance variables of the class. This reduces the number of parameters to the method.

The parsing process is fairly repetitive, the **builder** returns a **Document** object which contains the tree of elements in the file. The **getHistory()** method then converts the string data of this tree back into **Move** objects for the strategy subsystem.

restore can then be defined as:

```
public List restore(String file)
{ try
  { HistoryParser hp = new HistoryParser();
    return hp.parse(file);
  }
  catch(Exception e)
  { System.err.println("Error reading history"); }
  return new Vector();
}
```

The **replay** operation can be expressed in pseudo-code as:

```
public void replay()
{ clear the board;
  start a new ReplayThread thread, which calls
  replayMove with successive moves from the
  history, at 1 second intervals;
}
```

```
public void replayMove(Move mv)
{ int player = mv.getPlayer();
  Place pl = mv.getPlace();
  position.move(player,pl);
  gui.setPlace(pl.getX(), pl.getY(), symbol[player]);
}
```

Pausing a program can be achieved by using the **sleep** method of the **Thread** class:

```
import java.util.List;

public class ReplayThread extends Thread
{ private int delay; // suspension time between actions
  private List history; // of Move objects
  private Game game;

  public ReplayThread(int del, List hist, Game g)
  { delay = del;
    history = hist;
    game = g;
  }

  public void run()
  { int steps = history.size();
    try
    { for (int i = 0; i < steps; i++)
      { Move mv = (Move) history.get(i);
        game.replayMove(mv);
        sleep(delay);
      }
    }
    catch (InterruptedException e) { }
  }
}
```

The argument of **sleep** is the number of milliseconds to pause. Clearing the board can be done by calling the **clearBoard()** method of **NCGui**, within **actionPerformed** in the case that the replay button was pressed. Clearing the position can be done by creating a new **Position** object:

```
position = new Position();
```

Figure B.5 shows the GUI of the completed system. The complete classes of this case study are provided on the web site.

B.6 Other Term Projects

The above project was set as the main coursework of a first year, second semester programming course in 2002, with students working individually or in teams. Most students successfully completed it and found it useful in improving their Java skills. Alternative projects in the same style are:

1 Design a system which supports the playing of solitaire. This game is played on a board of 45 squares (usually holes) and with pieces (pegs) which can only move two positions vertically or horizontally into an empty square by jumping over an occupied square. Figure B.6 shows a typical position and move. The aim of the game is to eliminate as many pieces as possible from the board, using the least number of moves. A piece is removed when it is "hopped over"

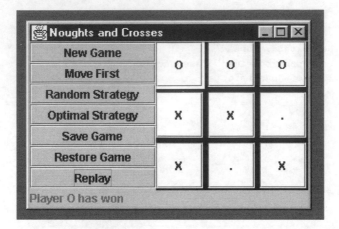

Figure B.5: Complete Interface of Noughts and Crosses Game

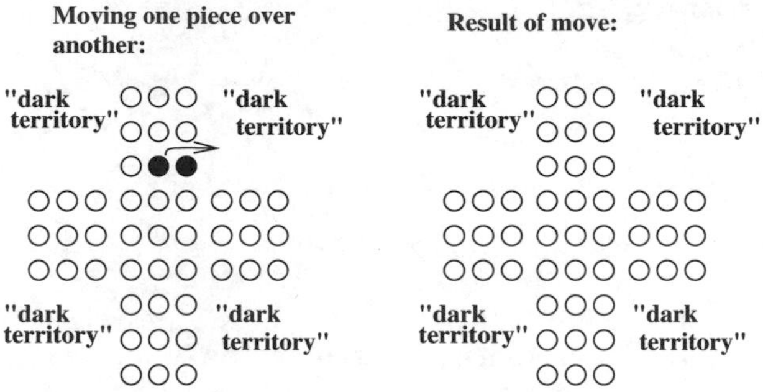

Figure B.6: Solitaire Game

by another piece, and a piece can also move off the board by jumping over another piece into the "dark territory" areas of Figure B.6.

The system should support:

1. A human player playing the game – by recording and showing their moves and the state of the board; by only permitting valid moves; and keeping track of the users best scores so far.
2. Strategies for playing the game by the software, from a starting position where just the center nine squares are occupied by pegs.
3. Strategies for playing the game by the software, from any possible starting position where a random set of squares are occupied by pegs.

Moves could be animated by a simple form of "drag and drop": the user clicks on the starting square, the peg mark disappears from this square and the cursor changes shape to a peg icon. When the user clicks on a valid target square or dark territory, the peg mark appears on the target and the cursor reverts to normal. To cancel a move the user clicks back on the starting square.

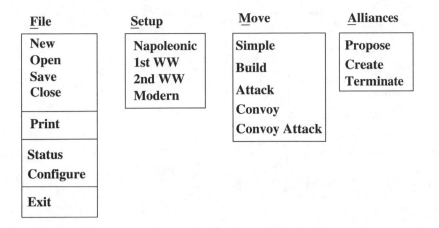

Figure B.7: Menus of Diplomacy Game Application

2 Design a system which supports the playing of "Diplomacy". The game involves the movement of pieces representing fleets and armies across positions of a 2-dimensional board. The players (2 or more) represent countries and engage in alliances or attacks with each other until there is a clear victor or a stalemate. If there are multiple human players (instead of program against one user) they take it in turns to use the console. Four basic board configurations will be supported, all based on maps of Europe: Napoleonic, 1st World War, 2nd World War and modern. It should be possible to create a new game with one of these configurations (players get assigned three pieces initially on their home territories, and can build more if their resources allow). Also it should be possible to save a game in progress and restore it from file later, and to print the board. The tool should display the board and positions and use menus to allow a player to make one of the 5 possible kinds of move. To make a move, the user clicks and drags the mouse over the board. Higher-level operations of proposing and creating and terminating alliances are also provided. A status function allows the state of various players to be summarised and to confirm if a game is close to being won. Finally a "configure" option allows changes to be made in the starting positions of a new board. Figure B.7 shows one possible menu layout. The system launches an initial dialog when a new game is started, asking the user which country they want to play as (the others will be simulated by the program or taken by other human players). This is shown in Figure B.8.

- A Diplomacy board consists of a 2D rectangle completely divided into a number of areas of "land" and "sea", of arbitrary shape.
- Each area can be occupied by at most one piece. Some areas can be designated as "impassable" (e.g. Scotland) and can never be occupied.
- There are two kinds of pieces: fleets and armies. Fleets may only occupy and move on sea areas and armies on land areas, although armies may be conveyed by a chain of adjacent fleets from one land area to another

Figure B.8: Initial Dialog of Game Application

provided all these fleets are owned by the same player as the army, and the army is adjacent to one of these fleets, as is the destination area.

- There can be two or more players.
- Each player is allocated a "home territory" of three or more adjacent areas.
- At the beginning of a game a player gets three pieces and can choose which three of their home territory areas they will initially occupy (if they have 3 sea and 3 land areas, they could choose to start with all fleets, or all armies, for example).
- Players take it in turns to move: an order of moves is decided before the game starts and the game consists of cycles of player moves in this order. A player may only move or build one of their pieces when it is their turn.
- A move can either be:

  1. *Simple move*: a player moves one of their pieces from an area to an adjacent unoccupied area, subject to the condition that armies can only occupy land areas and fleets occupy sea areas.

  2. *Attacking move*: if a player (or alliance of players) has three or more pieces surrounding an area occupied by an enemies piece, then one of these surrounding pieces can move into the attacked area, eliminating the attacked piece. An attacking piece may also be a conveyed army, but then the conveying fleet(s) do not count towards the 3 piece total needed for an attack although the conveyed army does.

  3. *Build move*: a player may build on any of their home territory areas, provided this area is unoccupied and their own pieces make up a majority of the pieces surrounding the build area (or there are no pieces surrounding the build area).

  4. *Convoy move*: a player conveys one of their army pieces from a land area to an unoccupied land area, across a sequence of adjacent fleet

pieces of theirs. The start and end areas of the move must also be adjacent to fleet pieces in this sequence.

- Players may form alliances in order to conduct joint attack moves, refrain from attacking each other, carve up enemy territory, etc. Alliances are informal agreements and may alter from move to move.
- A game is won by a player when that player has established a territory (number of occupied areas) larger than that which any other player can attain, no matter how long the game is prolonged. Games can also end in stalemate where no player can attain a winning position.
- The adjacency relation and the type of a position do not change during a game, nor can new players/countries join the game.

Figure B.9 shows the state of a board midway through a game. Player GB has white pieces, player NL has grey pieces and player F has black. NL has partially invaded F but cannot make any more progress without support from GB. Home territory areas for these players are marked with their names.

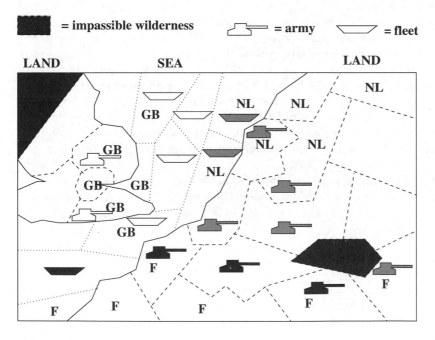

Figure B.9: Typical Diplomacy Game

3 Three-dimensional noughts and crosses: devise a system which supports the manual and automated playing of this variant of the game. The basic rule is the same: the first player to achieve a line of pieces is a row is the winner, however there are now 49 possible winning lines. The game could be made more interesting by requiring that a winning line has to involve all three sub-boards: front, middle and back. There are then 25 possible winning lines.

More advanced projects, suitable for a final year project, could be:

4   Develop an on-line travel agency system, which enables users to book flights between a set of given destinations, and to book car hires and hotels for their trips. The system should maintain a database of bookings, and connect where necessary to external websites to check availability and make reservations (these websites, e.g. for airlines, car hire companies and hotels, could be simulated).

5   Develop an on-line share management system, which enables a user to maintain a record of what shares they own, their current prices and their performance since purchase, and current price trends. They should be able to set warnings to alert them if a share changes in price more than a pre-set amount between two logins to the system. The system should read share prices from a free data feed such as that provided by **yahoo**, these feeds are typically 15 minutes behind current prices.

6   Develop an ambulance dispatch system, involving: (i) a dispatcher's interface, where the details of an emergency incident are entered (location, time, level of urgency, any special note/equipment), decisions are made to which ambulance station and destination hospital to allocate to this incident in order to minimise response and delivery time and provide medical resources needed; (ii) ambulance station interface, by which station managers provide up-to-date information on which of their vehicles are available/on call; (iii) ambulance crew interface, by which crews report their status back to the ambulance station.
Use a technology such as TCP sockets, RMI or JMS to enable communication between these subsystems when they are running on separate machines.

7   Cat tracking: develop a mobile computing system which allows an owner to track the location of their cat within 100 yards/metres of the base station. The tracking component on the cat should be small, light and unobtrusive and should fit on a normal cat collar. The system should have an interface which runs on a normal home PC and gives a position indication superimposed on a map of the neighbourhood. This interface should also be accessible via the internet to enable remote monitoring.

Bibliography

[1] C Alexander. *The Timeless Way of Building*. Oxford University Press, 1979.

[2] C Alexander, S Ishikawa, M Silverstein, M Jacobson, I Fiskdahl-King, and S Angel. *A Pattern Language*. Oxford University Press, 1977.

[3] A Ames, D Nadeau, and J Moreland. *VRML 2.0 Sourcebook, 2nd Edition*. John Wiley, 1999.

[4] B Anderson. The architecture handbook. In *OOPSLA Workshops*, 1991–1992.

[5] L Andrade, J L Fiadeiro, and M Wermelinger. Enforcing business policies through automated reconfiguration. In *Proc. International Conference on Automated Software Engineering*, pages 426–429. IEEE Computer Society Press, 2001.

[6] L F Andrade and J L Fiadeiro. Interconnecting objects via contracts. In R France and B Rumpe, editors, *UML'99 – Beyond the Standard*, number 1723 in LNCS, pages 566–583. Springer-Verlag, 1999.

[7] R Back and R Kurki-Suonio. Distributed cooperation with action systems. *ACM TOPLAS*, 10(4):513–554, 1988.

[8] K Beck. *Extreme Programming Explained*. Addison-Wesley, 1999.

[9] R Benson and J Perkins. The future of process control – a UK perspective. In *IEEE Conference on Process Control*. IEEE Press, 1996.

[10] B Boehm. A spiral model of software development and enhancement. *IEEE Computer*, May 1988.

[11] G Booch, J Rumbaugh, and I Jacobson. *The Unified Modeling Language User Guide*. Addison-Wesley, 1998.

[12] A Burns and A Wellings. HRT-HOOD: A structured design method for hard real-time systems. *Real-Time Systems*, 6(1):73–114, January 1994.

[13] M Buro. Improving heuristic mini-max search by supervised learning. *Artificial Intelligence*, 134(1–2), January 2002.

[14] S Cook and J Daniels. *Designing Object Systems: Object-Oriented Modelling with Syntropy*. Prentice Hall, Sept 1994.

[15] J Coplien. *Advanced C++ Programming Styles and Idioms*. Addison Wesley, 1991.

[16] J Crupi, D Alur, and D Malks. *Core J2EE Patterns*. Prentice Hall, 2001.

[17] T DeMarco. *Structured Analysis and System Specification*. Prentice Hall, 1979.

[18] A Dix, J Finlay, G Abowd, and R Beale. *Human-Computer Interaction*. Prentice Hall, 1998.

[19] J L Fiadeiro. On the emergence of properties in component-based systems. In *Proc. AMAST '96*, number 1101 in LNCS, pages 421–443. Springer-Verlag, 1996.

[20] The Financial Times Survey. Stock and Derivatives, Exchanges. Friday 31 March, 2000.

[21] E Gamma, R Helm, R Johnson, and J Vlissides. *Design Patterns: Elements of Reusable Object-Oriented Software.* Addison Wesley, 1995.

[22] D Gelernter and N Carriero. Coordination languages and their significance. *Communications ACM*, 35(2):97–107, 1992.

[23] M Goodland and C Slater. *SSADM Version 4.* McGraw-Hill, 1995.

[24] M Grand. *Patterns in Java, Vol. 1.* Wiley, 1998.

[25] Java 2 Platform, Enterprise Edition, http://www.java.sun.com/j2ee/, 2002.

[26] I Jacobson. *Object-Oriented Software Engineering: A Use Case Driven Approach.* Addison-Wesley, 1992.

[27] http://java.sun.com/j2se/javadoc/.

[28] JSci graphing package. http://fourier.dur.ac.uk:8000/~dma3mjh/jsci/api/Package-JSci.awt.html.

[29] S Katz. A superimposition control construct for distributed systems. *ACM TOPLAS*, 15(2):337–356, 1993.

[30] H Kilov and J Ross. *Information Modeling: an Object-oriented Approach.* Prentice-Hall, 1994.

[31] P Ladkin. The A300 crash in Nagoya. http://www.rvs.uni-bielefeld.de/ publications/Incidents/DOCS/FBW.html.

[32] K Lano. *The B Language and Method: A Guide to Practical Formal Development.* Springer Verlag, 1996.

[33] K Lano and H Haughton. *Object-Oriented Specification Case Studies.* Prentice Hall, 1993.

[34] K Rustan M Leino, J Saxe, and R Stata. Checking Java programs with guarded commands. In *Formal Techniques for Java Programs, technical report 251.* Fernuniversität Hagen, 1999.

[35] N Leveson. *Safeware: system safety and computers.* Addison Wesley, 1995.

[36] D Lightfoot. *Formal Specification Using Z.* Palgrave, 2000.

[37] T Mandel. *The Elements of User Interface Design.* Wiley, 1997.

[38] B Meyer. Applying design by contract. *IEEE Computer*, pages 40–51, Oct 1992.

[39] B Meyer. *Object-Oriented Software Construction.* Addison-Wesley, 1992.

[40] B Momjian. *PostgreSQL: Introduction and Concepts.* Pearson Education, 2001.

[41] D Notkin, D Garlan, W Griswold, and K Sullivan. Adding implicit invocation to languages: Three approaches. In *Object Technologies for Advanced Software*, number 742 in LNCS, pages 489–510. Springer-Verlag, 1993.

[42] The object constraint language. http://www-3.ibm.com/software/ad/library/ standards/ocl.html.

[43] R Pressman. *Software Engineering: A Practitioner's Approach.* McGraw Hill, 2000.

[44] B Randell. London ambulance service inquiry report. *The Risks Digest*, 14(48), April 1993.

[45] Robocup initiative. http://www.robocup.org/.

[46] W Royce. Managing the development of large software systems. In *Proceedings of IEEE WESCON.* IEEE Press, 1970.

[47] The Rational Unified Process, http://www.rational.com/products/rup/, 2002.

[48] Charles Schwab web site. http://www.schwab-worldwide.com.

[49] The user interface hall of shame. http://www.iarchitect.com/shame.htm.

[50] M Snoeck, G Dedene, M Verhels, and A-M Depuydt. *Object-oriented Enterprise Modelling with MERODE*. Leuvense Universitaire Press, 1999.

[51] OMG unified modelling language specification 1.4. OMG, http://www.omg.org/technology/documents/formal/uml.htm.

[52] L Vanhelsuwe. Jgl. http://www.javaworld.com/javaworld/jw-06-1997/jw-06-jgl.html.

[53] Web services architecture overview – the next stage of evolution for e-business, September 2000. www106.ibm.com/developerswork/web/library.

[54] Extensible markup language (xml). http://www.w3.org/XML/.

Index

IMPORTANT DOCUMENT – LICENCE AGREEMENT

By opening this package you agree to be bound by the terms of this Licence Agreement. If you do not agree to be bound by the terms of this Licence Agreement then you should promptly return the book, the CD ROM, the software contained on the CD ROM, this licence, its packaging and any other material received with it ("the Products") with the receipt for their purchase to your supplier for a full refund.

This document forms a legally binding agreement between you (as buyer or user of the Products) and Palgrave Macmillan Limited ("Palgrave") for the use of the software contained on the CD ROM ("the Software"). By using any of the Products you agree to be bound by the terms of this licence agreement.

You acknowledge that the Software is the property of Palgrave and/or its licensors.

You may:

(a) Use the Software for your personal private study purposes.

(b) Use the Software on one computer at a time only. You may not use the Software on a network of linked computers.

(c) Make one copy of the Software solely for back up purposes.

(d) Transfer the Software from one computer to another as long as you delete it from the computer from which it is being transferred.

Palgrave warrants that it has full rights and authority to grant the rights granted herein to you and that the use by you of the Software in accordance with this Agreement will not infringe the rights of any third party.

Palgrave may terminate this licence at any time by notice in writing.

Notwithstanding any other term of this Agreement Palgrave does not limit its liability for death or personal injury caused by its negligence.

Palgrave shall not be liable for any loss or damage whatsoever resulting from errors, omissions or inaccuracies in the Software regardless of how caused. Palgrave does not warrant that the Software will be free from errors or faults. In the event of a fault you should notify Palgrave in writing. Palgrave's sole liability for any fault or defect in the Products or any part thereof shall be replacement of the Product.

Without prejudice to the generality of the foregoing Palgrave shall not be liable for any claim arising from:

(a) Any failure or malfunction resulting wholly or to any material extent from your negligence, operator error, use other than in accordance with these terms or any other user documentation provided to you or any other misuse or abuse of the Products;

(b) The failure by you to implement recommendations previously advised by Palgrave in respect of, or solutions for, faults in the Products; or

(c) The decompilation or modification of the Software or its merger with any other program or any maintenance repair adjustment alteration or enhancement of the Software by any person other than Palgrave or its authorized agent.

THE SOFTWARE IS PROVIDED "AS IS". NEITHER PALGRAVE NOR ANYONE ELSE MAKES ANY WARRANTIES OF ANY KIND, EITHER EXPRESS OR IMPLIED, INCLUDING, BUT NOT LIMITED TO, WARRANTIES OF MERCHANTABILITY, QUALITY, ACCURACY OR FITNESS FOR A PARTICULAR PURPOSE. EXCEPT AS OTHERWISE EXPRESSLY PROVIDED IN THIS LICENCE AGREEMENT, ALL CONDITIONS, WARRANTIES, TERMS, REPRESENTATIONS, AND UNDERTAKINGS EXPRESS OR IMPLIED, STATUTORY OR OTHERWISE IN RESPECT OF THE SOFTWARE ARE TO THE FULLEST EXTENT PERMITTED BY LAW EXPRESSLY EXCLUDED. NO ORAL OR WRITTEN INFORMATION OR ADVICE GIVEN BY ANY REPRESENTATIVE OF PALGRAVE OR BY ANYONE ELSE SHALL CREATE ANY WARRANTIES.

The Agreement is governed by and construed in accordance with English Law and the parties agree to submit to the exclusive jurisdiction of the English courts.

Credits

This product includes software developed by the Apache Software Foundation
(http://www.apache.org/).
This product includes software developed by W3C Consortium
(http://www.w3.org)
This product includes software developed by Sun Microsystems, Inc
(http://www.sun.com)
This product includes software developed by Slava Pestov
This product includes software developed by Johannes Döbler

Minimum System Requirements

Java JDK 1.3